Butler's Battlin' Blue Bastards

BUTLER'S BATTLIN' BLUE BASTARDS

Thor Ronningen

Brunswick

Copyright© 1993 by Thor Ronningen

All rights reserved. No part of this book may be reproduced in any form or by any means, electronic or mechanical, including photocopying or by any informational storage or retrieval system, without written permission from the author and the publisher.

Library of Congress Cataloging-in-Publication Data

Ronningen, Thor, 1925–
  Butler's Battlin Blue Bastards/by Thor Ronningen.
     p.   cm.
  Includes bibliographical references and index.
  ISBN 1-55618-132-9 (pbk. : acid-free) : $19.95
  1. United States. Army. 395th Infantry. Battalion, 3d—History.
  2. World War, 1939-1945--Regimental histories--United States.
  I. Title.
  D769.31 395THR66   1993
  940.54' 1273--dc20   93-9515
                                                                            CIP

First Original Edition

Published in the United States of America

by

Brunswick Publishing Corporation
Rt. 1, Box 1A1
Lawrenceville, Virginia 23868

Thanks

This book would not have been possible without the continual support and steadfast encouragement I received from Lt. Col. McClernand Butler; from the many men from the 3rd Battalion who shared their war with me; and especially from my wife, Ruby. It is their book.

The Title

BUTLER'S—Lt. Col. (then Major) McClernand Butler assumed command of the 3rd Battalion—395th Infantry on 1 February '44. He directed their training Texas, oversaw their trip to Germany and led them in combat from 9 November '44 to 30 April '45, when he left the Battalion for the hospital, and set up the unit for occupation duties. The great success of this battalion was largely due to the inspired and dedicated leadership of Lt. Col. Butler. For most of the men in the Battalion, he was the only commander they had.

BATTLIN'—The 3rd Battalion had an outstanding combat record and were recognized by friend and foe as a fighting unit. This is also a slight play on words with the word "Battalion."

BLUE—In the triangular organization of World War II infantry divisions, the code word for the 1st Battalion was RED, the 2nd Battalion WHITE and the 3rd Battalion BLUE. The 395th Infantry Regiment's code name was DANUBE, hence the 3rd Battalion—395th was called DANUBE BLUE.

BASTARDS—One accepted meaning of this word is non-standard or different from the norm. The 3rd Battalion was, in many ways, different from most rifle battalions. During much of their time in combat this battalion was separated from their parent organization, the 99th Infantry Division. During the Battle of the Bulge they were attached to the 9th Infantry Division; in the attack on Bergheim they were attached to the 3rd Armored Division. In the Battle of the Ruhr Pocket at various times they were attached to all three combat commands of the 7th Armored Division. Both the 9th and the 7th requested use of the 3rd Battalion because of its very special (different) fighting abilities. The Germans called this battalion "Nighthawks" because of their proficiency at night fighting and the French Army requested Col. Butler to write a treatise on battalion-size night attacks. (The Infantry School at Fort Benning, GA teaches that a battalion is too large a unit to control in night attacks.) From their unyielding defense of Höfen, Germany, in the Battle of the Bulge, through their great success in attacking cities and towns, overcoming terrain and weather obstacles and carrying out their assignments, this Battalion was a very special, or different, fighting unit.

Glossary

AIB—Armored Infantry Battalion

AP—Anti-Personnel

A.S.T.P.—Army Specialized Training Program

AT—Anti-Tank

AWOL—Absent Without Leave

BAR—Browning Automatic Rifle

BN—Battalion

BLUE—3rd Battalion code designation

BURP GUN—German rapid-fire automatic weapon

C RATION—Canned food ready to eat cold or warmed

CCB—Combat Command B

CO—Commanding Officer

COL.—Colonel

CP—Command Post

DANUBE—395th Infantry code designation

D BAR—High calorie concentrated food bar

DP—Displaced Person (refugee)

DUKW—Amphibious Truck

FA—Field Artillery

FO—Forward Observer
GI—Government Issue
HQ—Headquarters
ITEM—I Company
KING—K Company
KP—Kitchen Police (Cooks' helpers)
LOVE—L Company
LTC—Lieutenant Colonel
MIKE—M Company
NCO or NON-COM—Non-commissioned officer
OP—Outpost or observation post
POE—Port of Embarkation
PW or POW—Prisoner of War
RAF—Royal Air Force (British)
RCT—Regimental Combat Team
RECON—Reconnaissance
SCR—Signal Corps Radio
SHAEF—Supreme Headquarters Allied Expeditionary Force
SOP—Standard Operating Procedure
S-1—Staff Officer – Personnel
S-2—Staff Officer – Intelligence
S-3—Staff Officer – Operations
S-4—Staff Officer – Supply
TD—Tank destroyer
TOT—Time on Target (Artillery timed to explode before impact)
WP—White Phosphorous

Table of Contents

Prologue xiii
    Chapter 1   The Beginning 1
    Chapter 2   En Route 8
    Chapter 3   Höfen 22
    Chapter 4   The Battle of the Bulge 39
    Chapter 5   Off the Line 83
    Chapter 6   Bergheim to the Rhine 95
    Chapter 7   The Rhine and The Weid 111
    Chapter 8   The Ruhr Pocket 137
    Chapter 9   To the Third Army 158
    Chapter 10   The Altmühl, Danube and Isar Rivers 164
    Chapter 11   Aftermath 174
Epilogue 179
Bibliography 183
Appendix 185
Index 221

Prologue

At 0525 on the morning of December 16, 1944, men of the 3rd Battalion—395th Infantry—99th Division were in their usual positions. Guards manned each position and the off-duty men were sleeping. It was cold and dark and quiet. Five minutes later the world seemed to come to an end as ten battalions of German artillery opened fire on Höfen, Germany. High explosive shells whistled in; nebelwerfer rockets, aptly called "Screaming Meemies," came in with an ear-piercing, almost heart-stopping, shriek before they exploded thunderously. The very earth trembled. Houses burned. Debris filled the streets. All communication lines were severed. Each position was cut off and in each hole the men prepared to defend themselves, to the death if necessary, not knowing what was happening around them. For twenty minutes the 3rd Battalion endured one of the heaviest artillery barrages the German army had ever fired prior to an attack.

When the artillery finally stopped firing, three battalions of the German 326th Volksgrenadier Regiment began their attack. It was an eerie scene as the Germans shined aircraft searchlights against the low hanging clouds to aid their troops. Of course these lights also aided the defenders, as the enemy was silhouetted as they plodded through the snow towards Höfen. Remembering their training, the defenders held their fire until the oncoming Germans were almost on top of them and then opened up with every weapon they had, inflicting massive casualties on the enemy.

The Battle of the Bulge had begun. This was a last, desperate effort by the Germans to regain the offensive and became the largest pitched battle the American army had ever fought. Over 600,000 Americans were eventually involved and they suffered 81,000 casualties (Charles B. MacDonald—A Time For Trumpets). The Battle of the Bulge was also the first of many pitched battles the 3rd Battalion was to have with the enemy.

The Battalion (836 officers and men) is the basic unit of Infantry and is the largest infantry unit to be controlled by one man. Division commanders plan their tactics based on battalion units. The battalion is designed to be a separate fighting unit that can be attached to various commands as needed.

This is the story of one infantry battalion and what they went through.

CHAPTER 1

The Beginning

*T*he 99th Infantry Division was activated on November 16, 1942, at Camp Van Dorn, near Centreville in southwest Mississippi, with Brigadier General Thompson Lawrence commanding. Camp Van Dorn, named after a Confederate general, was typical of the army camps hastily thrown up at the start of World War II. The buildings had tar paper roofs and siding, were not watertight and were difficult to heat. During construction, the area had been pretty well cleared off so the camp area was mostly dust and mud, depending on the weather. Since there were no cities of any size near the camp, it was difficult for the men to find relaxation in their off hours. This situation worsened when both service clubs in the camp burned down. The division cadre came largely from the 7th Infantry Division and the balance of the troops were largely raw recruits with no previous military experience.

In January 1943 basic training began, complete with marches in the rain and mud. There was weapons training, first aid and hygiene, map reading, military courtesy and discipline, vehicle driver qualification, physical conditioning, inspections ad infinitum, KP, more marching and all the details necessary to take a group of recruits and make soldiers of them.

"Our camp was near Natchez, Mississippi, not too far from Baton Rouge, Louisiana. I was homesick, scared and unhappy. For over a year I was to learn to shoot an M-1, a

BAR, crawl under machine gun fire, climb ropes, walk mile after mile and run the same distance. Do close order drill, salute and say 'Sir' to every shavetail I met. I peeled potatoes and cleaned latrines. I picked up cigarette butts and polished shoes. I pitched tents in woods filled with ticks, chiggers and snakes. That's not all. When I left Camp Van Dorn, I was sent to Camp Maxey, Texas, where I had to do the same things all over again."

Warren Wilson—I Company

On April 3, 1943, there was a division review marking the "graduation" from basic training. In May everyone took physical fitness tests. In June the first WACS came to Van Dorn. On August 2, 1943, Brigadier General Walter E. Lauer took over as Commanding General of the 99th Infantry Division. From August 15th to September 9th the Division was on D Series maneuvers in Mississippi. From September 17th to November 15th the Division participated in the largest U.S. Army maneuvers ever staged, which started in Louisiana and ended in Texas with a mock battle between the Red and Blue armies. Later in November the 99th sent about 1500 men to the 85th Division and another 1500 to the 88th Division to bring these units up to full strength.

On November 19, 1943, the 99th entered Camp Maxey, near Paris in the northern part of Texas. This was a camp with "real" buildings, service clubs and towns near-by with lots of off-duty recreation. A far cry from their original home at Camp Van Dorn.

On February 1, 1944, shortly after his return from attending the Command and General Staff School at Ft. Leavenworth, Kansas, then Major McClernand Butler assumed command of the 3rd Battalion—395th Infantry Regiment. On March 21, 1944, he was promoted to the rank designated for a battalion commander, Lieutenant Colonel. Thus began a very successful melding of a commander and his men into the fine fighting unit it became.

In March 1944 more than 3,000 A.S.T.P. (Army Specialized Training Program) men joined the division to replace the men sent out in November. This brought the division up to full strength. The Army had set up the A.S.T.P. as a method of producing a large supply of highly educated specialists. To enter this program required a high IQ, maximum age of 20 and good physical condition. These men had been given standard infantry basic training and then sent to a number of colleges and universities for an accelerated course of instruction in several fields. However, as the war progressed, the need for more soldiers became pressing and this program was disbanded with most of the men being sent to infantry divisions. In the 99th these men were assigned to units throughout the Division, although most of them went to infantry regiments. Even though these men had had basic training, they were formed into a provisional regiment under LTC Jack G. Allen for a three month course of basic infantry training. LTC McClernand Butler commanded the training battalion for the 395th Regiment. Because these men absorbed this training so quickly and easily, the training schedule was abbreviated and the men soon joined their individual units.

Paul Putty, I Company—395th, was working on some charts at the 395th Regimental Headquarters when two full Colonels visited Col. McKenzie, the 395th CO. Since the door was open, Putty could not help but overhear the conversation. The visitors asked Col. McKenzie how the regimental training was progressing and how well the young troops were doing. McKenzie stated that in all his army career and experience, he had never encountered a group of enlisted trainees as smart and intelligent; as eager and willing to learn as this group. He said that more often than not, this group of men mastered the different training tasks in half the time allotted for such programs. He stated that discipline problems normally encountered with basic training groups were non-existent with this group. He even stated that all reports from Battalion and Company officers were effusive with their praises of these young men. Putty, of course, lost no time in passing this report on to his fellow trainees.

This basic training consisted of all the basic instruction needed by combat soldiers. There was weapons training on the fixed and variable distance ranges with the M-1, the BAR (Browning Automatic Rifle), the .30 cal machine gun, .50 cal machine gun, 60mm and 81mm mortars, .45 cal automatic and the .30 cal carbine. They fired on the Close Combat Course and the Combat in Cities course and crawled under live machine gun fire. There were marches, physical training, hygiene courses, first aid instruction and map reading.

After this basic course, the men returned to their companies where the training continued. There was unit training so the men would learn to fight as a unit. There were field problems from squad size to division size. There were problems with tanks working with infantry, night attack problems, problems that lasted an hour to problems that lasted several days. All the men qualified as Expert Infantrymen.

On June 6, 1944, the 395th Regimental Combat Team (395th Infantry Regiment plus attached units such as artillery, quartermaster, etc.) boarded trucks and traveled to Camp Barkley, Texas, to engage in a "fight" with the 12th Armored Division. This was D-Day in Normandy and as the men were boarding their trucks, newsboys were hawking special editions about the invasion of Europe. The papers had little detail about the invasion and the men wondered if the war would be over before they completed training. Not to worry. There was plenty of war left!

It was a two day trip to Camp Barkley and each way the men spent a night camped at Bridgeport Marine Base at Bridgeport, Texas. Many of the men from the northern parts of the country got a real lesson in what a problem chiggers can be. This was the first of many long motor marches these men were to make. The "war" was a complete success for the 395th RCT. The 12th Armored was considered to be ready for a combat assignment, but after this exercise were taken off the "ready" list.

The 395th set up a defensive position and the 12th attacked. Three hundred and fifty miles of barbed wire were used in the construction of tactical and defensive obstacles and some 15,000 anti-tank mines were laid, containing puff charges. In addition, all buildings, windmills and other places that might be used by the armored force were thoroughly booby-trapped. It was hot and dusty and positions were hard to dig because of the stony soil. Snakes, largely rattlers and copperheads, added to the men's discomfort. Col. A. J. McKenzie commanded the 395th RCT, with L. Col. James A. Gallagher as Executive Officer.

In a memorandum issued to each member of the Combat Team, Col. McKenzie said, in part, ". . . you did your job in a superior manner. You set up a defensive position which thoroughly balked a superior force. The Commanding General of the XXIII Corps, Major General Craig, told me, 'I am highly pleased with your regiment in every respect.' The Commanding General of the Fourth Army, Major General John P. Lucas, told me, 'It's a pleasure to inspect troops like these.' Let me say in closing that I am thrilled with the privilege of commanding such a regiment."

In July there was another motor march, this time to southeastern Oklahoma for small unit exercises. This time the enemy was the climate and the topography. It was very hot and humid with clouds of biting and stinging insects as well as an abundance of snakes, mostly copperheads. The area was so desolate that the men had to cut trees down so the vehicles could move. It seemed to many of the men that training in an area like this was done to prepare them for combat in the Pacific Theater.

In August the training period ended and the 99th Infantry Division was considered "combat ready." The men had learned their craft as soldiers as well as training could teach them. The officers and men had gotten to know each other, combat procedures had been worked out and a group of individuals was now a team. Only actual combat would show if their training had accomplished what it was meant to do. All leaves were canceled and the men were put to work crating and packing the many tons of equipment for shipment. None of the men knew where they were going, but they all knew they were on their way to war.

On September 15, 1944, the 3rd Battalion boarded trains for their journey to a Port of Embarkation. The weather was good as the train wound its way up through Oklahoma, Missouri, Illinois, Indiana and Michigan. Many men passed close to their homes and wondered what their loved ones were doing as they headed toward an uncertain future. The train crossed into Canada at Detroit/Windsor, through the lush farmland of southern Ontario

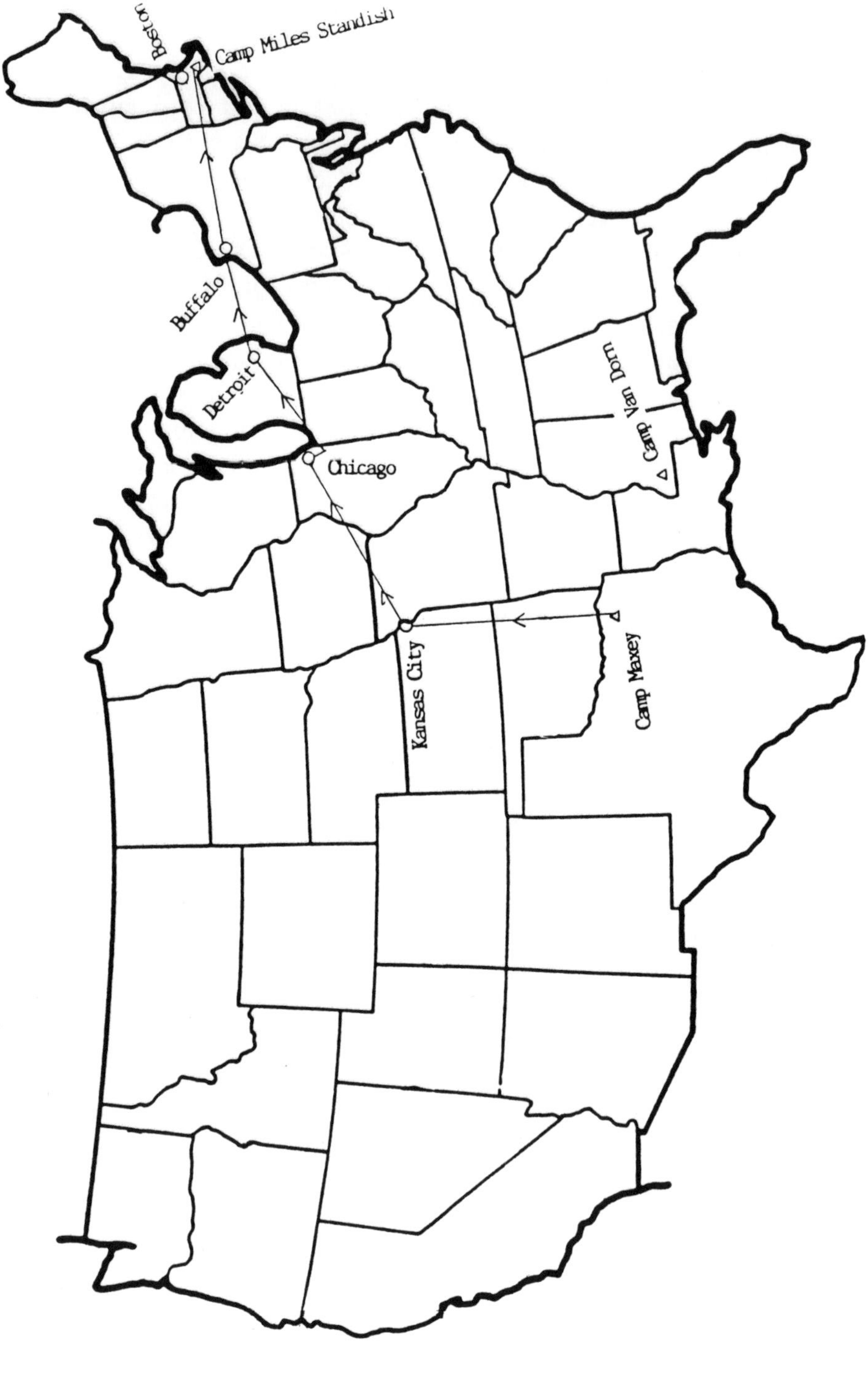
Boston
Camp Miles Standish
Buffalo
Detroit
Chicago
Camp Van Dorn
Kansas City
Camp Maxey

and back into the U.S. at Niagara Falls, New York. It was a typical troop train movement with an exercise stop each morning and each afternoon. Meals were cooked in baggage cars by the unit's cooks and the men used their regular mess gear as china. The men passed the long hours in many ways—reading, playing cards, writing letters, sleeping, etc. By this time they were experienced soldiers and were used to killing time for extended periods. Most of these men were in their late teens or early twenties with the optimism of youth and each man worked out his own way of facing the unknown future.

The 3rd Battalion arrived at Camp Miles Standish, just outside Taunton, Massachusetts, on September 18, 1944. The entire 99th Division had traveled in three trains traveling different routes to their assembly point at this camp. The camp was extremely well run. Guides met the units in the train marshaling yards and led each unit to its assigned quarters with a minimum of delay. All troops arriving at a POE are quarantined for 48 hours. During this quarantine period the men got inoculations and physical inspections, which were perfunctory at best. There were numerous administrative details to be taken care of, but no formal training. When the quarantine period was up, 50 percent of each unit was issued passes each day and the men scattered to Boston, Providence, Rhode Island, and to Taunton for a last "fling" before they headed overseas. Some of the men who lived in this area had the opportunity to visit their homes. Sadly for some, this was their last visit home. All the training was over. It was time to put that training to use.

Chapter 2

En Route

The 99th Division left Camp Miles Standish on September 29, 1944, boarding trains at the train yard for the short trip to Boston Harbor. The 3rd Battalion boarded the USS Marine Devil. This was a new ship built for the United Fruit Company, a "banana boat," and far more useful for hauling bananas than for handling troops. The bunks for the men were flat canvas hammocks in pipe frames which were stacked seven or eight high. This left about eighteen inches vertical space per man with aisles about two feet wide. Into this minute space each man had to put himself and all his army equipment—rifle, duffel bag, steel helmet, overcoat, pack, spare clothes, etc. Only an infantry soldier could make a home out of a situation like this. Some of the top tiers were directly under ventilators and the men in these bunks were continually cold while the men in the bottom bunks were too warm in the fetid air.

Meals were served cafeteria style at stand up tables. When a man would get sick at meal time, the men at his table would decide they were through eating. As with any sea voyage, some of the men never were sick and some were seasick the entire way. Most of the men were soon acclimated to the sea motions and functioned normally. As they sailed out of Boston Harbor in the evening, some of the men could almost see their homes—unfortunately for some it was the last time they would see home. Many of the men had never seen the ocean before and of course all

USS Marine Devil—Source unknown

of them were somewhat apprehensive as they did not know what the future would bring. It was a time of reflection.

Fortunately the weather was relatively calm with no major storms. This was one of the largest convoys of World War II. Ships changed their positions within the convoy, but during daylight hours there were always ships in view—cargo ships, troop ships and tankers with destroyers circling their charges and baby flat-tops near the periphery. There were rumors of enemy submarines in the vicinity, but none of the troops spotted any. The Marine Devil, like many of the ships, had deck guns and anti-aircraft guns and their crews held practice almost daily. The ship personnel were rather a mixed bag with the troops as passengers, navy gun crews and civilians operating the ship. It was surprising to the first-time sailors that each day the ship's crew would hose down the decks and wash great quantities of dirt overboard. This was the maiden voyage of this ship and yet when it got to England there was a great deal of rust all over it from the salt water.

The salt water showers, even with the salt water soap, did not do much of a job and the men never really felt clean. Of course with this many men aboard ship, the gambling games started almost as soon as the ship left the harbor. Blackjack, poker and crap games went on around the clock with all three groups of men participating. The prices were steep with thousands of dollars changing hands. These games were not for amateurs!

With time on their hands, there was a lot of conversation and speculation among the men as to what the future would hold. Each man, in his own way, struggled to condition himself for the uncertainties he was facing. A few officers and a few enlisted men assured their listeners that they were "tough." Usually in loud voices, they would tell everyone within earshot that they were going to "kill every German I see," and that they could handle whatever the enemy threw at them. In many cases, these were the first ones to fail when faced with the reality of actual combat. The majority were quietly determined to do the best they could, whatever came. All of them knew they were facing possible death or injury, but most did not fully accept the fact that it could actually happen to them.

Many hours before land was sighted, the men saw the English fishermen at work in their little double-ended dories. The troops were on their way to war and yet they felt sorry for these men who went to sea in such small craft. Several hours after spotting Lands End, the ship steamed into Plymouth Harbor. It was great to see land again after 12 days at sea. These men were soldiers, not sailors! The lush green hillsides were a balm to the eyes. As the ship pulled into its assigned docking space, an RAF Mosquito bomber made several low passes over the harbor as he engaged in target practice. The men aboard ship would track him with their M-1's, simulating shooting at him. It was a good rehearsal for the real thing.

After de-barking, the men formed up and marched several hundred yards to a waiting train. Uniforms were clean and pressed and they were a smart looking group. A far cry from their appearance several months later. The English train was novel as it was so different from American trains. The cars were much smaller and the individual compartments were entered through side doors. The ride across southern England was a relaxing time, as the men were more like tourists than soldiers as they drank in the green hillsides and the small towns.

It was raining lightly as they arrived at their destination— Camp Marabout near Dorchester in southeast England. This camp had last been used as a staging area for the troops involved in the invasion on D-Day, June 6, 1944, and had a rather rundown appearance. The men set to with a will and soon had it looking like a viable military base. The barracks were mopped and swept out, mattress covers were filled with straw for mattresses and the mess halls were set up. Even though the Battalion was to be here for a month, this was just a staging area and training was minimal. The mornings were devoted to group games such as volley ball and pass-and-touch football, and the afternoons to long marches through the countryside to keep the men in shape. It rained every day. The men were issued passes and many went to London and some as far as Edinburgh, Scotland.

The war felt a little closer here as there was some evidence of German bombing raids and Dorchester had some of the tank obstacles and defenses that Winston Churchill was talking about when he said, "We will fight on the beaches, we will fight in the streets, etc." Over the main intersection there was a small blue light and to the natives this meant that the blackout had been somewhat lifted even though it shed little illumination. At night the lights inside the stores and pubs that were open could only be seen from directly outside their doors.

At one meal each man was given several oranges as they were beginning to spoil and the cooks did not want them to go to waste. A young English boy, about 12 years old, had come to visit with "The Yanks" and one of the men offered him an orange. The boy thanked the man and put the orange in his pocket. When asked why he did not eat it, he said he was going to take it home to share with his family—his parents and a younger sister. When asked if he had ever had an orange, he replied that, yes, he had had one once. Imagine a 12 year old child that had had an orange only once in his life! With typical American generosity, the men then tied both of his trouser legs at the ankle and loaded his pant legs with oranges. The poor fellow could hardly walk when he left for home.

The English people had difficulty realizing the size of America and found it hard to believe that the men from New York City were closer to home in Dorchester than they had been in Camp Maxey. While they were there the troops learned all about fish 'n chips and 'alf 'n 'alf and of course got acquainted with some of the local young ladies. Rumors about the future flew thick and fast.

> "Snafus continued. We uncrated and de-cosmolined our guns and then got orders to re-cosmoline them for turn in to get new ones. Of course the new ones were packed in cosmoline too. We all had a bad case of cosmoline burn-out when finished."
>
> Homer Kissinger—M Company

On October 21, 1944, Aachen, Germany, surrendered to the American 9th Army. This was the first major German city to surrender to Allied forces.

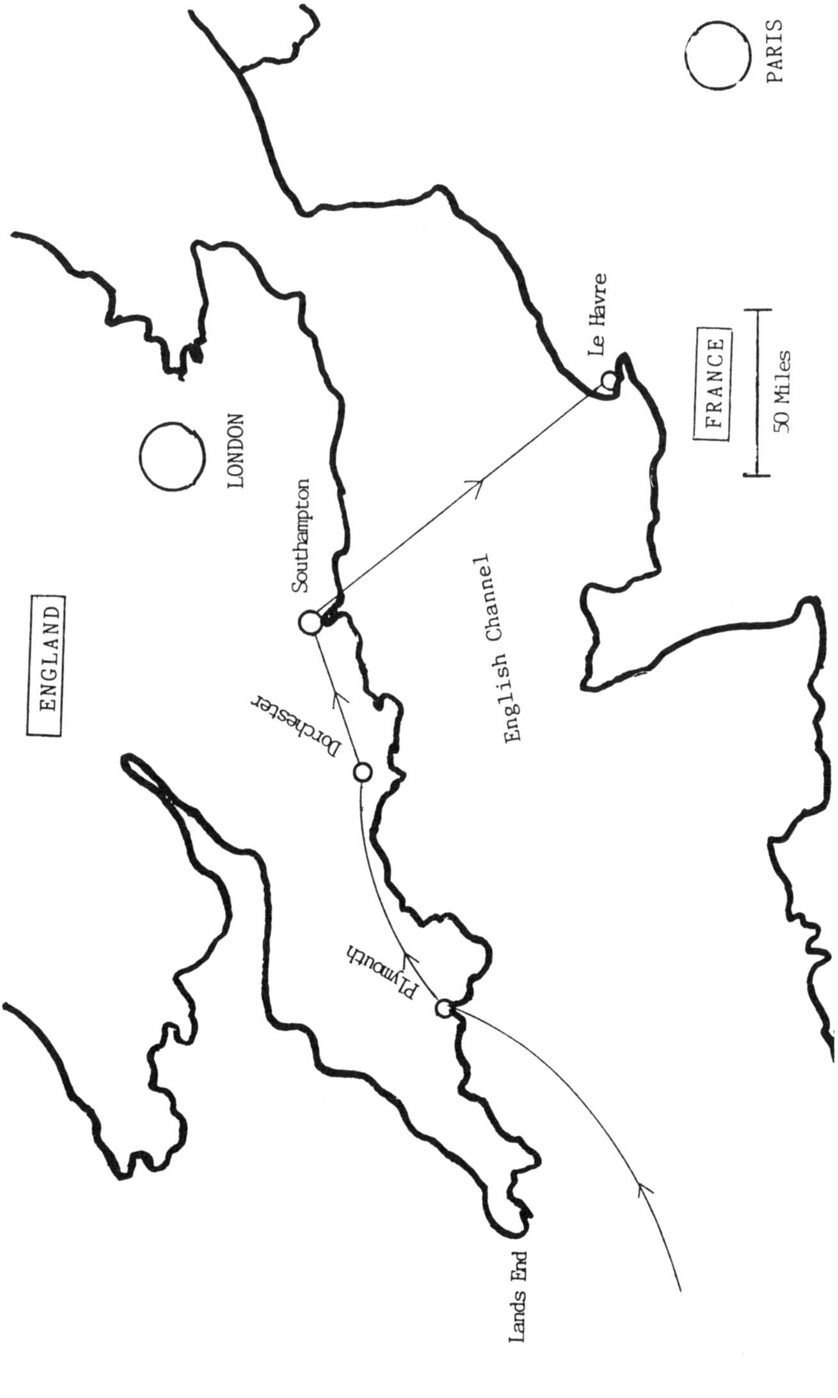
PARIS
Le Havre
FRANCE
50 Miles
LONDON
Southampton
English Channel
ENGLAND
Dorchester
Plymouth
Lands End

It was time to get down to business and on October 31, unit organic transportation left for Southampton and was followed the next day by the troops.

"When we were in the loading area of Southampton preparing to leave jolly old England for adventures unknown, we began to realize it was cold and winter was coming on. Somebody reported that a railroad boxcar was nearby with Red Cross supplies aboard. One of my group climbed in and took a box of turtleneck sweaters that had been knitted by volunteers in Connecticut for the British army. They looked like the proverbial 'manna from heaven.' We each grabbed one and put it on. Of course this was discovered, and as we went up the gangplank we were pulled out of line and I spent the entire trip across the English Channel cleaning pots and pans in the galley. I wore that sweater until the spring of '45, so the episode was definitely worth it."

Robert Parks—K Company

The 3rd Battalion boarded HMS Empire Lance and set sail across the Channel. The food was poor and the accommodations left much to be desired, but the men were only aboard for 24 hours so they took it pretty much in stride. Blackout rules were strictly enforced and even a lighted cigarette was not allowed on deck after dark.

What a surprise to sail into LeHavre the next evening and see floodlights on the piers and a waiting truck convoy with headlights on full. Although they had seen some bomb damage in England, LeHavre was the first view the men had of the total destruction of war. The harbor was a shambles. The entire port had been bombed and shelled and the piers and moles were masses of shattered concrete. Sunken ships abounded with their superstructures forlornly showing above the water. With the harbor in this shape it was impossible for the ship to get to a pier so the men were off-loaded down cargo nets into LSTs for the short trip to shore and the waiting trucks. By truck the men were taken to an open field camp site about five miles east of Forges,

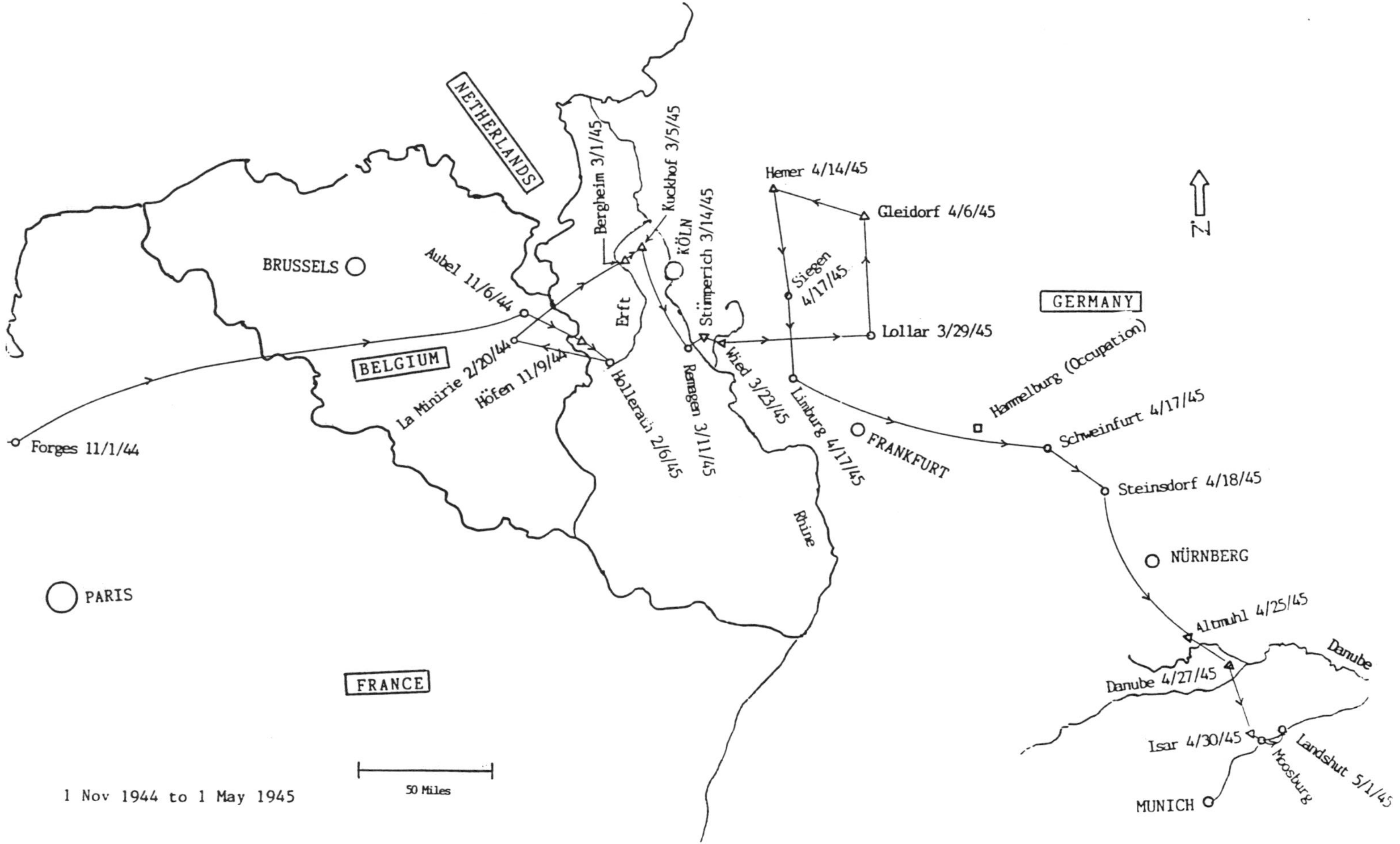
NETHERLANDS
BELGIUM
FRANCE
GERMANY
BRUSSELS
PARIS
KÖLN
FRANKFURT
NÜRNBERG
MUNICH
N
Forges 11/1/44
Aubel 11/6/44
La Minirie 2/20/44
Höfen 11/9/44
Hollerath 2/6/45
Erft
Bergheim 3/1/45
Kuckhof 3/5/45
Remagen 3/11/45
Stümperich 3/14/45
Wied 3/23/45
Rhine
Lollar 3/29/45
Gleidorf 4/6/45
Hemer 4/14/45
Siegen 4/17/45
Limburg 4/17/45
Hammelburg (Occupation)
Schweinfurt 4/17/45
Steinsdorf 4/18/45
Altmuhl 4/25/45
Danube 4/27/45
Danube
Isar 4/30/45
Moosburg
Landshut 5/1/45
50 Miles

1 Nov 1944 to 1 May 1945

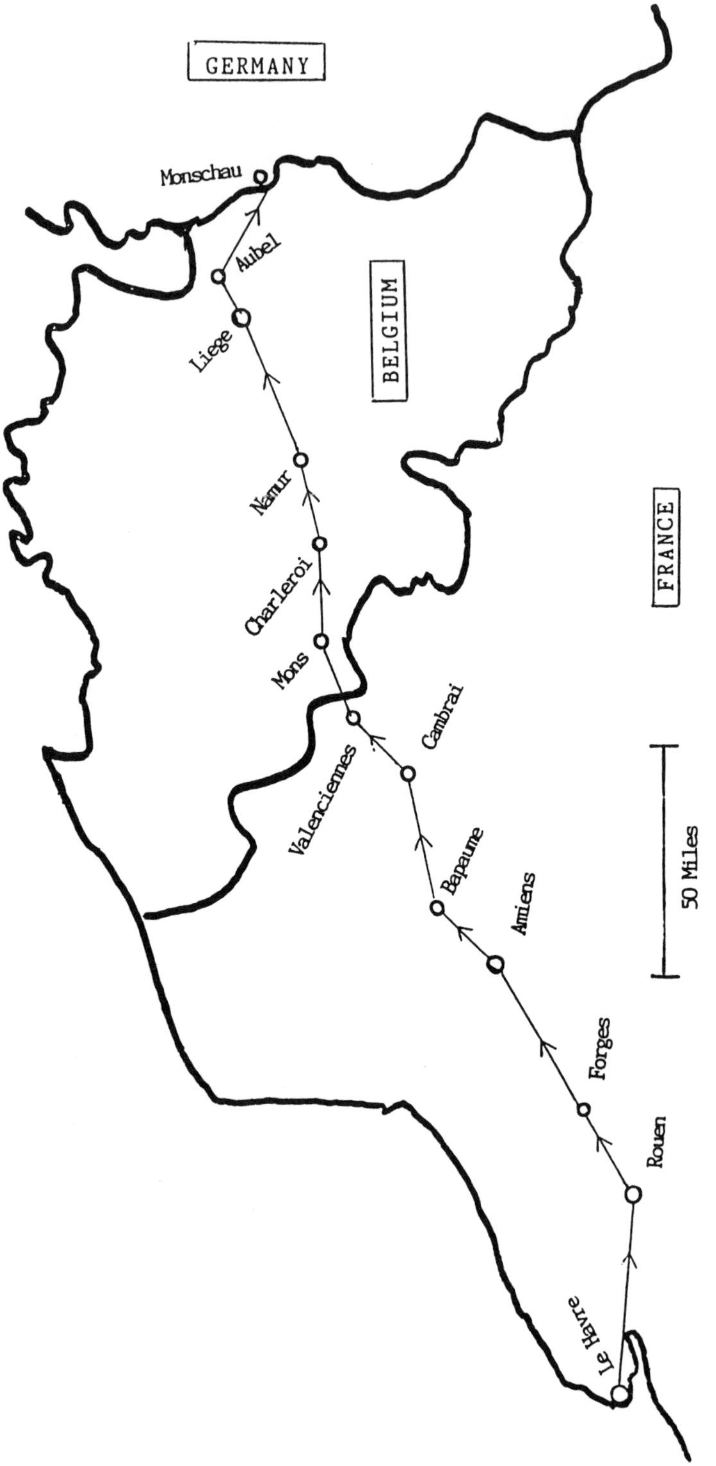
GERMANY
BELGIUM
FRANCE
Monschau
Aubel
Liege
Namur
Charleroi
Mons
Cambrai
Valenciennes
Bapaume
Amiens
Forges
Rouen
Le Havre
50 Miles

France. For the first time the men met civilians who had experienced war at first hand.

> "We were a little shocked when we bivouacked in an apple orchard and found local people, both male and female, using our open latrines and 'accepting' food."
>
> John R. Tabb—I Company

> "Two men from our platoon were detailed to unload the officer's bedrolls and spread them out. One of the two took deep offense at this assignment and commenced mouthing off. The more he talked, the madder he got, until finally he began describing the retribution he intended to exact when the bullets started flying. That did it. The next morning he was gone as if he had never existed. I never heard from him or found out what happened to him. Weak mind, powerful mouth; an unfortunate but too common combination."
>
> Homer Kissinger—M Company

When all was organized, the Battalion went by truck through Normandy to Amiens, through Picardy, Flanders, Bapaume, Cambrai and Valenciennes to Belgium and then through Mons, Charleroi, Namur and Liege to Aubel. Overall the trip was 285 miles. As the 3rd Battalion arrived in Aubel on November 6th, other units of the 99th Division were just leaving England.

> "As we traveled I was impressed with the debris of war as we saw knocked out German and American tanks and trucks, torn up villages, splintered trees, etc. It had only been a short time since the area had been contested and things had not been 'tidied up' yet."
>
> John R. Tabb—I Company

On November 7, 1944, Franklin D. Roosevelt was elected to his fourth term as President.

> "At that time it was election day 1944 and we were told if we wanted to vote, you could go back in a booth there, just

behind where we were bivouacked. We were all 19. We were too young to vote. (Minimum voting age then was 21.) I made up my mind that if I ever came through this thing and got home, I was going to vote. So far (1992) I have never missed an election."

Richard Gorby—K Company

Men of the 99th will remember this church at Höfen, especially the men of the Third Battalion, 395th Infantry. Photo sent in by Dr. John Reid of Indiana, PA.

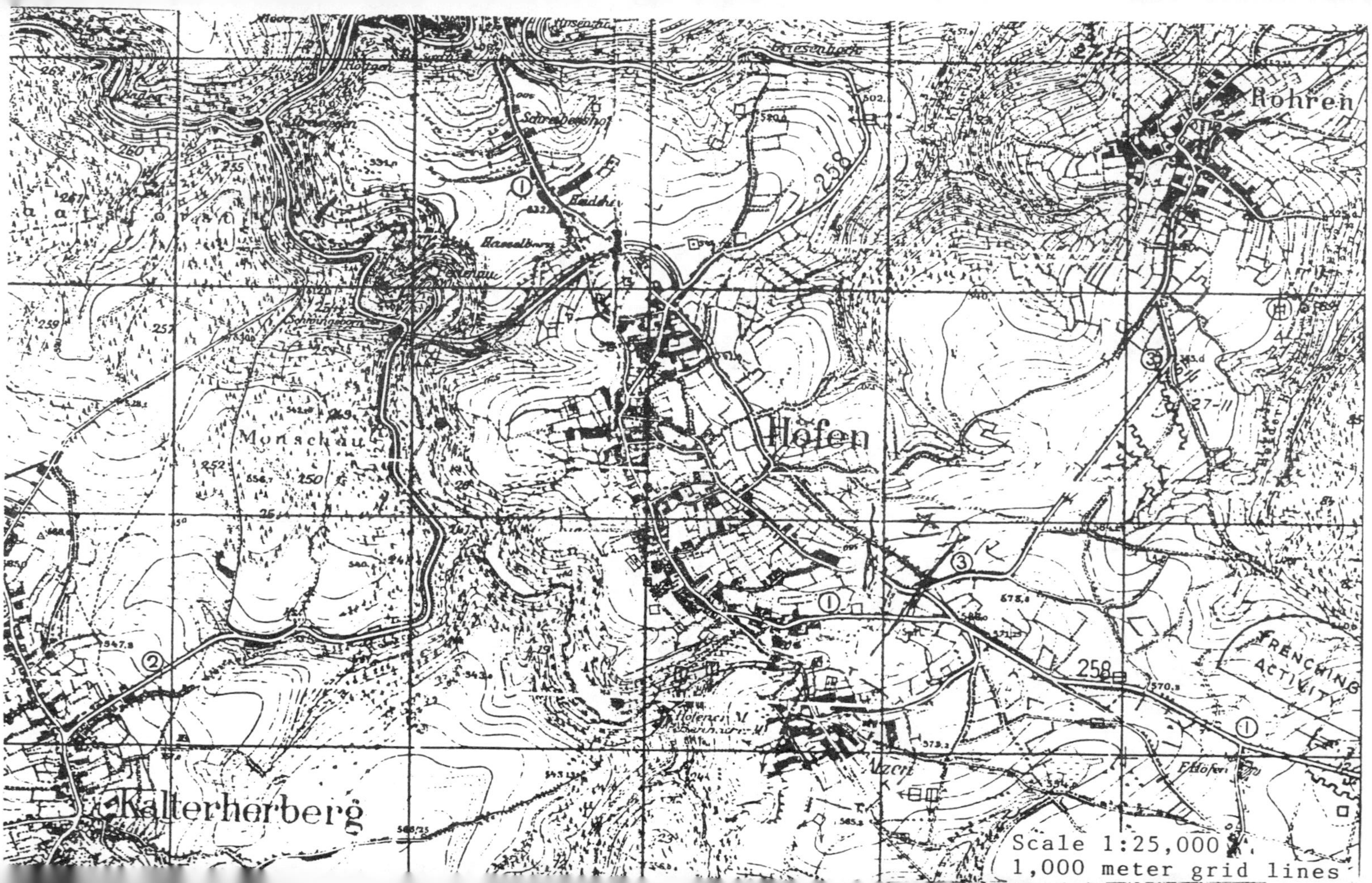

Rohren
Höfen
Monschau
Kalterherberg
TRENCHING ACTIVITY
258
Scale 1:25,000
1,000 meter grid lines

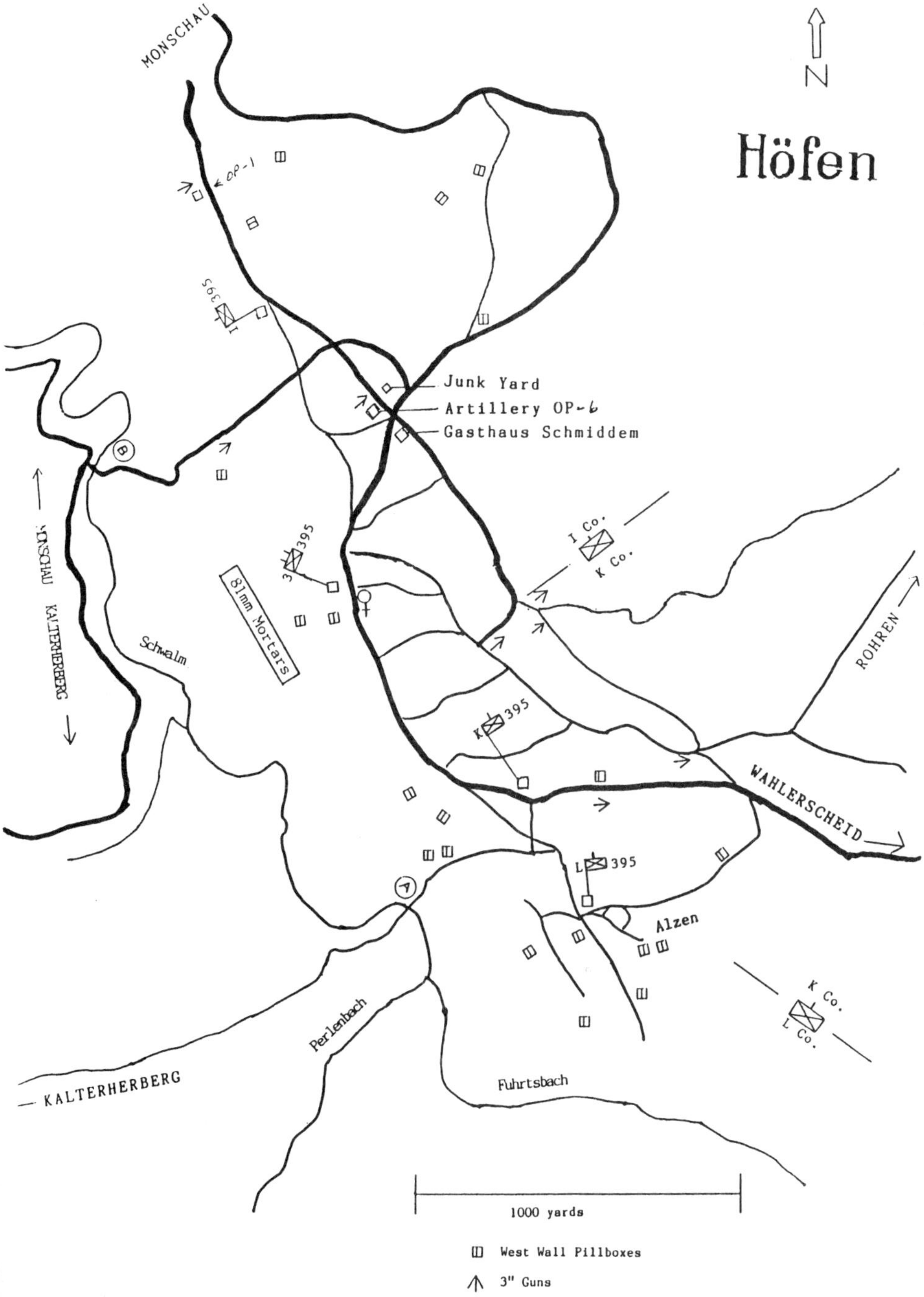
N
Höfen
MONSCHAU
OP-1
I 395
Junk Yard
Artillery OP-6
Gasthaus Schmiddem
MONSCHAU
KALTERHERBERG
I Co.
K Co.
3 395
81mm Mortars
Schwalm
ROHREN
K 395
WAHLERSCHEID
L 395
Alzen
K Co.
L Co.
Perlenbach
KALTERHERBERG
Fuhrtsbach
1000 yards
West Wall Pillboxes
3" Guns

Chapter 3

Höfen

Leaving his executive officer, Major Luther D. Allison, in command, on November 8th Lt. Col. Butler and his staff went to Höfen, Germany, to reconnoiter the area the Battalion was to occupy. Early the next morning the balance of the Battalion boarded trucks in Aubel for their assembly area in Kalterherberg, just across the German border. It began to snow. The last part of the trip was made in half-tracks which proved to be very uncomfortable. At Kalterherberg the men de-trucked and moved the rest of the way on foot.

> "As with many of my memories of World War II, the scene comes back in black and white, with our olive drab uniforms and vehicles, and the undersides of the fir boughs standing out in dark contrast to the falling snow covering and veiling everything else. I remember also the silence, with snow tending to muffle sound and the absence of any battle noises from the front on top of a ridge a mile or so away, hidden by a curtain of snow."
>
> James Crewdson—M Company

As the men headed for the front they were as well or better dressed than any soldiers in history. Long underwear was wool, two piece; wool socks; leather high top shoes and canvas leggings or high top shoes with an attached leather cuff; wool shirt and trousers; some men had wool pull-over sweaters; a field jacket that was hip length; wool overcoat; a wool knit cap covered by a plastic helmet liner which in turn was covered by a steel helmet. Most men had wool gloves and many of them soon added their own variations of protection because of the severe weather.

> "The ingenuity of the infantryman is unbeatable. No matter how tough the weather or what have you—he can fix himself up pretty comfortably. It is really amazing."
>
> Robert Snevily—I Company

In spite of how they were dressed, the weather and conditions soon showed that there was much room for improvement. The boots were not waterproof so frozen feet and trench foot were a constant problem during the cold months. None of their clothing was waterproof so that when the men later had to ford streams and rivers they got soaked to the skin and thoroughly chilled. Each man used his own ingenuity to aid him in staying dry and retaining body heat.

The infantry travels basically by foot and each man had to carry his share of the necessary tools and supplies. The primary item was an M-1 rifle (9 pounds) or a BAR (20 pounds). Around his waist he wore a woven canvas rifle belt which had pockets filled with spare clips of rifle ammunition. Attached to the belt by wire hooks was a canteen carrier which held a canteen and cup, a first aid pouch, and a bayonet scabbard and bayonet. On his back he carried a field pack which held a wool blanket, poncho, shelter half with rope and pegs, mess kit, entrenching tool, emergency rations, spare socks and toilet articles. Many men also carried personal items such as stationery, photos, etc.

In addition to all of this, he had a gas mask under his arm with a carrying strap over the shoulder, extra cloth bandoliers of ammunition and hand grenades in his field jacket pockets and hanging from his jacket lapels.

> "There we were issued ammunition and prepared to go up to the front. I remember having a full field pack, a gas mask, two bandoliers and a full belt of ammunition and

then picking up a musette bag full of ammo for a BAR. I remember it must have weighed 700 pounds."

William Blasdel—K Company

On reaching Höfen, the 3rd Battalion relieved a part of CCB (Combat Command B) of the 15th Armored Infantry Battalion (AIB) of the 5th Armored Division. The Battalion was the first unit in the 99th Division to reach the front line and be in contact with the enemy. One position at a time, the new troops took over positions that had been manned by the 15th. The changeover was completed by 1700 hours.

"When we first entered the front line it was a cold, dark night. We were soaked to the bone, nearly frozen stiff, scared and confused. We were divided into groups of four and slowly led, by personnel being relieved, to various fortified foxholes and defensive positions. When we finally reached our foxhole, it was filled with four other GI's who obviously were in a great hurry to be relieved. They climbed out of the dugout enclosure and quickly disappeared into the darkness. They neither said 'hello' or 'good-by'—or gave us any clue as to the direction or distance of the enemy."

Paul Putty—I Company

The 9th Infantry Division under Major General Louis A. Craig, had captured this area in September 1944. The historic town of Monschau was taken on September 16th. On September 17th the 60th Combat Team, under Col. Jesse L. Gibney, attacked Höfen from the north and Task Force Buchanan, under Brigadier General Kenneth Buchanan, attacked Höfen and Alzen from the south. They encountered fierce opposition from strong German forces, but by the 18th had secured the area. In the I Company area there was a mute reminder of this battle in the form of two knocked out tanks, one American and one German, that apparently had destroyed each other in the fighting.

"I was duly impressed as we relieved infantry units of the 5th Armored Division. We took over their positions and were 'briefed' (10 minutes and they were long gone) by that group. When a 745 (rifleman) is briefed by another 745 it is probably mostly an exchange of ignorance. We were relieved when they said the area was 'quiet' but to me it was scary enough just to be there."

John Tabb—I Company

While that first night was a frightening experience, it served to bring the men closer to each other as it emphasized how dependent they were on each other. From their training they had gained confidence in each other, as well as in their officers. This confidence and reliance on each other was an essential part of their success in combat.

"Just a few days from England and the company is bivouacked in a pine forest near Aubel, Belgium. Duffel bags containing items that do not fit in a full field pack are stacked in a building. In the dark the Colonel told the company commanders we were to move out at 0600. We hastily rolled up our gear, donned our packs and, loaded with extra ammo, stood around in the dark trying to rest our packs against trees. Snow was silently drifting down through the branches. When the order came, there was a scramble for good seats on the trucks. After what seemed like a long trip through little villages and the city of Eupen, we stopped. Unloading, we saw a number of dugouts, low log huts and canvas covered half-tracks. We relaxed when we were told we were still a couple of miles behind the front at Kalterherberg. Pap Larson and Joe Hallman set up the kitchen and began to cook a meal. The company was digging in when I Company was told to move out. As we filed by the kitchen, we looked longingly at the chow and loaded quietly into the waiting half-tracks. Through the slits the road is only a scar of black against the snow leading up a long hill. A few buildings and a church steeple are visible in the last grey light on top of Höfen hill. 'End of the line,' the driver said.

"As the company filed by, the long line of familiar faces are quiet now and serious for a change. No one seemed to notice the weight of the weapons and the extra bandoliers and grenades. Headquarters group finally moved out past fresh, ugly black scars in the blanket of snow, by two burned out tanks and stopped in front of a house and barn that was to be the I Company CP.

"I am left standing guard. I felt the safety of my carbine and reached down into my overcoat pocket to feel the grenade. I stare into the dark, wiggle my cold toes and quietly try to stomp my feet. I wonder; Which direction is the enemy? How far? How active is this sector? Are there likely to be patrols? Shivering here in my big overcoat and helmet I stand out like a sore thumb against the snow and the white house."

Jack Randall—I Company

"I and two other members of my BAR team were taken to an out-in-the-open, uncovered, dug in position about 100 feet from the farmhouse. It faced a flat, cleared, 500 foot wide snow covered valley that ended with a tree line that began at the foot of steep, heavily wooded hills. As I replaced his machine gun with my BAR, I asked the departing gunner, 'Where are the Germans?' He replied, 'Behind those trees in front of us.' Then they departed, leaving us alone."

George Neill—L Company

The next morning, under the direction of the Battalion and Company commanders, a concerted effort was begun to improve positions, establish lanes of fire, zero in the mortars on potential targets and do the many things necessary to strengthen the integrity of their defensive lines.

I Company (Captain Charles Burgin) held the left flank facing north and east from Monschau to about the center of Höfen with the 2nd, 3rd, and 1st platoons in line from left to right. K Company (Captain Keith Fabianach until 11/23 when Captain

Horace Phillips II took command) extended this same line southeast to the edge of Höfen and curved around to the south toward Alzen. L Company (Captain Paul Price) extended the line around the Alzen area to the west. The 1st and 3rd platoons set up headquarters in West Wall pillboxes and the 2nd platoon set up defensive positions near a bridge over the Schwalm (position A on the Höfen overlay). Several days later the 2nd Platoon moved down the Schwalm to point B on the overlay. M Company (Captain Ernest Golden) positioned their heavy machine guns (water-cooled) at strategic points in the rifle company areas and their 81mm mortars behind Battalion headquarters. Since some of the 15th AIB mortar bases had been frozen in, the two groups swapped baseplates which speeded up the zeroing in process. M Company had also managed to acquire some extra 81mm mortars so that at least two mortars could fire in support of any position on the Battalion line.

Liaison was established with the 38th Cavalry Squadron on the Battalion's left flank and with the other two battalions of the 395th Infantry Regiment across a long gap on the right flank.

The total Battalion front was about 6,000 yards, which is more than four times a normal battalion front. Because of the extensive area to be covered, it was not possible to set up a solid front. Instead, a series of strong points were established along the entire perimeter. Only one platoon from L Company was able to be held out as a reserve force. Behind Höfen, as well as to the right, the nearest friendly troops that might be able to support the 3rd Battalion were miles away. They were quite isolated and alone. Butler's plan was that any attacking force would be contained between the strong points and that the reserve force would finish them off. This proved to be the exact tactics needed when the Germans did attack.

Höfen is a small rural town. It is situated on a high hill, about 1800' elevation, surrounded by a number of open fields. There are valleys, mostly wooded, on all sides which are up to 300' deep. In 1936, the Germans began construction of the West Wall, often called the Siegfried Line, which consisted of a series of concrete blockhouses or pillboxes, tank obstacles and gun emplacements from the Swiss border to the Netherlands. Höfen was an important link in this line of fortifications with one line across the southern edge of the town and another just north of town. In 1938 construction efforts were increased, but after the German offensive in 1940 they began to remove troops and weapons from these fortifications. By 1944, no troops or weapons were permanently stationed there, but in late 1944 German soldiers reoccupied some pillboxes. In 1991 these pillboxes are still evident in many places, although partially destroyed, as well as many of the "dragon's teeth" concrete anti-tank obstacles. As mentioned above, L Company used some of these pillboxes in setting up their positions.

In front of the I Company lines (north of Höfen and east of Monschau) there were pillboxes occupied by German troops as well as some that had been dynamited. The 99th Reconnaissance Platoon was stationed east of Kalterherberg, but Germans occupied pillboxes between them and Höfen. L Company faced enemy occupied pillboxes across the Fuhrstbach valley.

"We were in OP-1, the extreme left flank of the 99th Division. Our gun position was in the basement with a window looking out on a valley with a pillbox-studded hill on the other side. These were German pillboxes with real live enemy soldiers inside. To our left was Monschau, close enough we could look down on their streets. A squad of I Company riflemen occupied the first floor while an artillery observer had the attic."

Homer Kissinger—M Company

About 50 or 60 yards in front of I Company was an unoccupied pillbox. It had a wide anti-personnel minefield in front of it. A couple of cooks walked up from Kalterherberg to look at "the front line." While the front line may be well defined in the movies, it is not well defined in actual combat. These two cooks walked out through the minefield and past the pillbox before they realized it was much too quiet and there must be something wrong. They turned around and walked back through the minefield to return to Kalterherberg. When they got back to I

OP-1 as seen from the rear. Sketch made by James Crewdson of M Company. Note shell hole in roof at right and basement wall knocked out to afford entrance from the rear so as not to be exposed to the enemy.

Company, a GI grabbed them and bawled them out for what they had done. He got through and a sergeant bawled them out and then Capt. Burgin showed up and he bawled them out. At this time Col. Butler showed up and he bawled them out. Quite frankly, when the GI told them what they had done, nobody really needed to bawl them out. The day before, this minefield had killed an engineer company commander, his second in command and his first sergeant. They had all been on their hands and knees probing for mines. The Captain and the Lieutenant had both missed a mine, but the sergeant following them hit the mine. When it exploded it blew his arm off and he fell forward and hit another mine. This mine exploded and killed all three men. This is the minefield these two cooks had walked through both ways.

Höfen is located at more than 50 degrees north latitude, which is farther north than Winnipeg, Manitoba. This far north, night comes early in the wintertime and the nights are long. Snow, sleet and cold weather are the norm. The men manned their positions around the clock, but at night more positions had to be manned because of the poor visibility. After dark any moving object was considered enemy so the nighttime outposts had to be in place by 1600 p.m. and the men could not leave them until after 0900 a.m. This made for many long, lonely nights.

> "I was kind of surprised at how early it became dark and how long it stayed dark in the mornings. That put a lot of stress on the men who were there. We were required to remain quiet all during those hours 'cause German patrols were constantly coming into the area to try to plot our positions."
>
> William Blasdel—K Company

"Soon after we arrived, Col. Butler came up and told us just where to dig our hole in the ground. We did it and it was the most magical hole a person could imagine. It was on the north side of a hill overlooking a fork in two very small roads. We built a large sleeping room, large enough for six men, completely inside the hill and a firing room with a roof outside the hill. It was perfectly placed and when we got through with it, it was everything a person with normal intelligence would want. It had everything except running water and a heated living room. We called it 'Hubert.'"

John Martin—K Company

All along the line the men continued to improve their positions. The improvements were limited only by their imaginations. Logs were put over the top of some existing positions and covered with earth. New positions were dug. Sound powered telephones were run to every location so that all would be in communication with each other. Some of the men even brought rugs and pieces of furniture from the houses in the village to make themselves more comfortable. In a few places stoves were installed, but this was not a general practice as the smoke would give locations away.

> "The 1st Platoon had a machine gun section in the center of the Battalion, within the K Company section. As time went on we improved our position by adding logs, brush and sand bags to our dugout. We put limbs with leaves on 'em across paths of possible approach to give us warning. We made foxholes for the ammo bearers on each side of the heavy machine guns. Sound powered phones were installed in all positions and we had a SCR-300 radio to keep us in contact with Battalion Headquarters. To our front, down a hill, were fences and hedgerows running nearly parallel to our lines. We pulled all tracer ammunition from the machine gun belts and replaced them with ball ammunition to avoid giving our positions away. We were ready."

William Bartow—M Company

Aggressive patrolling was started at once and various sized patrols went out daily to reconnoiter enemy positions, capture prisoners and gain intelligence information about enemy actions and intentions. The Germans reciprocated and sent patrols into Höfen regularly to probe defensive positions and take prisoners if possible. There was sporadic artillery and mortar fire from both sides.

As early as November 11th the Battalion suffered its first battle death when an artillery round killed PFC Samuel P. Gibney from L Company, a runner at Battalion Headquarters. He was the first fatality the 99th Division suffered in combat. This same day the Battalion captured the first German prisoners the division had taken.

Captain Burgin of I Company led one combat patrol that had unexpected results. The purpose of the patrol was to get some prisoners for intelligence purposes. The patrol went out some distance and encountered a group of Germans holed up in a log bunker. Small arms fire did not drive them out, but one of the men dropped a white phosphorus grenade down the chimney and that brought them out on the run. Several of the enemy were killed and some taken prisoner. By radio, Capt. Burgin informed Col. Butler of the success of the patrol and was ordered to return at once. Burgin informed him that there would be a slight delay, but would not explain further. After the patrol returned safely, the full story came out. It seems that one of the Germans had a machine pistol and two members of the patrol got into a fist fight as they both wanted the gun as a souvenir.

A large three story building (OP-6) right on the front line in the I Company area was an important part of the defense. It was the highest building around and, with a good view looking north, was the perfect position for artillery and mortar observer teams. Shortly after the Battalion occupied Höfen, Maj. Gen. Walter E. Lauer, Commanding General of the 99th Division, and some of his staff visited the area to check on the Battalion's progress in establishing defensive positions. Gen. Lauer called for his binoculars and walked up to a window to scan the enemy area from the top floor of OP-6. One of the men told the General that the hole in the window he was looking through had been made the day before when a German sniper killed a man looking out that same window. The General promptly decided that he had seen enough and he and his staff left the area. It was his only visit.

"The river canyon below us (OP-1) had been fog-filled until quite late, but when it cleared out, it did so in just a few minutes, exposing a crew of Germans industriously hand pulling one of their 'Baby 88's'—the little high velocity 75 with the big muzzle-brake—along the road below us. The German gun crew by now were making strenuous efforts to heave their gun off the road, into the woods out of sight. The forward observer called for fire and found his battery was out of action, moving to a new location.

"His only alternative was the 81mm mortars in Höfen. They fired one WP round and the FO adjusted their fire. In another half minute four rounds came in smack on target, destroying the gun and most of the crew. It was fantastic shooting but, for the FO's sake, we let on that it was only commonplace mortar work."

James Crewdson—M Company

Work continued on improving positions. Booby traps were put in likely avenues of approach, as were trip flares. These were designed to be set off by trip wires or pull wires in the positions. Because of the ingenuity the men used in placing these booby traps, several men, including the Battalion Commander, inadvertently tripped them and were fortunate to escape serious injury. Not all of those who set off these traps were that fortunate and several men were injured. Mine fields were put in place and barbed wire entanglements set up.

"We were not particularly well equipped for winter warfare and lost a lot of people to frostbite and trenchfoot. I found a lady's fur neckpiece, cut it up and placed it in the bottom of a pair of galoshes. I took my shoes off and never wore them again until we pulled back from Höfen in February. I never had any foot trouble at all."

Robert Parks—K Company

November 23rd was Thanksgiving Day. The cooks sent the men on the line a typical Thanksgiving meal of turkey, dressing, cranberries and sweet potatoes. To this many of the men added their own touches. One man made apple sauce with apples from a local orchard. Several cows had been killed and butchered so a number of the men had some beef. Some had found wine in the houses and added this to the feast. The first squad, third platoon of I Company even had a wind-up Victrola and some records and listened to the Hermann Goering Symphony Orchestra as they ate. It is natural that all soldiers become good "scroungers" and this group of men had a table set with a linen tablecloth and napkins, crystal glasses and fine china dishes. When the meal was over, four men picked up the four corners of the tablecloth and threw the entire thing out the window—glasses, linen, plates and all. It was a memorable meal.

> "Once we drank toasts from very expensive crystal glasses and then threw them into the fireplace just like they do in the movies."
>
> John Tabb—I Company

On November 25th Lt. Robert P. Rohrs led a patrol of the 1st platoon of L Company southeast from Alzen up the Fuhrstbach valley in an attempt to capture some prisoners from the pillboxes they occupied. They reached the designated pillbox, but were unable to secure any prisoners and returned to the L Company area without suffering any casualties. The men on this patrol were awarded the first Combat Infantry Badges in the 3rd Battalion. Later all of the men in the Battalion received this same award.

> "Next morning the Lieutenant called me to go outside and see the dead German soldier lying along the road. I mentioned to him that it was the first time I had ever seen a dead human being, not even at a funeral."
>
> Angelo Vicari—K Company

Each day these men were becoming more hardened as combat soldiers. They had seen friends wounded and killed. They were learning the hard way that their ingrained sense of "fair play" no longer was appropriate behavior. They were in hostile territory where people were trying to kill them and their only hope for survival was their reliance on each other. The rules they had grown up with did not apply here. Behavior that would not be acceptable in a peaceful situation became the norm out of necessity.

> "In our first early days up on the front we were in an old house—there were two or three of us—and we had a sound powered telephone. We were awake, someone was on guard, when we saw the telephone moving toward the wall. We were sure there were German soldiers outside trying to pull our phone out or cut the lines. I'm not sure how many holes in the wall there were, but I feel confident there were some bullets fired. On investigation, however, it turned out to be a cow. A loose cow had gotten its legs tangled up in our phone wire and pulled the phone all the way across the floor. Quite an introduction to the front lines!"
>
> Thornton Piersall—I Company

There were three houses across from the I Company defensive line. Because they were on the enemy side of the road and could be used for cover and concealment by approaching enemy troops, Col. Butler sent down word that he wanted those houses burned and the area cleared. The men set to with a will and with the aid of various combustibles, soon had the houses burned to the ground.

During this time, word came down from higher headquarters to be on the lookout for a civilian coming into the Battalion lines. No explanation was given, but the men were told that he would be wearing a black and white checkered scarf, had gold teeth and that when challenged by a sentry he would reply, "My name is Victor." If and when he showed up he was to be sent back to headquarters as quickly as possible. No word was ever received as to whether or not he ever showed up.

> "We were on patrol one night. The snow was about eight inches deep with about an inch and a half crust. There wasn't a breath of air stirring and a perfect moonlit night.

Oh, it was beautiful; just like a spotlight. Here we were on patrol and every step you took could be heard for 200 yards. On this patrol we had to step in the same footprints as the guy in front of us or we would have sounded like a herd of cattle. There was only one guy making noise and that was the guy in the lead. It was all hair-raising, but that was the most hair-raising night. I guess some people wonder why I got grey prematurely. That night did some of it, right there."

William Blasdel—K Company

Near the end of November the men of the Battalion had another strange experience. A German civilian, an older man, appeared at the I Company line. He made it known that he had been the schoolmaster in Höfen and said he wanted to get records from the school so they would not be destroyed or lost. With approval of the Battalion Commander, this man was blindfolded and led to the school building across the street from the church. When he reached the school, the blindfold was removed and he was allowed to take several boxes of records that had been shoved in a corner. The blindfold was replaced and with his boxes in hand he was led back to the line where he had first appeared and was released.

With no plumbing available, army troops make their own sanitary facilities by digging a long, narrow trench that a man would straddle when answering the call of nature. Cpl. Harvey Lipshitz, a wire man in Headquarters Company, was in position over the straddle trench when a German mortar round landed and exploded nearby. Fortunately, a pile of lumber took most of the impact but the concussion was sizable and Lipshitz rushed for the HQ building, holding his trousers at half-mast with one hand and dragging his M-1 by the barrel in the other hand. He stumbled into the message center and cried out, "I'm blind. I'm blind!" One of the men in the room looked at him and replied, "Open your eyes, you damn fool." He did and said, "By God. I can see better now."

He had been so frightened by the explosion so near him, he had instinctively closed his eyes and forgot to open them. This exchange and his appearance were the occasion for a lot of laughter among those present. However, Lipshitz complained about a severe pain in his chest although there was no obvious wound. A medic had him strip to the waist and on closer examination found a small bluish puncture wound under his left armpit. Knowing this could be very serious, the medic had him evacuated and he never returned to the Battalion.

"We were lucky if any one of us got more than two hours sleep any one of the 40 plus nights we were there. One day a fellow was brought to me complaining of difficulty in breathing. I walked him back to the Medical Aid station in the late afternoon. Sitting in an old chair, he stopped breathing altogether. I gave him artificial respiration for quite a while until he came around. (Mouth to mouth resuscitation was unheard of then.) He received a sedative to induce sleep; and he did—for three days!"

Angelo Vicari—K Company

Army regulations specify that the troop be paid the first of every month, so on December 1st the Paymaster arrived with his records. The procedure was less formal than garrison paydays in that the men reported to the Paymaster as they were able to be relieved, instead of the formal alphabetically, by rank, manner used in camp. This first payday in Germany the men were paid in foreign currency. It was a unique experience for these men as there was no place to spend their money and the only value it had was to pay off debts or use for gambling. No one had a clear concept of the value of this foreign currency and most of the gambling just went by the number of bills they had at hand. This was another lesson learned. In combat situations money has no value.

About December 14th Col. Butler had a strong premonition, or as he put it, a "voice" spoke to him and told him to move the Battalion Headquarters at once. This feeling was so real that he told Capt. Williams, Headquarters Company commander, to move to some other building at once. This proved fortuitous as the initial German artillery barrage on the morning of the 16th hit the original building, set it afire and it burned to the ground. This was the first of several occasions in which such a premonition served Col. Butler well.

On December 15th some "quad 50's" were moved up from Kalterherberg to the Höfen area. These units are four .50 caliber machine guns mounted on a half-track that fire in sequence from a single trigger and are designed as anti-aircraft weapons. They were support weapons for the anticipated reaction by the enemy to the attack toward the Roer River dams.

CHAPTER 4

The Battle of the Bulge

For 450 miles the Allied forces had been successful in driving back the German troops. The Germans were desperately trying to stop this assault before they were defeated. They were considering a counteroffensive to regain the initiative and in September it seemed to them that circumstances might be favorable for an attack. Their fronts in Italy and Russia were fairly well stabilized. The American, British and French forces were halted in front of the West Wall, their supply lines stretched to the limit. The port of Antwerp was still not available to the Allies. The German supply lines had shortened considerably and they had a supportive civilian population.

The German high command envisioned an attack to encircle the Allied forces east of the Meuse River, the so-called "small solution." However, Hitler overruled his advisors and decreed the "large solution," which was to attack westward to the Meuse and then turn northward through Liege to the English Channel which would divide the Allied forces and either delay their attack significantly or collapse it entirely. Many divisions would be trapped and with Germans on the Channel coast there would be a chance to negotiate from strength. On October 8, 1944, Hitler issued his orders and the planning began. Initial plans were for the 5th, 6th, 7th Panzer Armies to attack through the thinly held Ardennes sector, block the southern and northern shoulders with infantry and then turn the panzers loose to cross the Meuse and turn north to Antwerp. They planned to attack on an 89 mile wide front.

The Ardennes area of Belgium is heavily wooded, very hilly with many rivers and streams and a very limited road network. It is not terrain well suited for an attack. However, the Germans had successfully attacked through this area in 1940, so they knew the area well and were counting on speed and surprise to gain their objectives.

The Allied forces had halted their drive largely due to a lack of supplies and were in a static situation. The decision had been made that the next major attack would be through the Netherlands under General Montgomery and a major buildup of supplies was being made in that area. The Ardennes area was being held by a very thin line of troops in a defensive posture.

On December 13th the 395th Regimental Combat Team (RCT), consisting of the 1st and 2nd Battalions and the 2nd Battalion of the 393rd Regiment, joined with the 2nd Infantry Division in launching an attack from Krinkelt-Rocherath northwest in an effort to secure the Roer River dams. Their plan was to cross the German border at the village of Wahlerscheid, several miles southeast of Höfen. This same day Company A of the 612th Tank Destroyer Battalion under Capt. William S. Groff moved their twelve three-inch towed guns into Höfen and prepared to fire on the village of Rohren in support of this attack.

Numerous fragmentary reports of German troop movements had been received from front line troops, through intelligence sources and from captured PW's, but no one from local area commanders up through SHAEF headquarters in Paris anticipated anything like the attack that came. First Army G-2 (Intelligence) estimate dated 10 December 1944 stated, "It is plain the enemy's strategy in defense of the Reich is based on the exhaustion of our offensive to be followed by an all-out counteroffensive counterattack with armor between the Roer (River) and the Erft (Canal) supported by every weapon he can bring up." Estimated German strength against the First Army (US) at this time was 14 divisions and one armored brigade, about

100,000 combat troops and 500 tanks. This estimate proved to be woefully low.

The I Company—395th Infantry morning report (Höfen) for 15 December 1944 reads, "Company still in defensive position. Weather cold. Morale good."

At 0525 on the morning of December 16, 1944, the skies seemed to open up as German artillery rained in on Höfen in one of the heaviest barrages of the war. The very earth seemed to break open. Artillery and mortar shells fell with a roar accompanied by the ear-splitting, almost heart-stopping, scream of Nebelwerfer rockets. The latter were aptly named "screaming meemies" by the defenders and were rockets nine or more inches in diameter, about four feet long. They would explode on contact with little shrapnel, but tremendous concussion. "You could bury a jeep in the hole one of those things would make in that frozen ground," said William Bartow.

"I remember being in my foxhole and here came the screaming meemies. I guess you know how they sounded. I guess I pushed the ground in my foxhole down two feet."

Donald Gangway—I Company

"The artillery shelling we received on the morning of December 16 was the most horrifying experience I have ever had. I had not seen anything previously like it nor did I ever suffer through another as bad."

Robert Parks—K Company

Rubble filled the streets, buildings began to burn and shell holes were everywhere. The building that had been the Battalion CP two days ago burned to the ground. Telephone lines were severed and even radio communications were interrupted. This rain of fire and destruction went on for 20 minutes, but it seemed much longer to the defenders. Because they had built their positions well, there were few actual casualties in the 3rd Battalion.

"At the time of the bombardment, three men were sleeping in a slit trench below my foxhole. A shell hit and a splinter struck between two of the three men and killed the man in the middle. The shrapnel must have hit a rock because it hit him from underneath."

George Prager—L Company

When this horrendous barrage stopped, the Germans turned on anti-aircraft searchlights to shine against the low hanging clouds to provide artificial moonlight for their troops. Of course this worked to the advantage of the defenders as well and gave them almost 200 yard vision. It was a good thing that the men on the line reported this advantage as the artillery forward observers got a fix on the location of these searchlights and requested permission to fire on them. In view of the reports he was getting from his front line, Col. Butler denied them permission to knock out the searchlights.

The 2nd and 3rd companies of the 751st Volksgrenadier Regiment and the 1st Company of the 753rd Volksgrenadier Regiment attacked at five different points, but their main efforts were on the Battalion's extreme left flank near Monschau (I Company) and on the right flank at the boundary between I and K Companies. The defenders held their fire as the Germans advanced through the haze in their characteristic slow, plodding walk. When the enemy was almost on top of the American positions, the men of the Battalion opened up with a withering fire from every available weapon: rifles, automatic rifles, machine guns and mortars. So devastating was this fire that in at least three instances dying Germans toppled into the defender's foxhole.

"I know that what I have to say will not agree 100 percent with what others have to say. Oftentimes in the infantry, on the ground, sometimes at night and even in the daytime, individuals are not aware of what's taking place much beyond the fingertips of the arm extended."

Richard Mills—I Company

A fact of life in combat is that each man has a very limited knowledge of what is truly happening. He is very familiar with his position, the men he is with and a small area around him. Beyond this small area he has no idea at all as to what is taking place. Each unit commander has a wider area of knowledge based on his responsibilities, but even the Battalion Commander is limited in what he knows of the overall situation. Because of this, it is absolutely essential for success in combat that each man rely on his buddy and follow the orders he is given.

"There was a simple dignity about Col. Butler that commanded the respect of every GI in the Battalion. His junior officers swore by him. When he spoke, it was with friendly authority, never as issuing a cold military order. That didn't mean he was overly friendly, or gushy—he wasn't. He was solid—that was the word."

William Huffman—I Company

"Col. Butler was tough but not chicken. He would improvise and change weapons and unit combinations to suit the cause, as well as tactics. Some leaders are dictatorial, aloof and uncaring. Some rule by intimidation, domination or manipulation or by all, which shows flawed leadership. Col. Butler was not a flawed leader. He was, I believe after 50 years, the best battalion commander in the army."

William Blasdel—K Company

Since all communications had been lost, the men in each position felt that they were the only ones left alive and were determined to fight to the death if necessary. This feeling is superbly captured in a poem written by one of those gallant defenders.

Danube Blue

Von Rundstedt thought he found the spot
When he picked Höfen town
To fling his grenadiers and such,
He needed that high ground.

Events have proved that he snafued
When he hit Butler's men,
He really thought these "green recruits"
Couldn't take it on the chin.

Lord! It was a sight that day
The stuff they threw at us,
Freight trains, stove pipes and kitchen sinks,
I never heard such a fuss.

I looked at Stone; Stone looked at me.
I said, "Looks like we're stuck."
Ole Stone replied quite gloomily,
"Yeh, Biv. I think we're fucked."

Uncle John was silent,
But I knew there'd be some fun
Should a Kraut find himself
In the sights of John's M-1.

When the shelling finally lifted
I was sure as I could be,
There's no one left on Höfen hill
'Cept John and Stone and me.

Just then a mortar coughed
It was just around the pike,
I knew besides the three of us
There was someone left at Mike.

Item started firing,
Right then I nudged ole Stone,
It was just as clear as it could be
We three were not alone.

King and Love cracked down on them
The Heinies sure played hell,
When they tried to storm that Höfen hill
Five thousand Heinies fell!

The newsboys simply stated
"Monschau sector did not crack,"
But Butler's boys knew goddam well
Who kicked those bastards back.

When I get back to Georgia
And folks say, "Where were you?"
I'll point down to my combat badge
And say, "Right there with DANUBE BLUE."

T/5 Isaac E. Bivings, Jr. 12/21/44

"DANUBE BLUE" was written by an infantry soldier, T/5 Isaac E. Bivings, Jr., 34574685 on December 21, 1944. It tells of his feelings and that of his two foxhole buddies, John T. Mattix and Willie T. Stone, both over 40 years old, at the time the Germans attacked the American lines south of Monschau in the little town of Höfen. For the defense of this town, which is recorded in depth of almost every history of the Battle of the Bulge, President Roosevelt awarded the Battalion with the Distinguished Unit Badge, and every soldier was awarded the Bronze Star by special order of the War Department. To assist in understanding this poetic account of this soldier's experience, Danube Blue was the code name of the 3rd Battalion—395th Infantry Regiment, 99th Division. The references to Item, Love, King and Mike are the rifle and heavy weapons companies of the Battalion. Every soldier who participated in the defense of the Ardennes sector had similar or worse experiences and would understand completely and should have a copy of this most unusual piece of GI literature.

James W. Williams
Hq Co—3rd Bn—395th Inf., CO

"If a man had guts, and if he could shoot, he was a good foxhole buddy. In Höfen we all lived alike—and we all died alike. Brains didn't make your foxhole or your cellar any warmer. Brains didn't keep your feet from freezing if you didn't rub them every chance you got. And brains didn't get you any special ride to the Graves Registration folks when you died. The brilliant and the slow-witted looked the same lying in a jeep trailer or under the tarp of a 6 x 6 truck."

William Huffman—I Company

By and large, the Germans did not respect the Geneva Convention as it applies to medical personnel. The Battalion Surgeon, Capt. Herbert Orr, MD, maintained a battalion first aid station as part of Battalion HQ. One of his medical corpsmen was attached to each platoon. These "medics" carried only a medical kit, no weapons and wore helmets with a large red cross on a white field painted on their helmets, front and back and on each side. They were easily identified as medical personnel from a great distance. In spite of this, many were deliberately fired on by the enemy which resulted in a number of them being killed or wounded.

"Early in the morning of December 16 I was called to aid a man who had been hit. Grabbing my bag and wearing my helmet (now with red crosses we painted ourselves) I ran out to find our men placed along a hedgerow in a draw. Snow had fallen during the night, an inch or so—enough to blanket the ground white. Dunkin was laying face down, part way down the hill. I climbed over the fence and walked down there. There was absolutely no cover except for a tree stump. I hit the ground when I realized the enemy was at the bottom of the hill. At this moment a German opened fire with his machine pistol, sweeping the ground near me. I could see the snow being kicked up by the bullets coming closer and closer to me. Evidently I was the target! Within a matter of seconds, I was hit. The force of the bullet entering my right side rolled me over to the left, my arms and feet flying into the air."

Angelo Vicari—K Company

Hit in the lower back, Vicari suffered temporary paralysis of his legs, but after more than four months in hospitals in France and England, was restored to health. Dunkin also recovered from his wounds.

Contrary to the tactics taught on employment of mortars in a draw, Lt. Arthur Decker, Reconnaissance and Executive Officer of M Company, had placed his 81mm mortars just below the crest of a hill rather than at the bottom of the hill which is standard practice. They also placed some empty ammunition boxes and other gear at the bottom of the hill to make it appear that the guns were there. This served them very well as much of the original heavy barrage was directed at the bottom of the hill and would have wiped them out. As it was, they were practically unaffected and were able to fire at once. Since they were without communications, the mortarmen took it on their own initiative to fire in support of their comrades and laid down a withering wall of fire in front of the rifle companies. Since they had arrived in Höfen, Howard Denhard, platoon sergeant, had reported 3 rounds expended for each round they actually fired and in this way was able to build up his supply beyond the prescribed inventory. The combination of extra mortars and extra available ammunition allowed them to fire without let-up. It was not until about 0650, almost an hour after the attack began, that radio communication was established with supporting artillery, the 196th Field Artillery Battalion, and they could add their support to the battle.

"On December 15th I had been temporarily assigned as liaison officer with the 38th Cavalry Squadron in Monschau. In the pre-dawn of the 16th, the screaming meemies hit us like they did everyone else. This was closely followed by artillery, especially near the Roer River where it turned eastward. This was very near the 38th Cavalry and the 3rd Battalion boundary. There were reports of a heavy penetration on the north flank of the 38th. I had to get this information to the 3rd Battalion. My driver had to change two wheels on the jeep as shrapnel had flattened them. Dodging artillery, we headed for Höfen."

James Hare—I Company

To add to the Battalion's problems, the breakdown of communications led V Corps headquarters in Eupen to believe that the enemy had been successful in capturing Höfen and the corps artillery began to shell the area with 155mm guns. This continued until Col. Butler was able to map some of the impacts and gathered some shell fragments which he sent back by messenger. When V. Corps received his report and the fragments, this artillery was ordered to stop shelling the Höfen area. On page 265 of his book, "Hitler's Last Offensive," Peter Elstob refers to the Americans "giving up Höfen in favor of a better position a couple of miles west." The fact is that the 3rd Battalion never gave up Höfen.

Initially the fighting was fierce on the left flank, but the line held. It was not without cost, however, as Lt. Ernest J. Chiodi of I Company was killed.

The attack at the boundary between I and K Companies raged on and 30 or more Germans succeeded in penetrating the line and got into houses in Höfen. S/Sgt. Robert L. "Bud" Craft had half of his squad from the first platoon of I Company in a house with a barn attached. They had been here since they first reached Höfen on November 9th and had built up quite a large supply of ammunition (rifle and machine gun rounds, grenades and bazooka rounds) which they stored in the barn. The barn had a thatched roof, like many of the buildings, which had been set afire by the German artillery. When the flames began to get near the stockpile of ammunition, they felt it was no longer safe to stay in their positions. Craft and one of his men, Robert E. Crist, dove out a back window only to discover about a platoon of enemy soldiers aiming at them from across the street. Realizing they had no other options, the two men surrendered to the Germans. There were a number of German wounded laying in the intersection to the south and machine guns from the 612th TD Battalion were firing down this street. A German non-com tried to tell Craft and Crist to go into the intersection to retrieve these wounded men. Both of the Americans pretended they could not understand what they were being told to do. As a German officer called the non-com over to ask him something, Craft told Crist to get ready to run, as he felt they had a better chance running from the Germans than they did in going out into that intersection. Crist said "What?" so loudly that the Germans realized something was afoot. About this time the non-com realized that Craft had hand grenades hanging from his lapels and came over and snatched them off. As he turned to throw the grenades down a hole, Craft pushed Crist through the door of the house, grabbed a burp gun and both men ran through the house and leaped out a back window. They were now exposed to machine gun fire from the TD men, but fortunately the machine gun jammed. Craft yelled to identify himself and the machine gun ceased firing at them.

Craft then got several men to return with them to their original position and they succeeded in capturing their erstwhile captors. However, the other four men from Craft's squad in their house had been captured during the fight and Ralph M. Barnes, George W. Barr, Martin S. Belefant, and Edward W. Broadbent were in German POW camps until they were liberated by American troops in April 1945.

Barnes was wounded when he was taken prisoner, but did receive attention from the German medics. Belefant had a special problem in that he was Jewish and the Germans treated Jewish POW's worse than their standard harsh treatment of all POW's. Belefant's comments about his experiences are very pertinent.

"Apart from the systematic starvation of the POW's—two slices of ersatz bread and a bowl of watery soup each day—another aspect of captivity made me even more miserable than normally miserable. I was a Jew. In the first minutes of my capture I was painfully aware that the U.S. Army had caused me a problem by putting an 'H' on my dog tags. I disposed of the dog tags quickly, deciding I was in a lose-lose position with or without dog tags. In two different camps I was interrogated and asked my religion, once by a bogus 'Swiss Red Cross' representative. Seeing no value in being a dead hero, I answered 'Protestant.' As a child I was sometimes embarrassed by my name because it wasn't simple like 'Cohen' or 'Pincus,' but when the Germans segregated all American POW's with Jewish-sounding names for 'special treatment', I became very thankful for my unusual name.

"A unique experience of all POW's is being shot at by friend and foe alike. In addition to being shot at by the Germans, I know what it's like to be bombed by the RAF (Limburg Stalag), machine gunned by Americans (Höfen), shelled by Russians (Lukenwalde Stalag) and strafed by the RAF (en route).

"I learned to love Great Britain, bagpipes and tea while a POW. A large group of Americans, including me, had just arrived in Luckenwalde after several hours of being transported in locked boxcars with only a can in the corner as the sanitary facility, occasionally attacked by Allied aircraft. As we dragged ourselves into the camp, a few British POW's welcomed us with a bagpipe serenade as they ladled out of GI cans the most delicious hot tea I have ever tasted."

"At one point behind enemy lines I was being taken from one place to another along a road with heavy traffic going both ways. My guard was a soldier even younger than I. Using the universal thumbs up signal at a passing truck, I was surprised to see the truck stop. I hopped aboard leaving my guard standing there encumbered by his rifle. I instinctively reached down and he handed me his rifle so he could climb aboard. The wheels in my mind spun furiously. I decided that an escape attempt at that point was futile and handed him back his rifle. I can still hear his sheepish, 'Danke Schein.' "

Martin Belefant—I Company

By 0745 the enemy had been pretty well driven back except for a number of them who had holed up in one of the houses, which was quickly surrounded. Although armed with automatic weapons, rocket launchers and rifles, the Germans were no match for the fire from rifles, machine guns and 3" rounds loosed at them by the men of I and K Companies and the 612th TD Battalion. Those Germans still alive were soon captured and sent back to PW camps. The initial attack had been defeated and the front line completely restored.

From about 1028 to 1033, a German artillery barrage again hit Höfen, but was not followed up by troops. At 1235 there was a determined attack on the right flank of K Company, but it was successfully beaten off. Sporadic artillery fire continued to come in, but there were no further attacks on the 16th.

The results of the day's fighting were amazing. The 3rd Battalion had taken 19 prisoners and estimates of German dead ranged up to 200. No count of German wounded was possible, but at least 20 percent of the attackers were lost to the 326th Volksgrenadier Division. In contrast, the Battalion casualties were amazingly light: 4 killed, 7 wounded and 4 men missing. From the German prisoners it was learned that their mission was to take Höfen "at all costs."

The defenders remained on alert for another attack as they replaced ammunition and supplies and repaired damage to their positions.

"The first morning of the Bulge fighting found me and two comrades in our hole in Höfen. We had downed a number of Germans early on but not before they had completely demolished a BAR I had my hand on. A burp gun volley in our faces shot the stock off the BAR and severed my jacket sleeve. Sand blew in my face and I had to be reassured by another soldier that my head was still attached. When daylight finally came, we three decided to try to make it to the platoon CP, probably about 50 to 100 yards away. We actually wondered if we were the only ones still alive. As one of my comrades climbed out of the hole, a wounded German soldier tried to raise his rifle and, at a distance of only about 20 feet, my comrade emptied his M-1 and never touched the German. The thought actually crossed my mind that he was firing blanks. I'll wager no soldier ever fired eight times at that distance and never touched the enemy. The German was summarily dispatched, but the incident still makes me wonder about the effectiveness of some soldiers at the killing game."

Robert Parks—K Company

The 2nd Division and the 395th RCT troops attacking through Wahlerscheid were also hit with a major attack on the 16th. At first they thought it was a localized counterattack, but as it progressed realized that it was much more than a local situation. They began to withdraw toward Rocherath and eventually fought their way to a defensive line on the Elsenborn Ridge, suffering many casualties from enemy action and the bitter winter weather. This left the rolling wooded area southeast of Höfen (right flank of the 3rd Battalion) wide open to the enemy and gave him easy access to the Schwalm Creek and Perlbach River valleys south of Höfen. Now the Battalion was truly cut off and on their own.

On December 16, General Kaschner, commander of the 326th Volksgrenadier Division, had had some success in breaking through north of Monschau while being decisively defeated at Höfen. The 38th Squadron of the 102nd Cavalry Group had been able to restore their lines only after a bitter battle. On the 17th Kaschner sent his 751st Regiment north of Monschau, determined to break through.

The town of Monschau, a favorite destination of pre-war honeymooners, had been spared from German artillery fire on direct orders from Field Marshal Model. The town itself had no real military value. It is located at the bottom of a deep, very narrow valley beside the Roer River. It is surrounded by sheer bluffs and high hills on all sides. The local residents had remained in their town.

The attack on the 17th resulted in a breakthrough by numerous German troops who penetrated a considerable distance. The 38th called for help and some elements of the 47th Infantry Regiment of the 9th Division came to their aid and by late on the 17th the original lines had been restored.

When word of this attack reached the 3rd Battalion, it only added to the concerns of Col. Butler and his staff. In part his report to the 395th Regimental Headquarters read as follows:

"Information at this time was received that paratroopers had been dropped behind our lines. That two companies of infantry had penetrated the unit on our left flank until they were in position to our rear and that heavy fighting was going on to the south (right flank of the Battalion) and on the right flank of the 99th Infantry Division. No friendly troops were in the area to back up the 3rd Battalion in case of penetration. (The 47th Infantry did not arrive until the next day.) The mission of the 3rd Battalion is to hold Höfen, Germany."

The paratroopers referred to in Col. Butler's report were part of an operation that was ill-starred from the start. The German command's intent was to drop a number of paratroopers well behind American lines on the night of the 15th of December. They were to seize bridges and road intersections and hold them until the attacking troops reached them. The troopers themselves were ill-trained and were not told what their mission entailed until they were boarding their Ju-52 aircraft. On the 15th trucks did not show up to get them to the airfield so they did not leave until the night of the 16th. Their commander, Colonel von der Heydte, was the only experienced paratrooper with combat experience. The pilot of the lead plane was the only pilot who had flown this type of mission before. To help keep their formation they flew with their navigation lights on which made them targets for anti-aircraft fire. Because of all this confusion, troopers and supplies were dropped all the way from the Rhine River to the intended drop area near Eupen, Belgium. Some were dropped as far away as Aachen. Some of their supply chutes dropped in the Höfen area. Only about 20 men showed up to meet von der Heydte at the designated rendezvous south of Eupen, although others straggled in later. Supplies for this group were as dispersed as the men and, although von der Heydte had a radio, it had been damaged in the drop so he had no way to communicate with his headquarters. His request for carrier pigeons had been ridiculed and rejected. For several days they moved around the area and gathered a lot of information but had no way to pass it on. Finally, realizing his mission was a failure, von der Heydte told his men to break up into groups of two or three men and try to infiltrate through the American lines and return to Germany.

Injured himself, sick and hungry, Col. von der Heydte surrendered to American forces in Monschau on December 22nd.

Only on the 17th did the Allied high command realize the extent of the German attack. Initially it was seen to be a local counterattack against the 2nd and 99th Divisions in their attack toward the Roer River dams, not the all-out offensive it really was. Also, only now was the situation of the 3rd Battalion fully appreciated. To the southeast of Höfen (the Battalion's right flank) there was a gap of almost 10 miles between them and the rest of the 99th. Any support to their rear was non-existent as the lead elements of the 9th Division did not reach Eupen until the 17th. In spite of the situation they were in, the men of the 3rd Battalion from Col. Butler down were determined to fulfill their mission, which was to hold Höfen.

After days of overcast weather, the skies cleared somewhat on the 17th and German planes strafed the area all day. Fortunately this was more nerve-wracking than lethal, as the only casualty was 1st Lt. Ralph Mizrahi who was hit by a single round and had to be evacuated. The men worked all day at improving their positions, disposing of the dead and bringing up ammunition and supplies. There were numerous dogfights in the sky as the American planes also took advantage of the weather to attack the enemy. German bombers hit the area north of Monschau as well as the 3rd Battalion area. One of these bombers was shot down and crashed near Rohren in a spectacular ball of flame.

Later in the day Col. Butler was informed that his battalion had been attached to the 47th Infantry Regiment, Col. George W. Smythe commanding, of the 9th Infantry Division. Company A of the 612th TD Battalion was attached to the 3rd Battalion as were the men of the 99th Reconnaissance Troop, who remained in their positions south of Kalterherberg. Capt. Golden was transferred to Battalion Headquarters as S-3 and 1st Lt. Arthur Decker took command of M Company.

This was the day that members of Kampfgruppe Peiper executed a number of men from Battery B, 285th Field Artillery Observation Battalion who had surrendered to the Germans at Baugnez, Belgium, just outside of Malmedy. The word of this slaughter swiftly became known to all front line troops and for some time German soldiers had great difficulty in surrendering. German troops in the Höfen area were using the Red Cross flag to protect themselves as they brought up guns and ammunition, but their perfidy was soon discovered and this flag no longer protected them.

During the hours of darkness several flares were dropped from German planes. Later the enemy ground troops fired an extreme number of flares, mostly white, perhaps presaging their renewed attack the next day.

"During a lull in the action about the second or third day of Bulge fighting I was sent with another soldier to investigate something, memory of which escapes me, in front of our lines. When we were about 100 to 150 yards in front of the lines a German artillery shell, probably an 88, landed close enough to knock us down. My buddy called out that he was hit bad in his right leg. I picked him up on my back and walking, crawling and dragging, got him back to our lines. Neither of us had the courage or the desire to inspect his leg. When we got into a cellar, with me still carrying him, we inspected the leg. Lo and behold, a piece of shrapnel about half the size of a fist had embedded itself in the stock of his M-1 and struck his leg so hard that due to the cold he got a terrible 'Charley horse.' No damage whatsoever was done. I called him every name imaginable since I had carried him to my complete exhaustion. Actually, we were both relieved he wasn't injured."

Robert Parks—K Company

On the 18th the Germans again launched a furious assault on the 3rd Battalion in a desperate attempt to fulfill their orders to "take Höfen, regardless of the cost." Despite heavy concentrations of defensive artillery and mortar fire, they were able to infiltrate some men through the I Company lines on the left flank in the darkness, about 0435. They managed to surround the Battalion CP, some 150 yards behind the front line. Because of the darkness, the enemy dispositions could not be determined and the fighting was very bitter, some of it hand-to-hand. With the coming of daylight the situation became clearer and a little after 0800 the area was cleared as the enemy withdrew. Almost immediately the force reappeared carrying white flags as though they would surrender, but at the same time placing heavy mortar and small arms fire on the defenders. Realizing that the white flags were merely a ploy, the 81mm mortars from M Company smashed this attempt.

A large measure of the successful defense of Höfen was due to the large volume of accurate and timely artillery fire supporting the defenders. From December 6th through January the 196th Field Artillery Battalion was in direct support of the 3rd Battalion with their twelve 105mm guns located near Kalterherberg. A forward switching center was established in Höfen to coordinate the forward observers in each of the rifle company areas. In the I Company area the Forward Observer Team set up shop on the third floor of the highest building in the village where they had a commanding view of the area. This was designated as OP-6 and there were observers for the 81mm mortars here as well. Initially led by 1st Lt. Stanley D. Llewellyn, Capt. George W. Looney assumed command of the team on December 17th. In this same building there were riflemen and machine gunners on the first and second floors as well as a 3" gun against the outside wall.

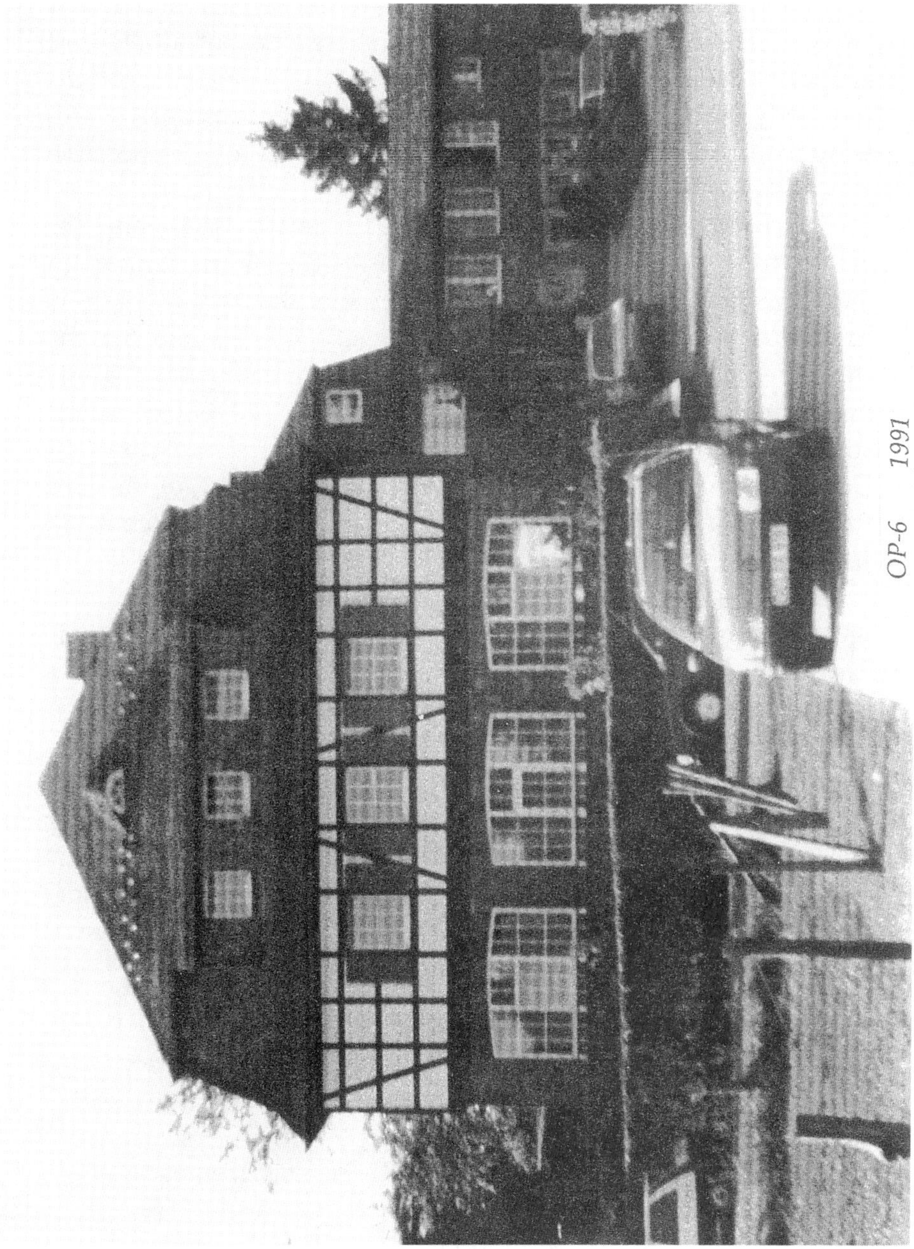

OP-6 1991

In addition to the 196th, the 863rd Field Artillery had twenty-four 105mm guns south and north of Kalterherberg and Corps artillery (155mm's) were in range. In all there were 36 battalions of artillery that could support the 3rd Battalion. Because of the relatively static situation from 9 November on, artillery pieces were well zeroed in and concentrations mapped for any possible situation.

On the 16th the artillery support had been vital in keeping the enemy from penetrating Battalion lines as their guns ranged up and down the Battalion front as the Germans attacked. In addition to this, the 196th had also been largely responsible for the capturing of 14 prisoners. The intense fire from their guns not only killed or drove back the enemy, it had also prevented enemy soldiers in front of the barrage from retreating so these 14 Germans only had the choice of staying in front of the 3rd Battalion lines and being killed or surrendering. They chose to surrender.

The observers directed fire up and down the line in front of the defending troops, often impacting within a few feet of their own men. There was a junk yard across the street from OP-6 and a group of attacking Germans made the mistake of coming through here in an attempt to penetrate the lines. When artillery rounds began exploding among them, the carnage was indescribable. In addition to the shrapnel from the shells, pieces of junk were flying everywhere and they were soon decimated. (When front line soldiers speak of "artillery" they are including the 60mm mortars from their weapons platoons and the 81mm mortars of the Heavy Weapons Company.)

"I cannot say enough good things for American artillery. Those guys were easily the world's best."

John Martin—K Company

"During the Battle of the Bulge there was tremendous artillery, tremendous noise, tremendous firing, tremendous troops all around us."

Thornton Piersall—I Company

Prior to the German attack, as a part of his tactical plan, Col. Butler had had the artillery observers plan concentrations on his Battalion's positions so that in case of a break-through no time would be lost in adjusting their fire. This proved to be prescient as he did have to call his artillery in on his own troops.

At 0830 another enemy artillery and rocket barrage began to fall on the Battalion's lines. This barrage was even heavier than the massive assault of the 16th. At 0900 the attack began with artillery leading the infantry into the 3rd Battalion lines. In addition to the 752nd and 753rd Regiments, General Kaschner sent the remnants of the 751st Regiment that had been so heavily punished on the 16th. Accompanying them were 12 tanks and 7 armored cars. The main effort was on the Battalion's left flank (I Company). The tanks and armored cars took part in an attack on the right flank (K Company) and a lesser attack was made at the boundary between I and K Companies.

"The Battalion Executive Officer, Major Allison, ordered me to seek help as tanks were supporting the German attack. I found a headquarters on the Eupen road, outside Monschau. I don't know what headquarters it was. A group of officers were bending over a situation map. A general officer was pointing to Höfen on the map and asked what was happening there. I explained what the Battalion positions were and also told him of the artillery concentrations and semi-automatic fire I had observed. I told him the Battalion exec had sent me to get help as they were sure the attack was being supported by tanks. I thought the needed help would have been anticipated and would be available almost immediately. The two star general thanked me and then turned to one of his staff and said, 'Well, if they break through there, we can set up here and hold them here,' and he designated an area on the map about 4 miles behind our lines. I was inclined to protest and argue in favor of sending help, but the two stars flashed in my eyes. So much for the tactics and strategy of higher headquarters. He didn't personally know the men in the squads and platoons. I guess that's why he could make the decisions I couldn't believe were right."

James Hare—I Company

The attack on the right flank came about 0900 with infantry leading the tanks and armored cars. The tanks had come from the Rohren area on the Höfen-Alzen road through the area vacated when the attack on Wahlerscheid was called back. As they loomed out of the fog, the defenders opened up with rifles, machine guns and mortars. The enemy kept pressing in spite of their losses and Col. Butler was forced to call his own artillery in on Battalion positions in one five minute concentration. The 3" guns added their voice to the battle, but could not hit the tanks which were in defilade. Finally the enemy began to withdraw. The tanks and armored cars were never really a factor as they began to retreat when their infantry protection was destroyed. By 0930 they were retreating. As the tanks headed back to Rohren they were no longer protected by the ridge and the guns of the 196th destroyed two of them.

The attack at the boundary of I and K Companies also came at 0900 and again Butler called friendly artillery in on his own positions, this time two five minute concentrations. The artillery and the small arms fire by the defending troops soon discouraged the enemy and they withdrew.

On the left flank the enemy pressed their attack in spite of furious small arms fire by the defenders and severe harassing fire from American artillery and mortars. At about 1000 a battalion-sized group managed to penetrate American lines in an area about 400 yards wide and 200 yards deep. Again they managed to surround the Battalion CP. With a planned artillery concentration, the gap was sealed. Yet again Butler was forced to call in his own artillery on his positions which pinned down the attackers in four buildings. This time three five minute concentrations were needed.

During this attack the artillery forward observation group and the riflemen in OP-6 exchanged small arms fire with the attacking

Germans. When Col. Butler ordered concentrations on his own positions, the observer's building was hit, blowing gaping holes in the roof and sides, showering plaster, bricks and shrapnel on these men. The radio operator moved to the basement and members of the team relayed fire commands to him to relay to the guns. At two different times the 196th fired 58 missions in 50 minutes. In nine and one half hours on the 18th they fired more than 3,600 rounds. The 196th history states that, "From the start of operations in Kalterherberg on December 6th until midnight 31 December 44, the battalion fired over 1,304 fire missions in support of the infantry at Höfen, Germany, with a total of 25,680 rounds of 105mm howitzer ammunition expended."

The only Battalion reserve, one platoon from L Company, was committed to the fight. Because the 100 or so Germans were in stone buildings, small arms fire was not enough. Butler had his 57mm anti-tank guns brought up and had them fire point blank into these buildings while riflemen and machine gunners kept the enemy pinned down so they could not fire on the 57mm's. Even though the armor piercing rounds of the 57mm's were demolishing the walls, these Germans did not give up until riflemen attacked with white phosphorous grenades. Twenty-five badly shaken enemy finally surrendered and about 75 enemy dead were found in the buildings. By 1130 the original line of defense was completely restored.

The complete success of the 3rd Battalion and the complete failure of the 326th Volksgrenadiers is evident in casualty figures, 326th, 50 prisoners and over 500 dead: 3rd Battalion five killed and seven wounded.

> "It got to the point where there were so many bodies out in front of us, that you could look at a body, look away and look back and you'd swear he moved. You'd also count fence posts to see if there's any extra out there. It was real hairy in that respect."
>
> William Bartow—M Company

There were numerous heroic actions by the Americans and two men from I Company were awarded the Distinguished

Service Cross, the first in the 99th Division for their individual heroism.

PFC Richard D. Mills "opened fire with his automatic rifle, killing many of the enemy and wounding others. Time and again he turned back their repeated fanatic attempts to pass his position. On the final attack his weapon jammed. With utter disregard for his personal safety, he left his foxhole and standing in the open, hurled grenades dispersing the hostile attack. By his superb personal courage and unhesitating action, Private First Class Mills contributed materially to the stemming of the German drive and protecting of his battalion's communication lines."

Sergeant Thornton E. Piersall "occupying a position in the path of the assault, held his ground. Wave after wave of hostile troops attacked him but he repulsed each attack by his intense fire. In desperation, the enemy brought up a machine gun and a rocket gun in an attempt to eliminate this threat to their advance. With his ammunition supply exhausted, Sgt. Piersall, with complete disregard for his life, courageously crawled from his emplacement, secured a grenade launcher and grenades from the enemy dead in front of him and returned to his position. Taking careful aim, he fired the rounds with devastating accuracy, knocking out both the machine gun and the rocket gun."

For the rest of the day the 3rd Battalion's positions were hit with heavy artillery and rocket fire. On December 18 the 99th Reconnaissance Platoon was attached to the 3rd Battalion, but they remained in their positions near Kalterherberg.

At 2030 a group of 30 to 35 Germans managed to penetrate the line in the I Company area, but they were contained and when daylight came the defenders had restored the line.

> "I've read about all the thousands of troops in the Battle of the Bulge. I believe I have the misfortune of being the only GI that was pissed on by a German patrol dog. It happened in the southeast corner of Höfen. I was with Sgt. Ziegler's squad as a forward observer for L Company's mortar section. My position was in a pillbox under the garage of an apartment house. I heard a noise and opened

the small embrasure and, seeing nothing, I opened the large embrasure just as he cocked his leg and hit me on top of the helmet. I had my rifle loaded and locked and a bare bayonet, but I froze with the piss dripping off my helmet and the dog taking off."

William Zellers—L Company

Although the weary defenders had no way of knowing it, this proved to be the last determined effort by the Germans to take Höfen. In their initial combat action the Battalion had done such a superb job of defending their positions that the Battalion was awarded the Presidential Unit Citation, the first one earned in the 99th Division. The Battalion was later cited twice in "The Order of the Day" by the Belgian army. In a letter from Maj. Gen. C. R. Huebner, V Corps Commander, to Maj. Gen. Walter E. Lauer, 99th Division Commanding Officer, he said, in part, "On December 18, the 3rd Battalion of the 395th Infantry gave a magnificent account of itself in the extremely heavy action against the enemy in the Höfen area and was the main factor in stopping the hostile effort to penetrate the lines of the V Corps in the direction of Monschau."

The 326th Volksgrenadier Division had been so badly mauled that they were able to offer only token help to the German drive the rest of the battle. Outnumbered five to one, the Battalion inflicted casualties on the enemy in the ratio of eighteen to one and were credited with destroying 75 percent of three German regiments.

"One night, shortly after the German attack, we heard trucks moving on the road behind us and in a little while we had the darndest fireworks display any of us had ever seen. It was spectacular. They fired several hundred rockets and were gone before anybody knew it. Just left some scorched places in the road."

George Prager—L Company

On the 19th the skies cleared somewhat and the Air Force was over Höfen in strength. German planes were driven off and enemy troops and supply lines were constantly attacked. It was a great morale booster for the ground troops to see this show of support. Sporadic enemy mortar and artillery fire continued to fall on Höfen as the defenders took care of their wounded and dead, strengthened their positions, and brought in ammunition and supplies.

"That night I had the hairiest personal experience of those eventful days. We had found that the enemy could be in our laps before we even knew they were around so that night we left our hole and pulled back to a house about twenty yards to our rear. There were six of us in the house ... doors barricaded, chicken wire on the windows, good visibility in the daytime and a 'feeling' of greater security as well as firepower. Two or three hours after dark we could hear considerable movement in and around our previous hole. We could hear shovels (digging in?), machine gun belts (metal) and even quiet voices. We had no communication with others but wished we had contact with our mortars. My guess at the time that there were at least 20 to 30 Germans. While we were trying to figure out just what to do, we realized that three or four of them had come to our house and were trying to get in. We followed our planned course of action which was for me, in the attic looking through a hole in the roof, to drop grenades on them. Those men on the second floor started shooting as did those on the ground floor. Promptly a German machine gun, mounted where our hole was, sprayed the whole building repeatedly. I dropped down to the second floor where one of our men had been killed. (PFC John R. O'Brien). After this short exchange they seemed to give up and move on. Then we heard the BAR in our squad hole to the right began to shoot steadily and for some time. The next morning I went to the attic and looked out the hole again and was very shook to find bullet holes all around where I had been standing—literally an outline—and I had not been scratched."

John Tabb—I Company

The BAR Tabb mentions above belonged to PFC George J. Nothwang. As the German patrol passed his position, Nothwang opened up on them. BAR men are taught in training to fire short burst of three or four rounds to conserve ammunition. Nothwang did this at first, but soon was firing a full magazine, 20 rounds, in each burst. His assistant, PFC Robert V. Snevily, and the other man in their hole loaded magazines as fast as they could. The enemy patrol dropped into a shallow ditch across the narrow road and tried to fight back with rifles, automatic weapons and "potato mashers" (German hand grenades), but were unable to stop this furious onslaught. After taking all they could stand, two or three of the Germans tried to flee down the road, only to be cut down by other units along the road. At daylight there were almost 20 enemy bodies laying in the ditch. Chunks of blacktop had been literally "chewed" out of the road surface. Bullet holes and blotches where grenades had exploded gave ample evidence of the intensity of this small battle.

Also on the 19th the 2nd platoon of L Company sent out a combat patrol to the southeast of Alzen. In the dark one of the men, George Neill, stepped in a hole and reinjured an ankle that he had broken in civilian life. The platoon medic, Warner Anthony, helped him back to a building where he would be safe until he could get further treatment. In trying to catch up with the patrol in the dark, Anthony blundered into a German sentry. The German challenged him with, "Halt! Who goes?" Anthony answered, "Amerikanser medic." The German told him, "You're lost." Anthony replied, "Right" and promptly retraced his steps to find his platoon.

Not all patrols had such benign results. Another L Company patrol sent out to make contact with an American unit near Kalterherberg was fired on by an American private. He hit an L Company sergeant in the upper leg and the man died in agony before he could be treated.

Position 7M facing southeast from Alzen. Sketch by James Crewdson—M Company. Houses in front manned by L Company. Church steeple at extreme right is in Kalterherberg. Heavy machine gun positioned to support L Company with overhead fire. Note range card and hand grenade hooked on telephone wire at the top of the embrasure.

An infantryman reported to Capt. Looney (196th FO) that he had seen movement in the junk yard across the street from OP-6. Looney fired some flares, but they saw nothing. An hour or so later the same man again reported movement there. This time a flare was fired followed by several rounds of mortar fire. No further movement was reported. In the morning a soldier went out to check and found a large, very dead rabbit.

For a number of days small battles took place along the Battalion perimeter as the Germans sent various sized patrols in, still hoping that somehow they could manage some success after the battering they had taken.

"The Germans were tugging at the cellar door that opened up to the street and we in the cellar were striving with all our might to hold those doors closed so they couldn't get in. That might sound like a rather comical situation, and it is in retrospect, but at the time we thought it was quite serious."

Richard Mills—I Company

Throughout this period the Battalion aid station under the direction of Major Herbert Orr, MD, was very busy doing emergency medical work to keep the wounded alive. Care beyond the normal was necessary as for a couple of days casualties could not be evacuated. When the roads cleared their load lessened and medical supplies could be brought in to replace those that had been used.

"One night someone shot one of the German paratroopers and he made it as far as 'our house' before he went down in the snow. We could see him, could clearly hear him pleading for help, but no one trusted him enough to go out and get him while it was still dark. He spoke very good English. We knew what was happening to him in those circumstances, but self preservation was a stronger instinct than any other at that time. When daylight came we went out. He could then be observed well enough so we felt safe and his hands and feet were so badly chilled he could do nothing. He told us he had gone to school in Massachusetts and told us how fortunate he would be to be where it was warm and dry."

Robert Kreuger—I Company

This exemplifies another of the lessons about combat these men had learned the hard way. Never, under any circumstances, trust the enemy.

"I thought the German would peek to see where his grenade had gone. I thought correctly. The edge of his helmet peeked around the corner of the building . . . then the side of his cheek. I aligned my sights where the corner of the wooden building met the protruding cheek and squeezed the trigger. The German screamed and pitched forward into the snow as the wooden corner splintered in his face. An arm stretched forward searching for the grenade he had dropped as he fell. I directed the sights behind the armpit of the outstretched arm and squeezed the trigger again. The German jerked once and then lay still.

"I was surprised at how little I did feel. I felt no remorse at all. A fellow creature had tried to kill me. Fortunately, I had killed the fellow creature instead. Now I calmly smoked a cigarette while a human being lay dead in the snow a few yards away. That was war. This brief interchange had been purely impersonal."

William Huffman—I Company

In supporting the 3rd Battalion, one platoon of the 47th Infantry—9th Division, had moved into a house originally occupied by the 2nd platoon of L Company. (Position A on the Höfen overlay.) The 81mm mortars of M Company were firing on German troops on the high ground northwest of Kalterherberg when the fins came off one round. This round went out of control and unfortunately hit the building occupied by the platoon from the 47th and it burned to the ground. The command of the 9th thought this was a deliberate action and it took some selling to convince them it was an accident.

Graves Registration units of the American army were very efficient at removing dead bodies from the field. American bodies were removed at once, both for morale and sanitary reasons. However, German bodies had a lower priority so the men of the Battalion were ordered to dispose of them. The ground was frozen so it was almost impossible to dig graves. Some of the men saved themselves a lot of effort by dumping these corpses down wells and cisterns. When Col. Butler got word of this after the heavy fighting was over, he ordered them removed for proper disposal.

From the 19th to the 24th of December German patrol activity continued as the Battalion prepared to defend themselves from another major assault, which never materialized. On the 22nd the 99th Reconnaissance Troop, southeast of Kalterherberg on Schwalm Creek, was attacked by two companies of the 277th Volksgrenadier Division supported by horse drawn artillery in a dawn attack. The 1st and 2nd platoons were forced to withdraw to Kalterherberg after dark, but the 3rd platoon was surrounded. They managed to hold out until the next morning when troops from the 3rd Battalion, 47th Infantry came to their aid. Seven Germans were captured and 50 killed. The Recon Troop lost four men killed.

A number of German paratroopers were killed or captured as they tried to infiltrate through Höfen and return to their lines. Men were still dying, on both sides of the line, but in much smaller numbers.

Ever since the Battalion had arrived in Höfen in November, German V-1 "Buss Bombs" had passed overhead heading for Liege in a vain effort by the Germans to inflict major damage. They were more nuisance than threat and it was common practice for ground troops to shoot at them.

"It was at that position that we were hit by a buzz bomb on the 23rd. It wasn't intended for us, I'm sure, but after flying around aimlessly for several minutes it dug its left wing into the stub of a wall remaining of the house we were occupying. Needless to say, we had to move! None of us got a scratch; we were so close to it that the blast went over us."

Hugh Ferris—HQ Company

On December 24th the 99th Recon Troop moved six miles north into the Battalion area and took up positions in a draw at the rear of the Battalion area, facing Kalterherberg. Some of their men moved into Höfen to support I Company.

One night one of the Recon men was on guard with an I Company man in a second floor corner room. They heard German voices directly below them from a German patrol and decided they would drop a grenade. Fragmentation grenades have a five second fuse, but this is not always reliable. Pulling the safety pin, one man let the lever fly off, counted to two and gently lobbed the grenade out a window. He had to toss it over a headboard and other furniture used to partially block the window and in the dark could not see several inches of curtain hanging from the top of the window. The live grenade hit this curtain and fell back into the room with them. Both men dove through doors to adjoining rooms while the grenade fizzled and then exploded throwing shrapnel and plaster all over the small room. Both men were very relieved to find that the other man had not been hurt.

On December 25th eighteen more paratroopers were killed or captured.

"As the snows got heavy we found some skis and devised a makeshift toboggan out of roofing tin and rope to carry litters on, thus exposing fewer men and no litter dropping when fire came in. However, it had its drawbacks as it was slower to get down from the skis and the colder it got, the noisier the sheet metal was on the irregular ground. On a clear night that sound carried forever it seemed. The colder it got, the noisier it got. We carried the skis with us until the March thaw."

Herbert Orr, MD—Battalion Surgeon

While all was relatively quiet in the Höfen area, the Battle of the Bulge continued to the southeast as Christmas came. The "Stars and Stripes" stated it well in their December 26 issue:

"There was no peace on earth for soldiers on the Western Front this Christmas Day. The only Christmas lights were the red and green flares splashing the skies to coordinate the relentless assaults and counterblows. There were no bells—only the roar of artillery, the thud of bombs and the chatter of small arms fire. There was no warmth; no cheer. There wasn't even time to think about what Christmas might have been.

"It was white along the front lines yesterday, but it wasn't Christmas."

Mail began to come in for the first time in many days. Until now, food, ammunition, supplies and replacements had taken up all available truck space and mail had to wait. In the heat of battle most of the men had not even realized it was Christmas.

"I got a Christmas package at that house. It had been a fifth of whiskey packed in a square tin with popcorn for packing, and the top completely welded shut. The bottle was broken, but the popcorn soaked up a good part of the booze. We didn't waste any! We lay on the floor behind our vision screen and sucked popcorn. It wasn't bad."

Robert Kreuger—I Company

"I was the company clerk for I Company and was assigned to the 395th Unit Personnel Section. A few days after the 'Bulge' started we were pulled back to a small town on the Belgium/Germany border. It was about the 18th or 19th of December.

"There wasn't room in any one building for all of us so permission was given for us to stay with civilians, if we were asked. A buddy of mine, Euart Scott, company clerk for L Company, was approached by a little boy, about 8 or 9, about staying with his family. Scottie and I moved in with this family of four—a man and his wife and two small children, a boy and a girl.

"Being the Christmas season, we asked them where their Christmas tree was. We were told that it was forbidden for any of the townspeople to cut down any of the pine trees, even though the town was surrounded by them. Not being registered citizens of this town, Scottie and I decided this rule didn't apply to us. So off we went and 'liberated' ourselves a Christmas tree. As we were carrying it through town, we came across a Major. After shifting the tree around and presenting the traditional salute, we figured we had had it, but all the Major said was, 'It looks like someone is going to have some Christmas spirit.'

"Our family was thrilled with the tree, but were quite concerned about what would happen to them when the local authorities found out. When the other 40 or 50 GI's staying with civilians heard what Scottie and I had done, they followed suit and 'liberated' trees for their families. This set our family's minds at ease—how can you arrest the whole town?

"Our tree was decorated and plans were being made for a big Christmas celebration, with Scottie and I being a big part of the family gathering.

"Unfortunately we were ordered to pull out on the morning of the 24th. When we told our family, tears came to their eyes, including 'Papa.' We had planned to put some presents under the tree for Christmas morning, but were forced to give them a day early. I think they appreciated our gifts of soap, candy, gum, cigarettes and even a pair of silk stockings that Scottie's sister had sent him for 'bartering' purposes. Our family had gifts for us also; homemade bread, preserves and some delicious honey-butter spread.

"It was quite a sight on the morning of the 24th of December, 1944. As we loaded into our trucks in the town square, I think the whole town turned out, with tears in their eyes, to say good-bye to us and to wish us a Merry Christmas."

James Whalen — I Company

German troops had captured a bridge over Schwalm Creek and at 0430 on December 25th 1st Lt. William K. Worley, Jr., from the 99th Recon, led an assault by two M-8 armored cars and a squad from L Company and by 0800 they had driven the enemy off and the bridge was once more secure.

On December 28th Company A—801st Tank Destroyer Battalion relieved Company A—612th TD Battalion who had helped in the defense of Höfen. Because of the bitter weather, most of the 3" guns were frozen in place so the two units simply swapped weapons.

To the south and east of Höfen the Battle of the Bulge continued to rage as the Germans fought a losing battle. On the 23rd of December the skies cleared and for five days the Allied air forces battered the enemy troops and supply lines. Morale soared among the men as they watched this tremendous display of air power. Military historians pretty well agree that on December 26 the initiative passed from the Germans to the Americans, although it would be several weeks before the original lines were restored.

In its first major combat engagement the 3rd Battalion more than proved its mettle. The German onslaught along a 70 mile wide front broke through everywhere, with one exception. That exception was at Höfen where the 3rd Battalion refused to let the attackers drive them from their positions. Since there were no troops in close support of this Battalion, a breakthrough would have meant that the enemy would have had easy access to the road to Eupen, Belgium, which was the headquarters of V Corps and would have put the Germans behind the defensive lines formed by the 2nd and 99th Divisions on Elsenborn Ridge. The end result of the battle would probably have been the same, but the actions of the 3rd Battalion were a significant contribution to the American victory. The men of the 3rd Battalion were

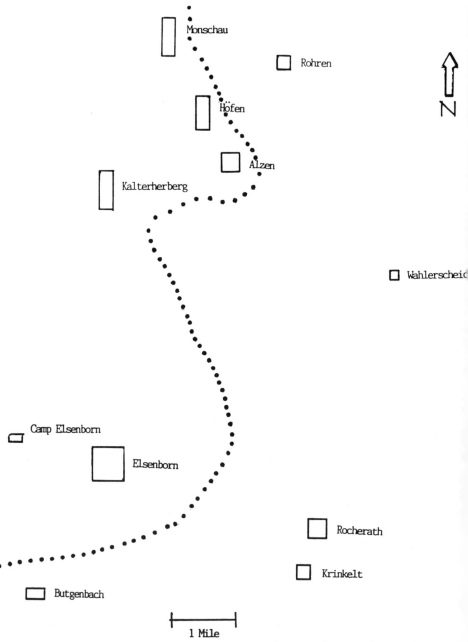

Dotted line indicates maximum German advances during the Battle of the Bulge. In addition, there were German troops north of Kalterherberg. The 3rd Battalion was almost surrounded.

justifiably proud to be called "The Rock of Höfen" in news dispatches.

It was only now that the men of the 3rd Battalion began to realize what a desperate situation they had been in. (See map, page 74). There was a German headquarters in Rohren. When the 2nd Division and the 395th RCT had been driven back from Wahlerscheid to Rocherath-Krinkelt and later to the Elsenborn Ridge, all of the area to the south and east of Höfen-Alzen was enemy territory. The attack of the 277th VG Division on December 22nd was only stopped near Kalterherberg by the men of the 99th Recon. There were also German troops in West Wall fortifications between Alzen and Kalterherberg as well as some north of Kalterherberg.

A Lt. Bemener had been commander of the 5th Company of the 753rd Volksgrenadier Regiment when it attacked Höfen. When he was captured east of the Rhine, Lt. Bemener asked his American interrogator for the name of the American unit that had defended Höfen. When told it was the 3rd Battalion—395th Infantry he stated that "It must have been one of your best formations." When asked what reason he had for this opinion, he answered, "Two reasons: one coldbloodedness; two efficiency."

On December 29, a cold front moved in from the north with heavy snow and blizzard-like conditions. It was so severe that wounded men would die from shock in a matter of minutes if not treated at once. In Höfen the men struggled to keep their positions open but the snow was too much for them and many of them had to be dug out of their positions in the morning. The roads were closed with snowdrifts and the next day only jeeps were able to move, and then only with great difficulty. Both armies had to devote their energies to clearing roads and positions and of course all air activity was grounded.

> "When the weather was bad we had much problem with frostbite and trenchfoot, pneumonia and flu. We also did a land office business with cough syrup since a cough carried so far and brought trouble. Unfortunately some

fellows learned to use the cough syrup—Elixir of Terpin Hydrate—as 'GI gin' to get drunk."

Herbert Orr, MD—Battalion Surgeon

"On New Year's Eve we had gotten a couple of rolls of concertina wire to string out in front of our gun positions to slow up any enemy troops who might come our way. We waited until dusk to start the job. About 200 yards to our front we stretched the wire and pegged it down as well as we could in the snow covered ground.

"With the job finished, the men started back. One man kicked off a parachute flare set there earlier as a booby trap by someone who never recorded it nor reported it. The flare struck and embedded itself in his groin and its white phosphorus and magnesium immediately ignited to white heat. Those with him quickly threw him to the ground and began to pack snow on the burning material but it was impossible to keep it from reigniting while the man thrashed and screamed in agony and fear. We finally got enough blankets and snow to keep the flare smothered.

"He was evacuated to the Battalion aid station where the Battalion surgeon was able to remove the flare. He survived to reach the States, but later died of his wounds."

James Crewdson—M Company

As the new year dawned, the men in Höfen sent out patrols on a daily basis to secure prisoners and gather intelligence data. Enemy activity consisted of sporadic artillery and mortar fire and some probing patrols. While there were no major battles, men continued to be wounded and killed. On January 3rd the American attack began against the shoulders of the German penetration and continued until the original lines were secured about the end of the month. Replacements came in to take the places of those men who had been injured or killed. The high command felt the situation was so urgent that some of these replacements had been flown from the U.S. and some had spent

Christmas with their families in "The States." Several non-commissioned officers received field commissions as 2nd Lieutenants. Some were transferred to other units. Weather was a continual problem as snow and cold not only made it difficult for the men to function at full efficiency, but meant that frostbite and trenchfoot would continue to plague them and many had to be evacuated. Several men were able to go back to V Corps headquarters in Eupen for 24 or 48 hour rest periods. Although the town was almost entirely military personnel, these short rests from "The Line" were most welcome.

These men were now combat hardened veterans and yet were very much the same men who had arrived here in early November, apprehensive and unsure. They now had the confidence that comes from successful experience in combat and the mental toughness that comes with it. Yet, many still did not swear, drink or smoke. Some men continued to read their bibles daily. When beer was sent in, only about half of them drank any. Very few picked up the smoking habit although cigarettes were readily available. They had learned that they could depend on one another and each respected the other man for what he was as a soldier. Most were in their late teens or early twenties, but these were MEN!

> "One man from M Company had been wounded on December 18. During the second week in January he showed up, having gone AWOL from the hospital in Liege to keep from being evacuated farther to the rear. His wound was not healed, but was coming along nicely.
>
> "He had been back with us for only a couple of days when a mortar round intended for the road junction fell 100 yards short and landed at his feet, killing him instantly. He was the first fatality in the company and this, along with the fact that he was extremely likable, hit us all very hard."
>
> James Crewdson—M Company

On January 25th the 2nd platoon of L Company was sent on a combat patrol southeast of Alzen for the purpose of knocking out a German strong point that had cut off a group of their men who had established a listening post near the enemy positions. Before they reached their comrades they came under fire from a German machine gun, artillery and mortar fire. Lt. Erskine Wickersham, L Company weapons platoon leader, led a small group of men to within earshot and he and Sgt. John Noonan began to put down a furious barrage with two 60mm mortars. They fired so fast that one of the mortars swelled from the heat to the point shells would not fit in the barrel. This barrage allowed the patrol and the men in the listening post to break contact with the enemy and withdraw down the hill. The two scouts, Duane Shipman and William Harmon, were the last to turn back and Harmon tripped an anti-personnel mine and was wounded to the point he could not walk. Shipman picked him up and carried him through the rest of the minefield—the trip wires were visible above the snow line—to safety. Shipman states that a German soldier watched the two men struggle through the minefield, but did not fire on them. When the patrol returned several men had been wounded and one man who did not return was listed as missing, but his body was later recovered.

As a part of their defensive efforts, in November the men of the 3rd Battalion had laid a number of anti-tank minefields in front of their positions. The army's Standard Operating Procedure (SOP) when laying mines is to lay them in a definite pattern and make a map showing the location of each mine. However, at Höfen most of these mines had been laid under fire from enemy artillery and as a consequence were laid in erratic patterns and it was impossible to make proper maps of their locations. This had dire consequences when the order came down on January 28th to remove these mines in preparation for an attack through the Battalion lines. The mines were buried under a foot or more of snow and, since no mine detectors were available, the men had to probe through the snow with pitchforks and bayonets to locate each mine. In addition, the continual freezing and thawing weather had frozen the mines to the ground and also swelled the trigger charges so that a safety fork could not be inserted when they found a mine and it remained "live" as they chopped it out of the ice. I Company had one man killed and several wounded when one of the mines exploded. After the casualties were attended to, other men had to resume this dangerous task until all the mines were removed.

Elements of the 47th and 60th Infantry Regiments of the 9th Division moved into Höfen and on January 30th they attacked through the 3rd Battalion toward Rohren and beyond. At 1200 the Battalion received orders to move to Kalterherberg where they were attached to the 39th Infantry, 9th Division.

"I remember standing a two-hour go deep in the night on the gun at the dugout with helmet cocked up to accommodate the sound-powered phone against an ear listening to dance music being piped down the line by Love 3 CP while the air temperature caused nostrils to stick together with each inhaled breath and drew body heat away through cheeks, fingertips and shoe soles. The background noise of high explosive was always present, from the stunning crash near at hand to the thump-ha-wung and summer thunder rumbles on out to the edge of hearing, and the realization that death could be with you at any time, even during the quiet time.

"But for all the monotony, fear, anger, frustration, sorrow, physical discomfort and a whole lot of other intense feelings, we were lucky in a way—or beneficiaries of good planning, hard work and determination. The Battalion gave much better than it got to a tough enemy; and we earned a Unit Citation in the process. Things could have been a lot worse for us than we experienced at Höfen and they got that way later on, a number of times."

James Crewdson—M Company

In recognition of their actions in Höfen, the 3rd Battalion received the following commendation from Col. George W. Smythe, Commanding Officer of the 47th Infantry Regiment:

"The 47th Combat Team was alerted and moved to the Monschau-Höfen-Kalterherberg line on 17 December 1944, at which time the 3rd Battalion, 395th Infantry, was attached to the Regimental Combat Team.

"Throughout the entire period of this attachment, from 18 December to 1300 30 January '45, the combat efficiency of the 3rd Battalion of the 395th Infantry was outstandingly apparent. On 18 December, at a critical point in the enemy counter-offensive, this battalion withstood the shock of a strong enemy attack and threw them back with heavy losses. The courage and steadfastness of this unit in holding the vital Höfen-Alzen area during a period in which our lines were fluid, is highly commendable. After the line had been solidified, the 3rd Battalion, 395th Infantry, continued to hold the Höfen-Alzen area and continually harassed the enemy with patrol action, taking a number of prisoners. During this period the Battalion was under continuous heavy enemy artillery and mortar fire.

"The superior combat efficiency of the Battalion, its excellent staff work and its cheerful attitude of cooperation with the 47th Reinforced Combat Team is deserving of high Commendation."

On 28 January 1945, the Allied High Command declared that the Battle of the Bulge was officially over. All penetrations by the Germans had been eliminated and the front line had been completely restored to what it had been prior to 16 December 1944.

The 3rd Battalion was now a veteran combat unit. The men had become combat infantrymen in the finest sense of the word. In the army only about 15 percent of the men in uniform are front line infantrymen and yet this small group suffers over 70 percent of the casualties. These men had seen friends die at first hand and had seen others leave due to wounds or illness. They had learned that there was no end to their trials and tribulations. Their training had shown them how to work together and actual combat had shown them how necessary it was to depend on one another for survival. Each man had learned that his only hope for staying alive was to rely on his buddies. The officers had proven they could be relied on, that they cared about their men and that orders were to be carried out as issued.

Being a combat infantryman is like nothing else in life. All these men know that their only destiny is the litter, the grave or survival until final victory. Fatigue is the norm as there is never an opportunity for a safe night's sleep. Fear is ever present. Meals are at irregular times and usually cold. Being cold in wintertime and hot in summertime is standard fare. Baths are a luxury not known to a combat man. Sleeping and fighting in wet clothes is accepted without comment. At any moment they may be called upon to fight for their lives, take care of a wounded comrade or seek shelter from bombs, artillery shells or small arms fire. Digging and marching while burdened with equipment become second nature. Those men who survive combat seem to develop a "sixth sense" about danger and instinctively take appropriate measures.

To offset all these problems a combat infantryman soon realizes that his only protection is the man next to him. It is common for one man to risk, and sometimes give, his life for his buddy as he knows the other man would do the same for him. Survival and success are only possible if the group acts as one body. The feelings these men have for each other are like nothing else in life. In so many ways they are closer than child/parent or even husband/wife relationships. Dependence on each other is absolute and demands absolute commitment. "Greater love hath no man than he who would give his life for another." Combat infantrymen demonstrate love for their fellow man in the highest sense of the word.

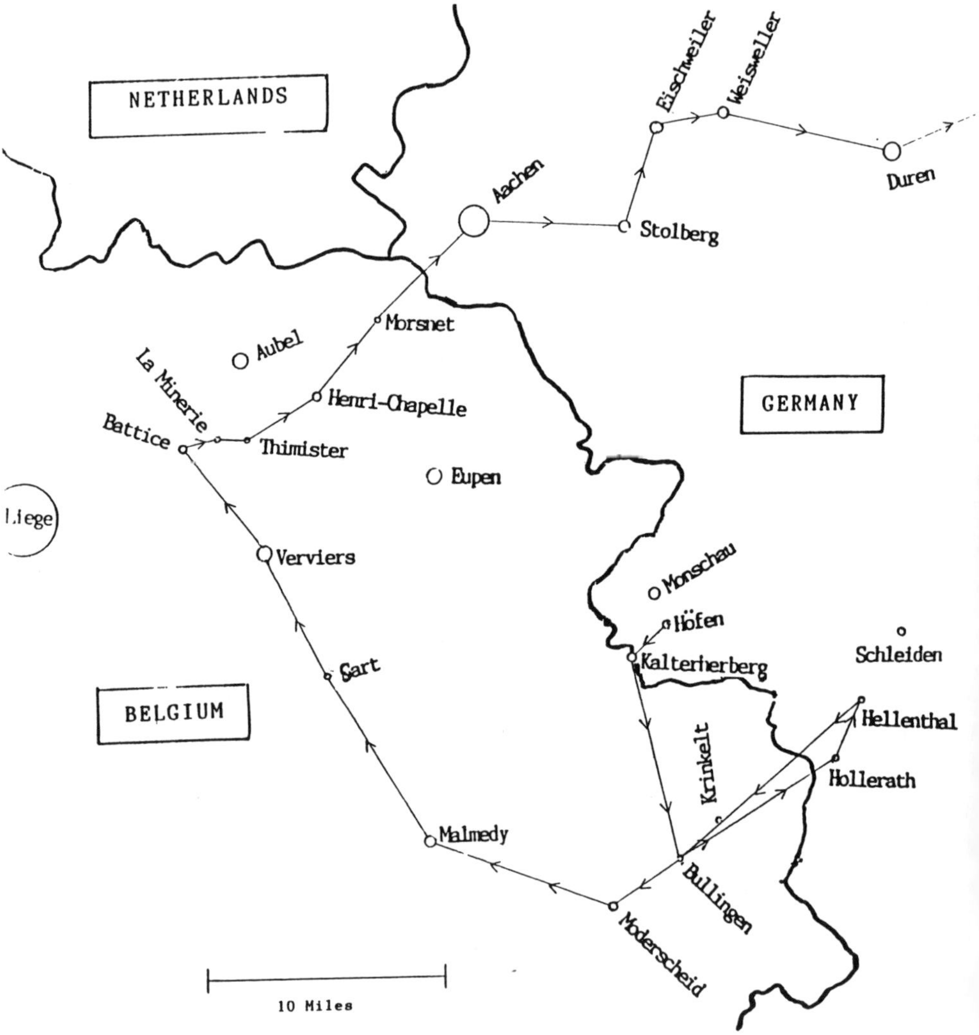
NETHERLANDS
GERMANY
BELGIUM
Aachen
Eischweiler
Weisweiler
Duren
Stolberg
Morsnet
Aubel
La Minerie
Henri-Chapelle
Battice
Thimister
Eupen
Liege
Verviers
Monschau
Höfen
Kalterherberg
Schleiden
Sart
Hellenthal
Krinkelt
Hollerath
Malmedy
Bullingen
Moderscheid
10 Miles

CHAPTER 5

Off the Line

At 0400 on January 30th elements of the 47th and 60th Infantry Regiments of the 9th Division jumped off on an attack through the 3rd Battalion lines toward Rohren. At about 1200 the 3rd Battalion moved out of Höfen to Kalterherberg and were attached to the 39th Infantry, 9th Division.

"As we left Höfen, we took all the stuff we had hauled up there. The snow was more than knee deep and we started strewing stuff as we went. I still have to chuckle about all the stuff we threw away. We stripped and it wasn't very long until this is what a combat soldier had. He had a blanket and a poncho draped over the back of his rifle belt. He had his extra socks inside his jacket. He had a toothbrush, maybe a razor and a spoon and a canteen cup. That was the extra gear. Most of the boys carried a New Testament."

William Blasdel—K Company

"As elements of the 9th Division moved through our positions we began to move back and close in at Höfen for the trek back to Kalterherberg, where we gathered about midnight in a large gymnasium. It was the first time M Company had all been together in three months. Some old faces were missing and some new ones were present, but it was a great family reunion."

James Crewdson—M Company

Remembering what problems they had had when they first came on line, the 3rd Battalion left some men as guides to show the incoming troops where things were and to try to pass along some of their hard-won knowledge.

"When the company was pulled back some of us were left to orient the incoming soldiers on the area. I remember that the first night they were there a platoon leader wanted to send out patrols. We advised against that and told them they needed to get better acclimated. They sent out patrols anyway and, sure enough, they collided during the night and engaged in a furious fire fight. Several were killed. These new people seemed to have to learn lessons the hard way."

Robert Parks—K Company

On January 31st the 99th Recon Troop and the 196th Field Artillery Battalion were attached to the 3rd Battalion for an attack on enemy strong points southeast of Kalterherberg. The attack was made with two companies abreast: K on the left and L on the right, with I Company in reserve. This was a wooded area that had been previously fought over and had been mined and booby trapped by the Germans and the Americans. Trees had been hit by artillery and were strewn about like matchsticks. It was difficult to advance at all, even with artillery and mortar support. However, the Battalion advanced 1,200 to 1,500 yards against mortar, machine gun and small arms fire until ordered to break off the attack. This was a very minor action in the overall scheme of things, but a very major action for the men killed. Again George S. Patton's statement proved to be true. "Riflemen suffer 90 percent of the casualties."

"We lost our first scout and my assistant BAR man moved up to first scout. Just about that time mortar fire started coming in. I heard that whistling coming in and hit the ground, face down in the snow. About 40 feet from me, off to my left and just a little bit ahead of me, I saw the scout go down on his back. I saw one of those shells come in and go right underneath him and explode. He never moved. All of a sudden, it must have been two or three minutes later, he just raised up to a sitting position and looked straight ahead. I looked at that man and he didn't have any head. He had a face. It looked like a body holding a false face above his shoulders. Then he just laid back down and was quiet. Before I left I went over to make sure he was dead. I kind of wish I had never looked at him 'cuz he wasn't a very good sight."

Richard Gorby—K Company

Returning to Kalterherberg the men were billeted in some of the buildings in town. Although they felt a little safer here than they had in Höfen, the men were still unable to get all the rest they needed as their billets were directly in front of some artillery pieces. Each time these guns fired, the concussion from the muzzle blasts shook these buildings as an earthquake might. For veteran infantrymen the sound of artillery meant instant alertness, even friendly artillery. Some had it even worse as some 240mm (16") guns were also firing and the concussion from these guns was even worse.

On February 1st the Battalion was released from the 9th Division and rejoined the 395th Regiment, which was Corps reserve. They remained in Kalterherberg but were on alert to move when ordered.

On the 2nd the 395th Infantry Regiment was told to prepare to attack Schleiden, Germany, and on the 3rd was attached to the 1st Division. On the 4th the 3rd Battalion moved to an assembly area north of Bullingen, Belgium. Here they saw some of the carnage from the fierce fighting that took place during the Battle of the Bulge. A frozen German crouched over his machine gun with his finger still on the trigger. Parts of corpses protruded from the snow. Transport, armor and horse drawn vehicles were smashed to junk.

"Farther along the scene was almost replicated but with the battle wreckage clad in OD. Prominent was a 99th Division jeep crunched V-shaped by passage over its front seat of a German heavy tank tread.

"In the lee of the hill, the snow seemed to be deeper and its mounds and hummocks gave only occasional glimpses of what lay beneath. Evening twilight cast a frivolous touch of fading pink and blue over the battlefield carnage until darkness closed it over.

"The sight of enemy dead and his broken equipage usually caused only an indifferent reaction in us. Bodies and abandoned materiél in OD, however, always brought a sudden, strong tightening of the throat."

James Crewdson—M Company

On February 5th the Battalion was assigned as regimental reserve. At this same time the 1st and 2nd Battalions of the regiment had been engaged in an attack on the pillboxes of the West Wall and had encountered very little opposition. Most of the enemy positions were deserted and a few enemy soldiers surrendered.

On the 6th the Battalion moved to Hollerath, Germany, on foot and took up defensive positions in the West Wall. The Battalion headquarters and some of the troops occupied pillboxes. Here they were able to fully appreciate what formidable positions the Germans had had. One emplacement was large enough to house an infantry battalion, but most had been built to accommodate eight to ten men. Fields of fire interlocked between pillboxes and all trees, bushes, etc., had been cleaned out to give the occupants large areas of observation.

On February 8, 1945, Col. Alexander J. MacKenzie was relieved as regimental commander of the 395th. Lt. Col. James A. Gallagher replaced him.

From February 5th through the 7th the Battalion had been engaged in setting up defensive positions in case of attack and policing the area for stragglers and dead. Great quantities of matériél were gathered up for salvage. On the 8th the 3rd Battalion relieved the 1st Battalion, 395th Regiment in the Hellenthal area.

On February 11, the Battalion was relieved by the 2nd Battalion, 271st Infantry, 69th Division. The weather had started to warm up some, which meant thawing of the ground and lots of mud. Because of the poor condition of the roads, it was difficult for the relieving troops to get in place and the transfer took several hours. All new units going into combat have to go through a breaking-in period. Having been in a fairly quiet area when they first went on line, the 3rd Battalion was fortunate in that they learned some of their basic lessons relatively free of casualties. The 69th was not that fortunate in that the Germans in this area had good defensive positions and a number of the new men were killed by artillery when they exposed themselves to the enemy observers. M Company had left a couple of men to help the new troops get settled in, but when some of the new men built a fire to warm themselves, the M Company guides left before German artillery hit the fire and those around it.

Late in the afternoon the Battalion left on foot for a rear assembly area in the woods west of Bullingen. When they started their march it was snowing and this later turned to sleet. Because of the strong wind, the men had to hold their helmets against the sides of their faces for protection. The sleet then turned to rain and by the time the men reached their assigned assembly area they were all soaked to the skin.

In the assembly area there were holes that had been made by some other outfit that could give some slight protection from the elements. These holes had been covered with logs, but were made as sleeping holes and were barely deep enough for a man to sit upright. As many as 15 men crowded into a hole made for three men to sleep in. Water dripped through the log roof. In an effort to generate some heat and light, C ration cans were filled with sand to act as a wick and gasoline poured over the sand for fuel. These makeshift lanterns gave off little light and less heat but did give off great quantities of soot. By morning the men were black with soot. Since there were not enough holes for all the men, some had to sleep outdoors and, because of blackout restrictions, did not even have the benefit of the makeshift lanterns.

> "We didn't have very many men left in our outfit. That night we moved to late evening and stopped in a woods. We were told to wait here all night and go back tomorrow morning. It was getting warmer and the snow was starting to melt. It was raining and wet. Everybody was half froze. A friend of mine who was a monstrous big fella, Grant Lintman, said, 'I'll tell you what you do, Gorby. Lay your poncho down and then your blanket. We'll lay on it and put my blanket and poncho over the top of us and we'll catch a little sleep.' That's what we did. I woke up sometime later and the weight of our bodies in that soft snow, and it was getting warmer, we had sunk in that snow. It was just like laying in a bathtub. All that water had run in and my poncho was holding it. Just like we were laying in a bathtub, soaking wet and cold."
>
> Richard Gorby—K Company

Sleeping problems were no respecter of rank. Col. Butler's staff had found a hole for him, but it had several inches of water on the floor. He slept as best he could, turning often to get at least one side of his body out of the water. Sometime during the night several of the logs fell in and in the morning he found himself trapped in the hole. His driver saw his predicament and got several men to help him get the Colonel out. Part way through their rescue efforts they had to pause as they were overcome by laughter at his forlorn appearance.

Morning was a welcome sight and it got better when the kitchen served up a hot meal, even though it was the familiar slightly green scrambled eggs. After eating, the men boarded trucks for their trip to Moderscheid, via Krinkelt, Bullingen and Amel. Evidence of the violence of the fighting that had taken place here during the Battle of the Bulge was very much in evidence. There were burned out tanks and trucks, both German and American, and the buildings that were standing were pocked with shell and bullet holes.

"To me this area had been worked over first by us, then the Bulge happened and the Germans came back through and now we're pushing them back out. You could just smell death in the air. I never saw so many dead people in my life, just laying everywhere. You couldn't mark off a 50' square, I'll bet, that wasn't shell marked."

Henry Thomas—M Company

"It'll get to ya. We went around this corner and they'd taken an American, stripped all his clothes off. He had his arms up in the air. He was frozen. His mouth was open and he was screaming. This was the thing we saw when we went through there. I saw a jeep run over up there. It was so flat it looked like a little toy car."

William Bartow—M Company

Even though all of the men in the Battalion were wet as they boarded the trucks, the only physical result was an epidemic of diarrhea. Arriving in Moderscheid, the men of the 3rd Battalion met some more of their replacements from the 69th Division. The contrast between the two groups was so great that one might have had difficulty believing they were members of the same army. The battle-hardened veterans were filthy dirty. They sported a variety of beards, sideburns, mustaches, etc. None of the non-coms had any stripes and there was not one division shoulder patch among them. Many wore parts of German civilian or military clothing for warmth and some were carrying German pistols. The green troops of the 69th were clean with pressed uniforms and were clean shaven. All their non-coms sported their stripes, all wore their division patch on their shoulders and all wore nothing but army-issued clothing and carried only U.S. Army weapons. To the men of the 3rd Battalion, their replacements seemed awfully young, yet the ages were the same.

The men were all billeted in buildings so they were dry and warm. Being in a rear area, it was not necessary to maintain guard posts around the clock and for the first time in many, many days the men could get a full night's sleep. They needed it as they had been in contact with the enemy for three months, much longer than most units experienced.

An engineer group had set up shower facilities, which were most welcome. There were long tents, floored with duckboards and many shower heads. The men entered at one end and stripped to the buff. There were baskets for their boots, wallets, watches and personal items, but all their clothes were dumped in piles. There was ample hot water in the showers which was a real luxury. Scrubbing themselves from top to bottom with the strong GI soap removed the layers of "combat dirt." At the exit end of the tent were piles of clean clothes, separated by sizes. The replacement uniforms were unpressed, but they were clean! An observer would not have believed the change in appearance. All the men looked so much younger! Some had to take a second look to identify friends as it had been so long since they had seen each other like this. This was the first time these men had really been clean since they went on line November 9th. A few had had a chance to bathe during rest periods, but the majority had had nothing but sponge baths out of a helmet. They had not even had a chance to change their underwear. All of them had gotten dirty at pretty much the same rate so the day-to-day changes had not been noticed, but here the change was dramatic.

Commissioned officers in the American army received a monthly liquor ration. Most of them shared theirs with the men in their commands in one way or another.

> "Every officer got a liquor ration—1 bottle of scotch, 1 bottle of gin, 1 bottle of cognac and a 1/2 bottle of brandy. Capt. Decker never gave the liquor ration out. He kept it all until we got to a rest area. I remember the first, in February, after the Bulge. That night after everyone got cleaned up and half rested, he called the company together for a 'cocktail party.' He had taken all the liquor—brandy, scotch, cognac—put it in a big wash bucket and mixed some strawberry ersatz soft drink with it. Everybody

dipped into it with their canteen cups. I don't know who was the last one to stand, but it wasn't me."

Fred Thompson—M Company

For the next four days the Battalion cleaned equipment and got things in order as well as doing some road repair. On February 20th the Battalion moved on foot to Malmedy, a distance of 18 kilometers. Just before this move they had been issued shoepacs; which are a leather topped boot with rubber lowers. Proper foot gear had been a continual problem. The shoe-pacs are great winter foot wear, but are not made for marching. Practically all of the men developed foot blisters on this march. They went by the crossroads at Baugnez, just outside Malmedy, where the "Malmedy Massacre" occurred during the Battle of the Bulge when German SS troops mowed down a group of Americans who had surrendered. At Malmedy trucks were waiting which took them to LaMinerie, Belgium, via Sart, Verviers and Battice, a distance of 37 kilometers.

The Battalion got to LaMinerie about 1700 and spent the first night in barns, but the next day they moved in with Belgian civilian residents, 2, 3, or 4 men to a family. It was a wonderful experience for the soldiers. The Belgians were on short rations, but they shared everything they had in an effort to show their gratitude. The Americans were all young men and the warmth of this welcome touched their hearts and made them think of home. It made their sacrifices very meaningful and the men were able to express some of their appreciation by giving the Belgians food and coaf from army supplies. Major Orr, the Battalion surgeon, was able to save a young woman's hand from the amputation recommended by the local doctor. She had gangrene in the hand from an injury inflicted by a German soldier. With debridement and sulfa, Orr was able to clean up the infection. Her thirteen year old brother was a soldier in his own right, as he had killed a number of Germans as a member of the local resistance group. Almost 50 years later some of the men are still in contact with their Belgian hosts.

The civilians had a hard time understanding that their beds were too soft for some of these combat men who preferred sleeping on the floor, as this was what they had gotten used to. The war was going well and at night in LaMinerie it was possible to look up and see the sky filled with vapor trails from Allied bombers on their way to Germany. One could even see flashes from the bomb explosions in Cologne and Frankfurt even though they were too far away to hear. This was a wonderful interlude in the midst of the death and destruction these men had come from and soon would return to.

Until the 27th the Battalion prepared for further action by repairing equipment, taking physicals and attending classes on such things as the proper use of flamethrowers. On the 24th there was a field inspection which did not go too well. The inspection was conducted by "rear area type" officers who had not experienced any combat action. They conducted a garrison type inspection and issued demerits for such things as a little rust on a rifle's butt plate. These military niceties were treated with disdain by these combat veterans and the inspectors lost whatever credibility they had had. An intelligence officer spoke to the men about the necessity of getting prisoners, pointing out how valuable they were to secured information. Since the massacre of American prisoners at Baugnez on December 17th by Pieper's SS troops, the number of prisoners taken by the Americans had gone down dramatically and SS prisoners were virtually nonexistent.

The 3rd Battalion left LaMinerie by truck on February 27 for Stolberg, Germany, via Thimister, Henri-Chapelle, Moresnet, Aachen and Eilendorf. At Stolberg all the men were quartered in houses. On the 28th they again boarded trucks and went via Eschweiler, Weisweiler and Düren to an assembly area one mile south of Elsdorf and dug in. Later that night orders were received to attack Bergheim and by midnight they were in an assembly area east of Paffendorf. For this attack the following units were attached to the 3rd Battalion: one platoon of Company C, 324th Engineers and one platoon of the 629th Tank Destroyer Battalion. Supporting artillery was the 925th Field Artillery.

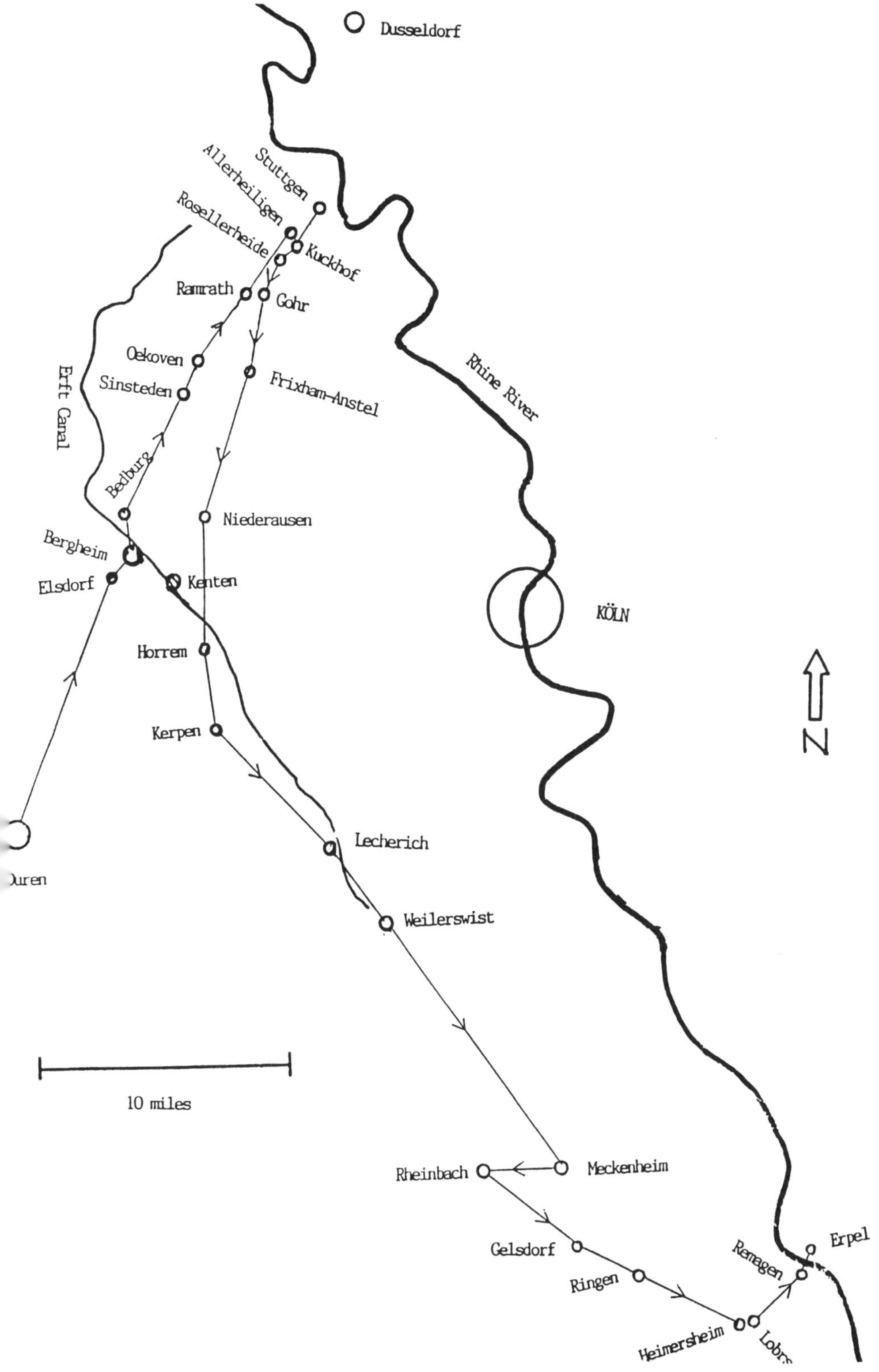

Dusseldorf
Stuttgen
Allerheiligen
Rosellerheide
Kuckhof
Ramrath
Gohr
Oekoven
Sinsteden
Frixham-Anstel
Erft Canal
Rhine River
Bedburg
Niederausen
Bergheim
Elsdorf
Kenten
KÖLN
Horrem
N
Kerpen
Lecherich
Weilerswist
10 miles
Rheinbach
Meckenheim
Gelsdorf
Erpel
Remagen
Ringen
Heimersheim

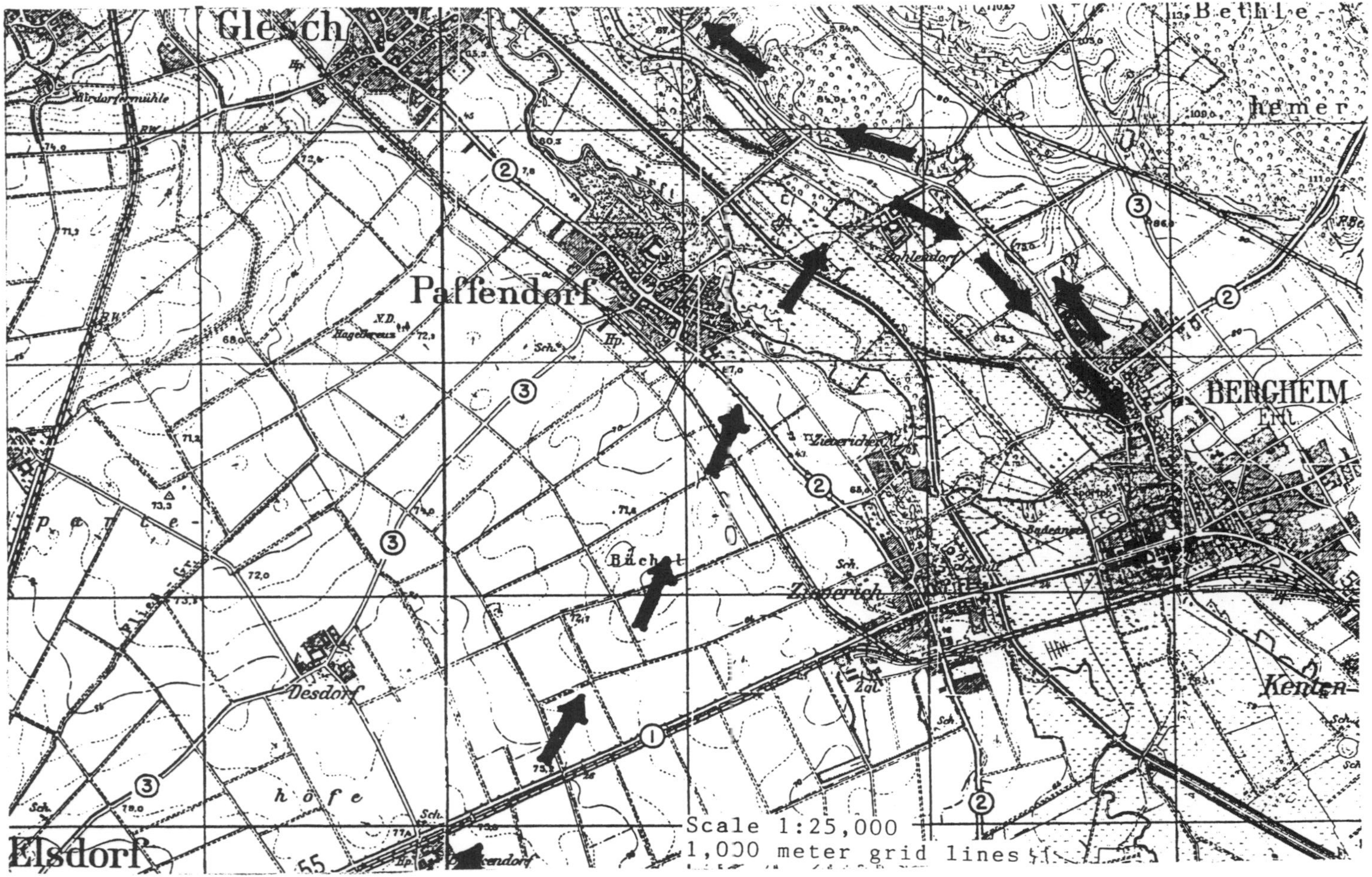
Glesch
Paffendorf
BERGHEIM
Erft
Bethle-
hemer
Zieverich
Büchel
Desdorf
Elsdorf
Kenten
Wiedenfeld
höfe
Scale 1:25,000
1,000 meter grid lines

CHAPTER 6

Bergheim to the Rhine

At Bergheim, a mid-sized city on the Cologne Plain, the 3rd Battalion made their first attack on a city of any size. Much of Germany is hilly, but the Cologne Plain is quite flat and is good tank country. Bergheim controlled access to the Erft Canal which is a natural tank barrier and it was necessary to secure a crossing over the canal for a successful attack toward the Rhine River and the city of Cologne. The 3rd Battalion was the first unit across the Erft and was far in front of other American troops.

For this attack the 395th Regimental Combat Team was under the command of the 3rd Armored Division. The attack was made in a southeasterly direction with the 3rd Battalion on the right and the 2nd Battalion on the left. The 2nd Battalion was stopped in their attack and the 1st Battalion took over the left flank.

At 0300 hours on March 1, 1945, the 3rd Battalion began their attack along the Bedburg-Bergheim highway. I Company was on the left, K Company on the right and L Company in reserve. Captain Burgin, CO of I Company, had been temporarily transferred to battalion headquarters as S-3 and Lt. James Hare acted as company commander during the attack on Bergheim.

"As the time came for the TOT (timed artillery fire) to be placed on the town, I called out for bayonets to be attached to the rifles. I was doing this in order to get the spirit of offense in the minds of the troops. I found out that only about 50 percent of them had bayonets. The rest of them seemed to think they weren't any good and had thrown them away or gotten rid of them in one way or another."

James Hare—I Company

This attack was unique. Conventional military wisdom, as taught by the Infantry School, is that a battalion is too large a unit to make successful night attacks. However, Col. Butler had had another premonition which told him to attack at night across a flat open field with a minimum of artillery preparation. This was the first of a number of successful night attacks that earned the 3rd Battalion such a reputation that the French Army asked Butler to write up his methods so they could use them in their training.

The attack was made across a flat, open field about 800 yards across. In the dark the men could easily hear artillery rounds passing overhead, going both ways, as opposing artillery engaged in counter-battery fire. At the edge of town a small outpost was overwhelmed by K Company and about ten of the enemy taken prisoner. When relating their actions after the fact, combat veterans tend to downplay their heroics.

> "We laid there for a few minutes. The word came along for my squad leader to take his squad off to the left, sneak down there, get across the canal and get behind those machine guns and knock 'em out. That's what we did."
>
> Richard Gorby—K Company

By daylight the men were in the town and by 1100 hours Bergheim was secured. L Company then passed through the attacking companies to clean out Kenten and the factory district to the southeast of Bergheim. At Kenten and the factory district there were a number of Russian and Polish "slave workers." No effort was made to control them other than to make sure they stayed off the streets. There were a lot of German civilians living in Bergheim and each house had to be searched and cleared.

> "L Company had not been able to clear the building they were in, so Col. Butler asked my buddy (Giles Tutt) and me if we would like to go with him to clear the building for them. The three of us went up a ditch to the position

and went from room to room, kicking in the doors and taking prisoners. I don't remember how many we captured—probably no more than six or so, but the point is that Col. Butler took his turn on the doors just like Tutt and I. I don't think he would ask a man to do anything he, himself, wouldn't do."

        Hugh Ferris—Headquarters Company

"The last house on the far side of town was cleared after sunup and we found a very strange thing there, an unusual occurrence. Just as we were coming up to the house, a little motorbike took off and the fellow who was on it went around a curve and was lost from our sight so he was safe. We went into the house with some caution and there we found a new-born baby. Just been born. A very unusual sight. Unusual things did happen."

        Richard Mills—I Company

  In clearing the buildings several hundred women and children and a few old men were rounded up. This was the first experience these men had in dealing with civilian non-combatants. They were rounded up and collected in a large church. While searching one house, Rollin Satler of I Company, saw a movement out of the corner of his eye and, turning quickly, he emptied his M-1 into a full length mirror!

  The Battalion had been so successful that they suffered no casualties at all in the initial attack and very, very few men were killed or wounded as they consolidated their positions. A single attack by a German plane was ineffective, but there was a German 88mm gun on the hill east of town that fired sporadically and caused some injuries. Two men were killed by this gun when they went into an open field to investigate a disabled German tank and exposed themselves. This gun continued intermittent fire on the area until it was knocked out by an American tank from the 3rd Armored.

  "There were 88mm shells screaming down the center of town, probably about 20 feet over my head. It sounded just like a rifle shot when you're in the pits. (The scorers position below the targets on a rifle range.) These were 88's so you got one hell of a bang when they hit."

James Hare—I Company

There was some sniper fire from time to time. One narrowly missed hitting Col. Butler, but the snipers were soon disposed of.

"Resistance became almost negligible except for a sniper in a second floor room. When we got down there I found some extra shells. They were not military shells. They were hunting rifle shells with soft points so whomever was up there as a sniper would have been a civilian rather than a soldier."

James Hare—I Company

Most of the houses were well built as this was a prosperous town. Those houses in the nicer part of town had been built after Hitler's rise to power and had been built with concrete bomb shelters in the basements. It was somewhat of a culture shock to the American troops that even these fine houses did not have central heating. There were stoves, many very elaborate with enameled finishes, in each room for heat and coal burning coil heaters in the bathrooms to heat bath water. Bergheim and Kenten were the first German towns to be captured by the 99th Division.

One of the houses was a perfumery and had a lot of expensive perfume about. The squad that searched this house began to play around and ended up spraying one another with perfume as well as appropriating some "souvenirs." For some days after this episode they could not be sent out on patrols as their odor would have given them away.

"I was with two or three fellows and we came upon what appeared to be a post office. There we were, 19, 20 years old, this battle we had just been through, after it was done, seemed like a piece of cake and were relaxed and curious. It was mainly out of curiosity rather than because of any military training we had had. There in the corner was a safe. Somehow or other we got into that thing. I think there was a minor explosion involved. When the smoke cleared, money was scattered all over the place. I guess you might expect to find money in a post office. We just took some souvenirs, stuck them in our pockets and went on."

Richard Mills—I Company

The town of Bergheim and the high ground behind it had been defended by approximately one understrength battalion which had orders to "delay and hold at all cost." This strategic point guarded one of the main approaches to Cologne as well as the Erft Canal. The 3rd Battalion captured about 100 POW's. Reports from these POW's showed that the 1st Battalion, 957th Infantry Regiment, 363rd Volksgrenadier Division had occupied this town on the morning of March 1st.

"We had an anti-aircraft soldier attached to our squad. He was not very experienced and not very dedicated to military life. We were in a building. I sent him upstairs to watch for a counter-attack which we were sure would come. Sure enough, across the field a group of tanks were coming and firing and hit my building. I yelled for him to get downstairs. He froze up there. I dashed upstairs to shove him downstairs for his own safety. In the meantime a tank shell came in through the building and exploded and that's how I got shrapnel in my spine. He grabbed me and I remember him shouting, 'Sgt. Piersall's been hit.' He grabbed me by the feet and tugged me down the stairs. I was alert enough to know that my head was hitting every damn step, all the way down to the ground floor. What a memory!"

Thornton Piersall—I Company

During the afternoon, considerable semi-automatic and self-propelled gun fire was received from the woods northeast of town. A reinforced rifle platoon from I Company worked well forward of the lines, but made no contact with the enemy. The Battalion set up defensive positions in Bergheim and Kenten while the 3rd Armored Division continued to attack toward the Rhine.

"All in all we came way out on top on that one."
Richard Mills—I Company

"I was very, very happy to see ol' Charlie Burgin come back to the company and take over. That man is one of the greatest small unit commanders that I've ever met and I believe he was responsible for a lot of our accomplishments."
James Hare—I Company

The Battalion stayed in Bergheim for another day and a half, while armored and infantry units kept up the attack toward the Rhine. There were no natural barriers that would afford the Germans good defensive positions and they were fighting a delaying action as they retreated to the Rhine River which was the last real barrier between the attacking forces and the German heartland.

Bergheim was a fairly prosperous city and the American troops found lots of civilian vehicles—cars, motorcycles and motorbikes. One group cut the top off a sedan and entertained their friends by driving around in the open car with a large bust of Hitler in the rear seat. By the time the Battalion was to leave, a number of German vehicles had American markings and the men thought that the extra capacity would be helpful. Two men from M Company were ready to proceed riding German motorcycles. However, their hopes were in vain as Col. Butler felt he could not permit this and all the civilian vehicles were left behind.

As the trucks were ready to leave, one man came running to catch up. In his haste he ran into and out of a slit trench. He was filthy and malodorous from the waist down and the other men on the truck would not let him aboard. The truck driver gave him some cleaner trousers and he cleaned himself up as best he could. The men then let him aboard, but insisted he sit on the strap across the back while they all crowded to the front of the truck to get as far away as possible from the odor.

At 1500 on the 3rd of March the Battalion moved by truck to an assembly area at Nanderath via Bedburg, Bucholz and

Heuhofchen, arriving about 1600. At 1700 they attacked with I Company on the left, K Company on the right and L Company in reserve. By 1800 they had secured Bongarderbo and Sinsteden against light opposition and organized defensive positions for the night. In this attack the infantry marched on each side of the road with the accompanying tanks in the center of the road. The tanks would draw artillery fire and when this would happen they would pull off the road and get near a building so they would be out of sight. In situations like this it was easy to separate the old soldiers from the replacements. The new men would instinctively head for the protection of a building, but the experienced men would run to get as far as possible from the tanks. As one of Bill Mauldin's characters said, "A moving foxhole tends to attract a lot of attention."

When official reports and news articles state that "opposition was light" it must be understood that this is a very relative statement. When a man was hit by enemy fire, he bled and died just as freely in a "light opposition" situation as he did in the midst of a raging battle.

> "After walking a couple of hours in a light rain, I started looking at the faces of the men I was with. Suddenly, I realized that I hardly knew any of them. Most of the ones I had come with in November were gone. I was shocked—my luck cannot hold out much longer. I had a feeling this could be the day.

> "As we approached a town, artillery started coming in. We scattered from the road, but continued to walk forward. I was in an open, flat field with no cover. All of a sudden the sound came closer and I knew I was going to be in the middle of it and attempted to dive to the ground. While in mid-air, I felt something hit my back as if I had been hit with a baseball bat.

> "Shortly thereafter, how long I don't know, I put my hand on my stomach to see if there was any blood there. I saw my hand was covered with blood. I thought my greatest fear had been realized—that I was shot all the way

through. No one could help me because of the shelling. I just laid there, thinking I would be dead in a few minutes.

"I laughed to myself at the shelling. For the first time in months I felt completely at ease. The shelling could not hurt me anymore."

John Laird—I Company

Laird recovered from his wounds, which turned out to be a large, superficial wound in the back. The blood running down his body had led him to believe he was shot through. He almost died from loss of blood and said he could literally feel life returning when he was given blood plasma. His comments about feeling at ease are somewhat typical of a wounded infantryman's thoughts when he is wounded. He knows that his war is over and that he will be out of harm's way, warm and cared for. Knowing that they probably would be hit sooner or later, infantrymen look forward to a "million dollar wound" which is loosely defined as a wound that is not fatal or crippling, but severe enough to require treatment at a rear area hospital.

Things kept moving. At 0700 on the 4th I and K Companies moved out and had captured Oekoven by 0900. L Company pushed through and by noon had captured Deelen. At 1330 the attack was renewed and the towns of Ramrath, Neukirchderheide, Gubisrath and Neuenbaum were occupied with little problem. All of these places were small villages, often only a few kilometers apart. The Battalion surgeon and his group of medical personnel would follow the combat units.

"Between Bergheim and Kuckhof we managed to take a wrong turn and take a town by mistake. The mayor surrendered to me and we took a collection of souvenir pistols and flags. When we got back to the front line, the Captain at the road block swore at the fool medics taking the town they were supposed to take the next day."

Herbert Orr, MD—Battalion Surgeon

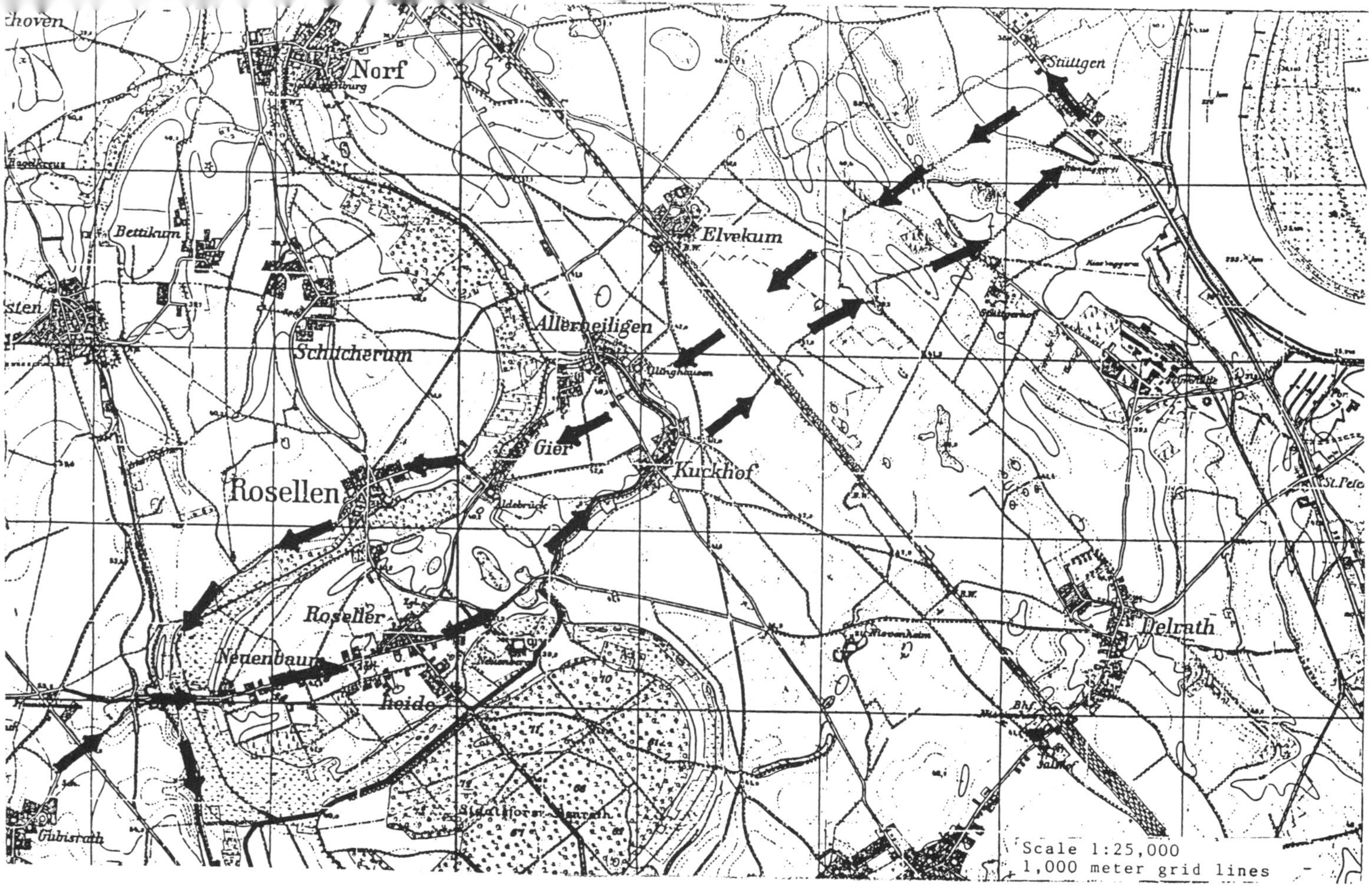

Norf
Stüttgen
Bettikum
Elvekum
Schlicherum
Allerheiligen
Gier
Kuckhof
Rosellen
Roseller
Neuenbaum
heide
Delrath
Gubisrath
Scale 1:25,000
1,000 meter grid lines

By this time the 3rd Battalion was so far out in front that other units of the 395th thought they were enemy and American artillery hit several men. Col. Butler managed to get this "friendly" fire stopped before his battalion suffered too much. At 1630 the Battalion was held up by machine gun fire outside Rosselerheid, but soon took the town and set up positions for the night.

"At one point in Germany we were attacking across an open field when a German machine gun opened up on us. We spotted the machine gun and called for mortar fire. One man had his 60mm mortar tube and some ammunition, but no base plate. He sat down, planted the tube between his legs, estimated the range and let fly, no increments on the shell. It hit the German machine gunner square on top of the helmet. Blew his head off as well as his blouse and peeled his skin to the waist. It also killed his loader."

George Prager—L Company

The attack was resumed at 0500 the next day and by 0700 they had secured the towns of Allerheilgen and Kuckhof. The entire front was moving so rapidly that the commanders of the various units had to stop the attacking troops occasionally so as not to lose control. At Kuckhof the Battalion was held up momentarily to get better organized for subsequent attacks.

Most of I Company was in a barn about 250 yards from the Battalion headquarters. A bazooka team was loading their weapon. The friction catch at the back of the tube which held the round until fired, did not work properly. The round slid through the tube, which was being held nose down, and hit the concrete floor of the barn. A bazooka round is theoretically not "live" until it has been fired which allows the safety tube to slide back and arm the round. In this case theory did not hold and when the round hit the floor it exploded. Both men of the team were fatally wounded and died within minutes. In a closed area like the barn the concussion was terrific and shrapnel from the bazooka round wounded a number of the other men. Because things had been moving so swiftly, the Battalion Surgeon, Dr. Herbert Orr, and the men from the battalion aid station were close by and were working on the injured almost immediately. Several of the injured men were in the doorway of the barn and those that were not seriously injured were quickly loaded on a jeep and taken out so as to give the medics more room to work. Those men taken out were very fortunate in that in a matter of minutes, German 88's began to shell the area. The enemy had left this area only hours before and were very accurate; at least one of the rounds hitting directly in the barn doorway. This artillery killed and wounded more men, some of the men injured by the bazooka round and even some of the medical personnel and men from the other companies that were aiding the wounded. In less than a half hour I Company suffered more casualties than they had suffered to date. Among others, Capt. Charles Burgin, the company commander, and his executive officer, Lt. James Hare, were wounded. Lt. Elroy Leming, third platoon commander, was one of those killed and the third platoon was reduced to five men. In all, about 14 men were killed or died of their wounds and about 40 men were injured, some crippled for life. Lt. Gene Stalcup took command of I Company and Lts. Peterson and Musser came from K Company to lead the 1st and 3rd platoons.

Robert Van Snevily from I Company was one of those men who were wounded by the bazooka round and hit again by the German artillery. As late as 1968 he had to have a major operation to remove pieces of shrapnel from his throat. Although severely wounded, it was typical of Snevily and his comrades that they downplay the severity of their wounds and try to reassure their loved ones back home. Following are excerpts from a letter to his parents a Red Cross worker wrote for him, March 13, 1944;

> "First thing—everything is OK. In case you haven't heard from the War Department, I have been wounded in Germany. I want to reassure you that it is nothing serious and I'm still in one piece. I am receiving the best of care and have everything I need.
>
> "The war will have to get along without me now."

In subsequent letters to his parents, Snevily said, "I'm feeling well. Sleep okay at night and just feel happy." Even though he came very close to losing his left arm, he wrote, "As to what extent function will return to my left arm I will be completely happy and content and ever so grateful."

Not all of the casualties were in I Company. M Company lost a platoon leader and a machine gunner. Headquarters Company had men injured as well. A machine gun had a water jacket torn by shrapnel and a jeep was destroyed.

"We were doing our usual thing. I can't remember how close our building was to the other company (I Company), but I was upstairs to see if I could see across the plain to get a position for an OP. They hit the building with an 88 or something. It blew me clear across the room and into the stairwell. It gave me a little dent and a little shake up. I didn't go to the hospital, but it gave me a wallop, I'll tell you. I thought this was all of it."

Fred Thompson—M Company

"It seemed like there would be no end to that day. The bazooka round went off just before lunch, artillery fell on us for sometime after that. I saw fellows in agony. There wasn't anything I could do except comfort with words and hold a hand here and there. The medics were very busy and doing an efficient job. We had just about gotten everybody cleared away and things kind of on an even keel. I had miraculously not been hurt in any way even though I was among the wounded while the artillery rounds came in. Some of the people I was with were taking shrapnel and I was blessed by not being wounded at all. That evening I was called to the company CP and told that we had some people who were out further toward the river, across this farmland. They had gone to do something and had taken some kind of a hit and been wounded. They wanted me to take a half dozen guys and go across this plain, at night, hook up with these people and give them the assistance they needed to get back to Kuckhof. I felt a little uptight about the whole situation. I was told to take the telephone line in hand and follow it for about two miles to find these people. It worked. I got to them. Finally, sometime in the night, we got back to Kuckhof and everybody was back together again who had not been evacuated and sent to a hospital. That was a black day for I Company."

Richard Mills—I Company

"The artillery in our whole area was intense. We got into the stairway just as a big shell knocked the brick wall down on us, damaging my left shoulder. We got into a hay bale shelter and took care of the wounded and shell-shocked, preparing for night evacuation. The daughter of the householders went into intensive labor so that night I delivered my first German baby—also my first in a hay bale shelter."

Herbert Orr, MD—Battalion Surgeon

At 1400 K Company attacked and by 1700 had secured the town of Stuttgerhof which is only 1,000 meters from the Rhine. They received heavy machine gun fire from Gincworke, which the adjacent unit had not been able to secure, and held in place until mortars knocked out those guns. Col. Butler's jeep took some of this machine gun fire and for the 7th time the windshield was shot out. Butler bailed out and his driver went into reverse for 500 yards at top speed to get out of the line of fire. There were about five tanks along the road and Butler worked his way back, tank by tank. As he came to each tank he would try to spot targets for the tank commander and by the time he got back to some protection, his company commanders were waiting for him. They had no hesitation in reminding him that he had always told them that they were to NEVER get in an exposed situation like this and enjoyed his discomfiture. By 0530 on the 6th Stuttgen was secured and the area from here to the Rhine River had been cleared of enemy troops. Junior Willis of K Company was the first man in the Battalion to reach the Rhine. At 1830 the Battalion moved back to Gier and Rosellen and were quartered in buildings. The Battalion headquarters remained in Kuckhof.

At noon on the 7th the Battalion marched to Rosellerheide where they boarded trucks and were taken to the town of Gohr. At 1500 the 99th Division Commander, MG Walter E. Lauer, presented Col. Butler and the Battalion with the Presidential Unit Citation they had earned for their staunch defense of Höfen during the Battle of the Bulge. It was a proud moment for the Battalion. This was the first time the Battalion had all been together since they left Boston. After the formal ceremony they returned to their company areas where each man was presented with his individual citation.

On the 8th the men spent their time resting and cleaning weapons. On the 9th they marched to Gohr and then moved by truck to Meckenheim via Frixheim-Anstel, Niederausen, Grossernich, Derkum and Rheinbach and were quartered in buildings for the night. Here they received more replacements for the men who had become casualties.

In World War II army policies had changed from those in effect in World War I. Instead of units being relieved from time to time to rest and re-equip, the units stayed in the line and individual replacements were shuttled in as needed. There are two negative aspects to this policy. One, the veterans achieve a very close feeling for each other because of their experiences and a "new man" is not part of this very close knit society and at first is treated as an interloper. The new man feels left out and the men who have fought together wonder if he can be trusted. The second drawback to this policy, from the standpoint of the individual soldier, is that he knows his chances of being killed or wounded increase the longer he stays. As a result, some men break under this continual threat and become fatalists, feeling that sooner or later they are going to be hit so they don't take all the precautions they should.

> "The drive across the plains to the Rhine River was a series of attacks when we took heavy machine gun fire, artillery

and mortar shelling. I remember one instance when the 'screaming meemies' pinned us down. We had to get out of there but every time we jumped up to advance, the machine gun fire started. I ran forward and jumped into a hole. In just a few seconds another body landed on top of me. I looked up and it was my company commander. In answer to his question as to how I was doing, I told him, 'Mrs. Park's little boy is scared to death.' He answered, 'Mrs. Phillips's little boy is scared too.' I told him that he was our intrepid leader and wasn't allowed to get scared."

Robert Parks—K Company

It is very common when discussing combat with front line soldiers to hear many stories with a humorous twist. A sense of humor is very necessary for them to maintain their sanity amidst the horrors they experience and the continual physical and mental abuse that is inherent in war. If you can find something to laugh at, you can persevere.

Major Orr broke regulations many times by sewing and litigating bleeders more than called for to save the lives of men who would otherwise not have made it to the rear and also by returning men to their units who wanted to stay with friends rather than being evacuated and coming back as replacements.

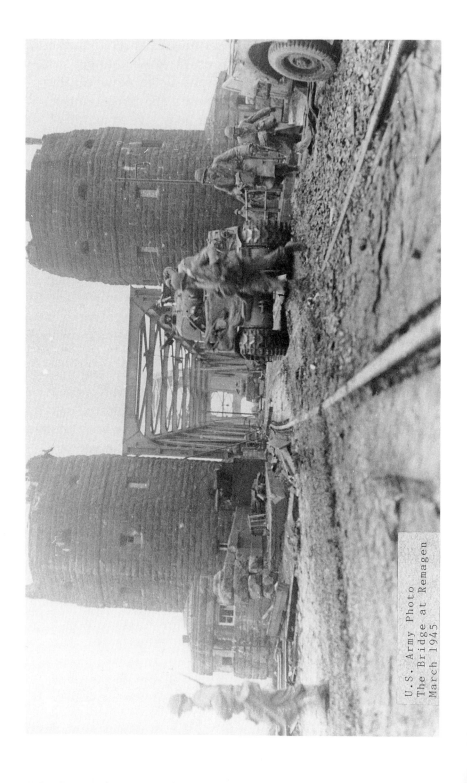

U.S. Army Photo
The Bridge at Remagen
March 1945

CHAPTER 7

The Rhine and the Wied

On March 7th leading elements of the 9th Armored Division reached the town of Remagen on the Rhine River. The Rhine was the final great natural barrier between the advancing Allied armies and the German heartland. If the Allies were not stopped here, the Germans knew the war was lost. To the surprise of the 9th, the Ludendorff railroad bridge was still standing. For some reason the charges planted to destroy this bridge had failed to explode. They were quick to take advantage of this unexpected break and immediately began to cross the river. The Ludendorff Bridge, 1,069 feet overall length, had been built during World War I to carry German troops and equipment to the Western Front and consisted of two rail tracks with a concrete pedestrian walkway on one side. The 9th put steel sheets over the railroad tracks so their vehicles could cross and other men crossed on foot.

The Germans were desperate to stop this incursion and used everything they could to destroy the bridge. Any artillery guns within reach were firing; the Luftwaffe sent planes to bomb it; frogmen were dispatched to plant explosive charges on the bridge piers. In their only attempt in World War II to use them as tactical weapons, the Germans fired eleven V-2 rockets at the bridge in a desperate effort to destroy it. The most accurate rocket missed the bridge by a mile and a half and this effort was abandoned. They even fired a 540mm gun with 2 ton shells. None of these desperate efforts were successful, although a shell was hitting the bridge on an average of every two minutes. American troops began to pour across and the engineers started at once to build pontoon bridges.

The high command of the American forces began to rush all the troops possible to the bridgehead at Remagen. On the 10th of March the 3rd Battalion moved by truck to Ringen via Gelsdorf. That night initial elements of the 394th Regiment crossed the bridge.

> "Somewhere below Düsseldorf, Bruce Waterman and I found a German telephone. Smart aleck that I am, I got on it and talked to a German soldier in German. I asked him if he knew where the Americans were and he told me about 100 kilometers from the Rhine, whereupon I informed him that he was talking to an Ami and I was looking at the Rhine. Dead silence and he hung up."
>
> George Prager L Company

At 0430 on the 11th the Battalion marched via Lantershofen and Bad Neuenahr to Heimersheim, where they received orders to continue their march across the Rhine. As they approached Remagen, they were in full view of the defending German troops who were on the high bluffs on the east side of the Rhine and were subject to heavy artillery fire as they moved up. For the last block or two as they approached the bridge, the men had to step over or around an American casualty at almost every step. Col. Butler was given the option of crossing on the railroad bridge or on a pontoon bridge. At the start of the pontoon bridge there was a truck full of mortar ammunition that had been hit and with the subsequent fire and explosions, the pontoon bridge was effectively blocked so he opted for the railroad bridge. They encountered a truck loaded with troops that had suffered a near miss from a big shell and the concussion had killed every man, including the driver, before they could move.

> "Just before we got to the river there was an army truck sitting along the curb with a tarpaulin all tied down. My buddy said to me, 'Gorby, I bet they got something good to

eat in there. Let's look under the tarp and see what we can find.' We untied the ropes from that truck to pick the tarp up and there was a whole truckload of American dead in there. We tied the tarp back down. The whole street along there was just lined with dead Americans."

Richard Gorby—K Company

It was a scene of chaos. Col. Butler had his Executive Officer, Maj. Ernest Golden, assemble the Battalion and bring them across as a unit. Because of all the confusion, units became separated rushing across and Col. Butler spent several hours on the east end of the bridge directing men to their units. Fortunately the 3rd Battalion did not suffer a single casualty crossing the river in spite of the enemy's desperate attempts to stop them. There was a large shell hole in the bridge deck and disabled vehicles were simply dumped through this hole after the men had gotten out in order to keep the bridge clear for following vehicles. Desperate circumstances demanded desperate actions.

"The next thing I remember was crossing the Rhine River at Remagen. On the west end of the bridge there was an American half-track knocked out and a soldier laying on top with his body slit half in two. We were under intense enemy fire and the Germans trying to bomb the bridge and the American ack-ack firing filled the sky with flak. There was a lot of dead and wounded on the bridge but my squad and I made it across okay. I will never forget that hour crossing that bridge because of the dead and dying soldiers."

Leo Humphrey—I Company

One young jeep driver had driven his commander across the bridge under intense fire and when they got to the east side, the driver informed his officer that he just couldn't take any more and wanted to quit. The officer told him that if that was the case, he would have to be evacuated which meant he would have to cross back over the bridge to get to medical help. The driver promptly decided that he was well enough to continue as there was no way he was going to go back across that bridge.

"The roads were choked with convoys of trucks and equipment from several divisions we had not seen before. For miles we had been passing Corps and Army eight inch, 155's and 240's firing almost continually. Trucks, jeeps, DUKW's (amphibious trucks), tanks and a couple of Navy LCI's rolled by in bumper to bumper columns. Major Golden was waiting to meet us and the road sign said 'Remagen 6 km.' For what seemed like a mile the road ran parallel to the river and a railroad and every few minutes an incoming round would sizzle across the river and hit with precision accuracy. The tanks and trucks were all bumper to bumper with motors running and the noise was deafening as we walked on each side of the road.

"As we reached the outskirts of Remagen, we waited behind houses and ran to the next cover between incoming rounds and tried not to notice the wrecked and burned out trucks, half-tracks and jeeps that smoldered at the curb where they had been pushed out of traffic. The medics were busy all around and a steady stream of ambulances tried to buck the traffic going back. We waited impatiently in a railroad underpass wishing to get on with whatever lay ahead.

"We finally moved out, edging ever closer to the bridge, passing scenes of horror and destruction. An ammo truck from the 394th was burning fiercely at the head of the bridge. We turned off the railroad and ran down through an old factory to the foot of the castle-like bridge towers. A big shell hit the water just before I got in the tower. We wound around on the steps going up for a few seconds and suddenly we were out and running, looking down at the planking underfoot. The route ahead looked a mile across and I felt something inside pushing me faster and faster. I ventured a glance over the rail at the muddy water way below and the trucks crossing the pontoon bridge downstream. I heard a big one coming but I had no place to duck. It hit in the water behind me by the bank. Finally, at long last, I was across."

Jack Randall—I Company

"My recollections of the Rhine crossing was as follows. Lt. Musser got our boys together, pointed to the bridge, and told us we were going to cross that baby. We had to get onto the bridge by going up through a tower. We were to cross with about 10 yards between each man. I do not remember seeing any steel plates the engineers put in for trucks and tanks. I do remember jumping across some big holes. I remember the big stuff from the Krauts was coming in heavy and, to this day, I still think of the Ludendorff Bridge as being the longest bridge in the world."

Dan Sullivan—I Company

"We crossed a pontoon bridge across the Rhine River. I was amazed at the swiftness of the flow of water in the Rhine. As we crossed on that pontoon bridge the truck mashed those pontoons down to the extent that the pontoons in front of us were at about eye level, or so it seemed. That gave me an eerie feeling.

"I saw a half-track with a 20mm mounted on it that had fired so many times at German airplanes trying to bomb that bridge, that the empty shell casings were piled up around it all the way up to the floor of the truck."

Richard Mills—I Company

Several German officers were court-martialed and executed on Hitler's orders for their failure to destroy the bridge before the Americans crossed. On March 17 the bridge collapsed from the battering it had taken, killing 28 engineers working on the bridge and injuring 93 others. By this time the American bridgehead was well established on the east bank of the Rhine and a number of pontoon bridges were in place.

With his battalion safely across, Butler reported to Gen. Craig, CO of the 9th Division, who had been designated as bridgehead commander as he was the senior officer on the east bank. Craig's headquarters were in a hotel in Erpel. Gen. Craig, an old friend, ordered Col. Butler to take his battalion 3 kilometers up the hill to Bruchhausen and relieve a battalion of the 9th Infantry that was down to less than 200 men. When he arrived there, Butler told his headquarters people to set up the Battalion Headquarters while he organized the troops to defend the area. The house he had selected, like many of the houses, had an outside entrance to the basement. This particular house had 27 steps leading to the basement which indicated that the basement was deep. The basement was filled with rubble and as they started to clean it out, the men discovered that this "rubble" was case after case of liquor of all kinds—cognac, vodka, wine, champagne, etc. After setting aside a few cases for himself, Col. Butler invited other headquarters to come and help themselves in an effort to get rid of it. He promptly forgot about the booze he had set aside until some weeks later when his driver asked him what to do with it.

Bruchhausen is on a hill overlooking the Rhine and the bridge. German planes attempting to bomb the bridge came over as low as 50 feet, strafing as they passed. To defend the bridge, the Americans had emplaced the largest number of anti-aircraft guns that were ever in one place in World War II. With all these weapons firing almost continually, spent shells and shrapnel literally rained down on the surrounding area and the 3rd Battalion lost several men a day from wounds caused by all this debris coming down. Some of these shells had delayed fuses and did not explode until they were falling on Bruchhausen.

On March 11, 1945, the 99th Infantry Division completed their crossing and were the first full infantry division in the U.S. Army to cross the Rhine. In 1990 a plaque was dedicated to this feat on the bridge towers on the west (Remagen) side of the river.

"The first platoon of I Company, Lt. Musser, was singled out (March 11) to represent the 99th Division at a First Army official flag raising ceremony in Cologne. Coming directly from front line action, they were filthy dirty and unshaven.

"Shortly after noon we arrived at the outskirts of Cologne. We were astounded at the tremendous damage our bombers had inflicted on the city. Not a single building was standing except the famous cathedral. After winding through this destruction for an hour, we arrived at what appeared to be a large concrete outdoor stadium. In very short order it became apparent that all the other units were cleanly uniformed—spic and span. A Major approached Lt. Musser from the reviewing stand and told him that we were the only ones taken directly from front line combat. As such, the Generals wanted us to be the honor guard and stand in front of the reviewing stand and have all the other units pass in review and salute us. When the parade ended, the American flag was raised on a tall flag pole located at the top of the stadium. The band played our national anthem and there wasn't a dry eye in the place.

"We were quickly loaded on trucks and told to rejoin our company near Remagen."

Paul Putty—I Company

On March 14 at 0015 the Battalion left Bruchhausen and marched to Dattenbergerwald via Erpel and Linz, a distance of about twenty miles. Regiment had told Col. Butler they were going to send trucks for this move, but Butler canceled the trucks and said his men would move on foot. It seems that with all the alcoholic beverages available, many of the men had gotten drunk. It was a rather sorry looking group that left Bruchhausen on foot and the column was pretty well strung out along the entire route. The men were pretty angry with Col. Butler, but by the time they reached Dattenbergerwald they were all sober and again were an effective fighting force.

The Battalion arrived in their assembly area at 0320. At 0830 artillery preparations began for an attack on Stümperich Quarry near the town of Halmer. The barrage lifted after twenty minutes

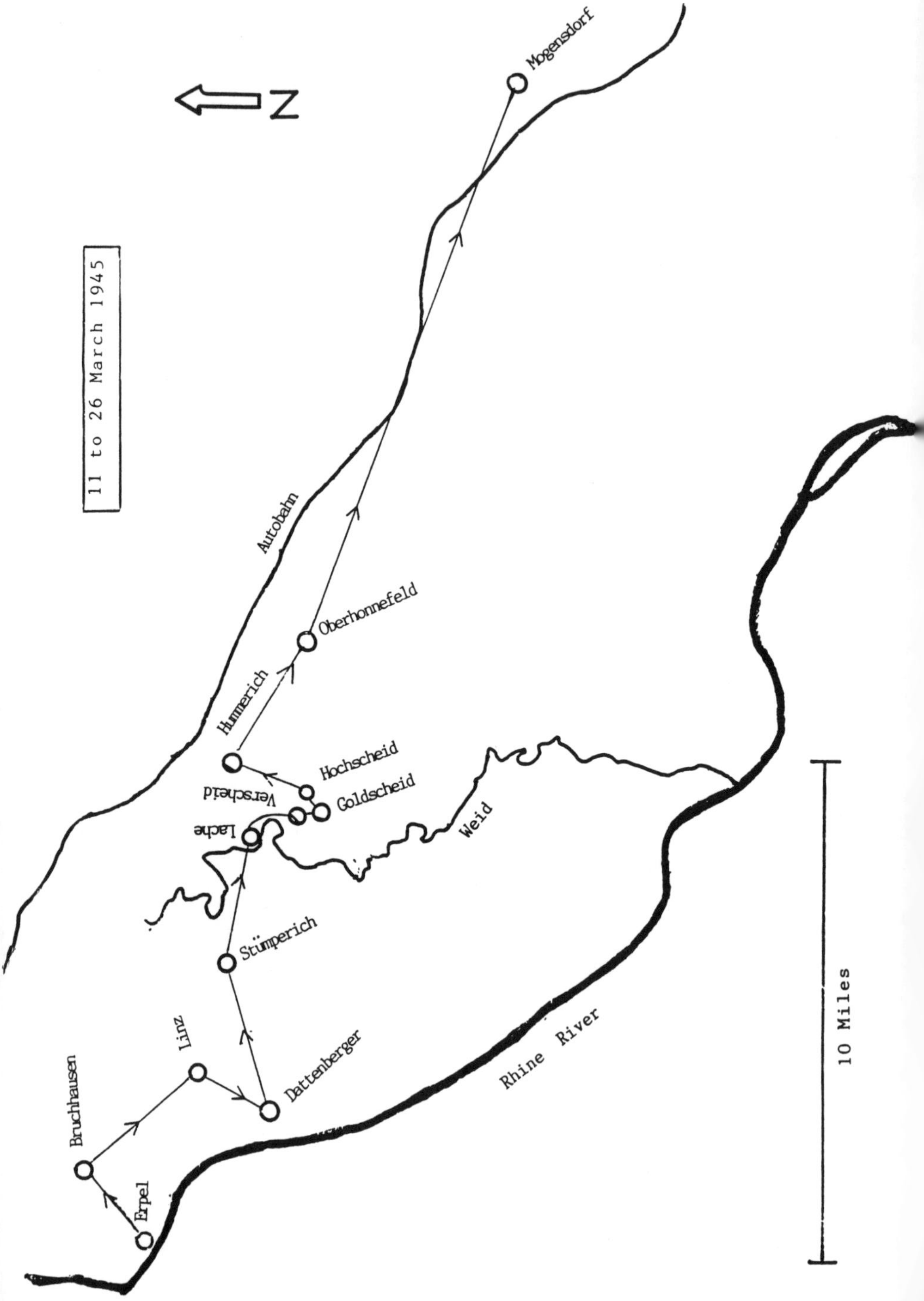
N
11 to 26 March 1945
Mogensdorf
Autobahn
Oberhonnefeld
Hummerich
Hochscheid
Verscheid
Goldscheid
Lache
Weid
Stümperich
Linz
Bruchhausen
Dattenberger
Erpel
Rhine River
10 Miles

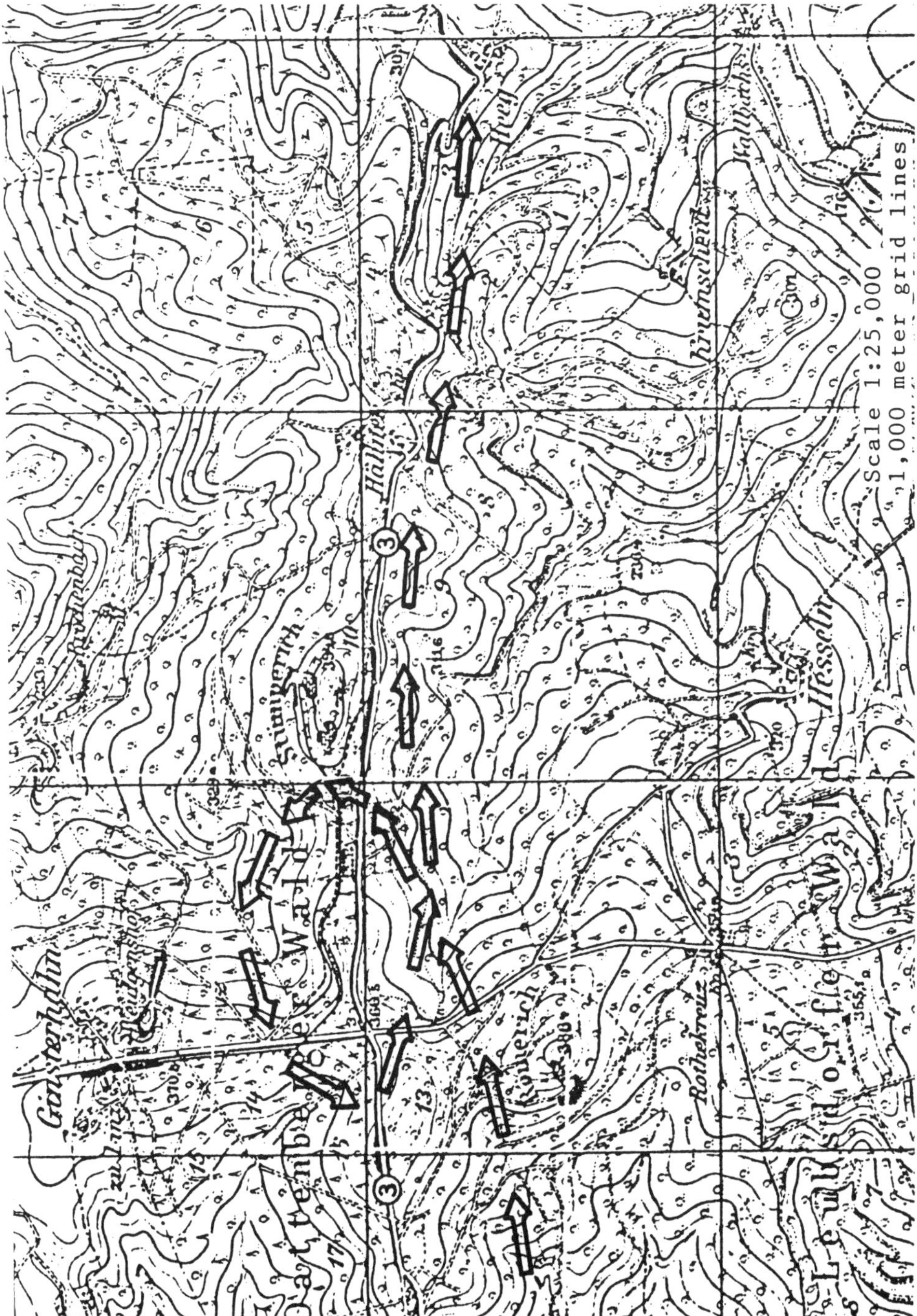
Scale 1:25,000
1,000 meter grid lines

and the Battalion attacked with L Company on the left, K Company on the right and I Company in reserve. At 0940 K Company was pinned down by automatic fire. From 0940 to 1330 progress was extremely slow against heavy automatic fire, artillery and rockets. Both K and L Companies were pinned down and I Company was sent forward to help L Company take the quarry, which was on high ground. They were to attack after a heavy artillery preparation which was fired from 1400 to 1430. At 1440 the attack was resumed with very slow progress. K Company was again pinned down by automatic fire and L Company made little progress until they were also pinned down by this same automatic fire. I Company worked around to the left and made some progress until 1730, when they too were stopped. The hilly terrain made it difficult to employ their accompanying tanks and tank destroyers. Because the regimental communications section had not moved forward, the only way Col. Butler could make radio contact and request artillery support, which was badly needed, was to move to the top of a hill. This area was clear which meant the German observers could direct fire on them and make the hill top untenable and they had to forsake the needed artillery support. The enemy was estimated to be one company, heavily reinforced with eight heavy machine guns and two tanks. They were well situated at the quarry and were later identified as a part of the 11 SS Panzer Division.

> "We had a tank with us and I remember Col. Butler going forward to see what was going on. The Krauts throwed a couple of mortars in, the tank fired a couple of shots back and we left. I recall the tank commander saying to me, 'You guys got a good officer. He's not a panty-waist.'"
>
> Dan Sullivan — I Company

> "On March 14, 1945, we were ordered to attack Stümperich Quarry. We were pinned down by two German machine gun nests plus artillery fire. I think all three companies were pinned down. I remember Col. Butler, Sgt. Malekos and I were in a rather large hole and Col. Butler was trying

to show us on a map how to go around the left flank and get to the German machine guns. While we were in the hole, a shell hit very close and threw dirt all over the map. Col. Butler calmly raked the dirt off and continues. He and Capt. Burgin both was good soldiers and not afraid."

Leo Humphrey — I Company

The above two quotes really epitomize the feeling and respect the men of the 3rd Battalion had for their officers. This was solid fighting unit with outstanding morale and solid cohesion from top to bottom. From what they had gone through together, they had been welded into soldiers who functioned as a single body. Each man felt he could rely absolutely on the man next to him as well as on his non-coms and officers.

At 2030 the Battalion received orders to attack again at 2200 after a seven battalion artillery barrage. The troops were ordered to withdraw 400 yards so they would be out of the way of the artillery. In spite of vigorous protestations from Col. Butler and Maj. Golden, the artillery fired too soon and caught all three companies on their move back, inflicting numerous casualties. L and I Companies were particularly hard hit. The artillery continued to fire for ten minutes before the Battalion could get it stopped. Many of the shells exploded just overhead and showered the men with shrapnel and white phosphorous. When the artillery finally stopped at 2155 both L and I Companies were thoroughly disorganized and the attack was called off.

"Just before the Battle of the Bulge I had a letter from my mother telling me not to be afraid and that God would take care of me and guide me. I never did seem afraid, just took it one day at a time. It was on this day that I didn't follow God's orders. I was standing just a few feet from a hole when it seems as though I got a message from above telling me to jump in that hole. I didn't do it and in just seconds I was cut down with shrapnel all through my body. My stomach felt like a ball of fire inside. It's possible that our own artillery hit me. I don't know, but there was shrapnel flying everywhere. I was given first aid and moved to a field hospital. I spent almost four months in hospitals over there and at home before being discharged."

Leo Humphrey — I Company

German artillery also fired in some propaganda leaflets claiming that the soldiers' wives and sweethearts were enjoying their absence and that within twenty-four hours there would be no Americans alive on this side of the Rhine. As with all propaganda leaflets the Germans sent in, these had no effect whatsoever on the morale of the men and were treated as great souvenirs or emergency toilet paper.

The Battalion organized defensive positions around Dattenbergerwald for the next several days. At 2300 on March 15th they were designated as Corps reserve. At 2200 on the 17th of March they reverted to regimental control and were designated as regimental reserve.

"One night I was told to take a jeep and get something or other, I forget what. I went down a light colored road when an ME-109 got after me. When I saw he was about to fire, I stopped and he overshot me and splattered the road in front of me with machine fun fire. he made another pass a few minutes later and this time I sped up and he shot behind me. We had orders not to fire ack-ack at night but by this time he had made me good and mad so when he made a third pass at me, I stopped the jeep, got behind the .50 cal and proceeded to empty the belt at him. After the war was over I was sent to a POW camp at Bachenburg to interview and process German POW's. I interviewed a Luftwaffe pilot and asked him if he had ever been hit by ground fire. He described the above action in detail as to time and place and informed me that whoever had shot at him had shot his tailplane to pieces. I then told him I was the fellow he had shot at. It's a small world."

George Prager — L Company

On March 21 Col. Butler received orders from regiment to prepare to attack across the Wied River the next day. Again he heard this "voice" which told him that a night attack would be successful and he made his plans accordingly. After dark a patrol led by the Battalion S-2 (Intelligence Officer) and consisting of four riflemen, one TD man, one tanker and one Ammunition and Pioneer Platoon member went on a reconnaissance patrol of the Wied River to locate fording sites for the attached armor. They returned at 0130 the next morning.

At 2030 one platoon of I Company was to secure the high ground across the river from the proposed crossing site at Lache. They were repulsed by small arms and artillery fire at 2330.

The U.S. Army history says of this time, "The 9th and 99th Divisions of III Corps profited from the shift of German armor to the north. On 18 March the 9th Division at last cut the Autobahn, while patrols from the 99th Division reached the meandering Wied River almost due east of Remagen. Other contingents of the 99th drove swiftly southward close along the Rhine River almost to a point opposite Andernach. By 20 March the III Corps had reached the prescribed bridgehead line."

Col. Butler had a company commanders meeting on the morning of the 22nd and issued his orders. I Company was again ordered to take the high ground opposite Lache immediately after dark. The attack was to start at 2400 with L Company crossing the river, clearing Lache and securing the high ground. Then K Company, with the attached armor, a platoon of TD's and a platoon of tanks, was to move to the right of L Company, take the hamlet of Hochscheid and then move south and take the hamlet of Verscheid. L Company was to leave a platoon at Lache to protect the flank and move into Hochscheid when K Company moved on to Verscheid. At 2400 I Company was to move across the Wied River and move southeast to take Wuscheid. Once Wuscheid was secure, they were to leave one platoon while the rest of the company moved north, clearing the road to Verscheid and be ready to provide assistance to K Company, if needed. All of these objectives were to be secured by 0300 on the 23rd. If K Company had secured Verscheid by 0300 it was to move on, with attached units, and take the hamlet of Goldscheid. The attached units were: one platoon of Company G, 786th Tank Battalion; one platoon of

Company G, 629th TD Battalion; two platoons of Company A, 90th Chemical Mortar Battalion. Supporting artillery was the 924th Field Artillery.

At 1630 on the 22nd I Company moved out and after a stiff fire fight had secured the high ground opposite Lache by 2030. Foot troops moved out of their assembly area at Dattenbergerwald at 2045 with L and K Companies reaching their jump-off points at the Wied River by 2200. At 2345 the artillery fired a light barrage on the immediate objectives for 15 minutes. The attack was launched at midnight.

While it is not very wide, the Wied River runs through very rugged terrain, which made it a real tank obstacle. Scouts reported that in most places it was only knee deep but where the Battalion crossed it was up to five feet deep. The water was the only protection the men had from the machine gun fire they received in crossing and they were soaking wet and chilled to the bone as they scrambled up the bluffs on the opposite side in the dark.

"God, what a night that was! One of the nights when we didn't stop and dig in. It was very dark. Sometimes we had to hold on to the guy in front because it was rough going and hard to see him. The Germans must have expected we'd be coming down a certain way. It was something like a hogback down this steep ridge. At that time we were a few yards apart. All at once mortars started dropping practically on top of us. We hit the dirt and I was scared! Then it let up a bit and we started again. BAM! Right in front of me a flash and one of our men flew up in the air. I can still see him. He seemed like a pile of laundry, dead and limp. He never knew what hit him. My squad leader was wounded and I had to take over the squad. I wondered if I was capable.

"Sgt. Lewis took us down that ridge, told us where we were to cross the river and told me where to put my squad 'til it was our turn to cross. Our machine gunners had routed the enemy so we got across okay. We had to push

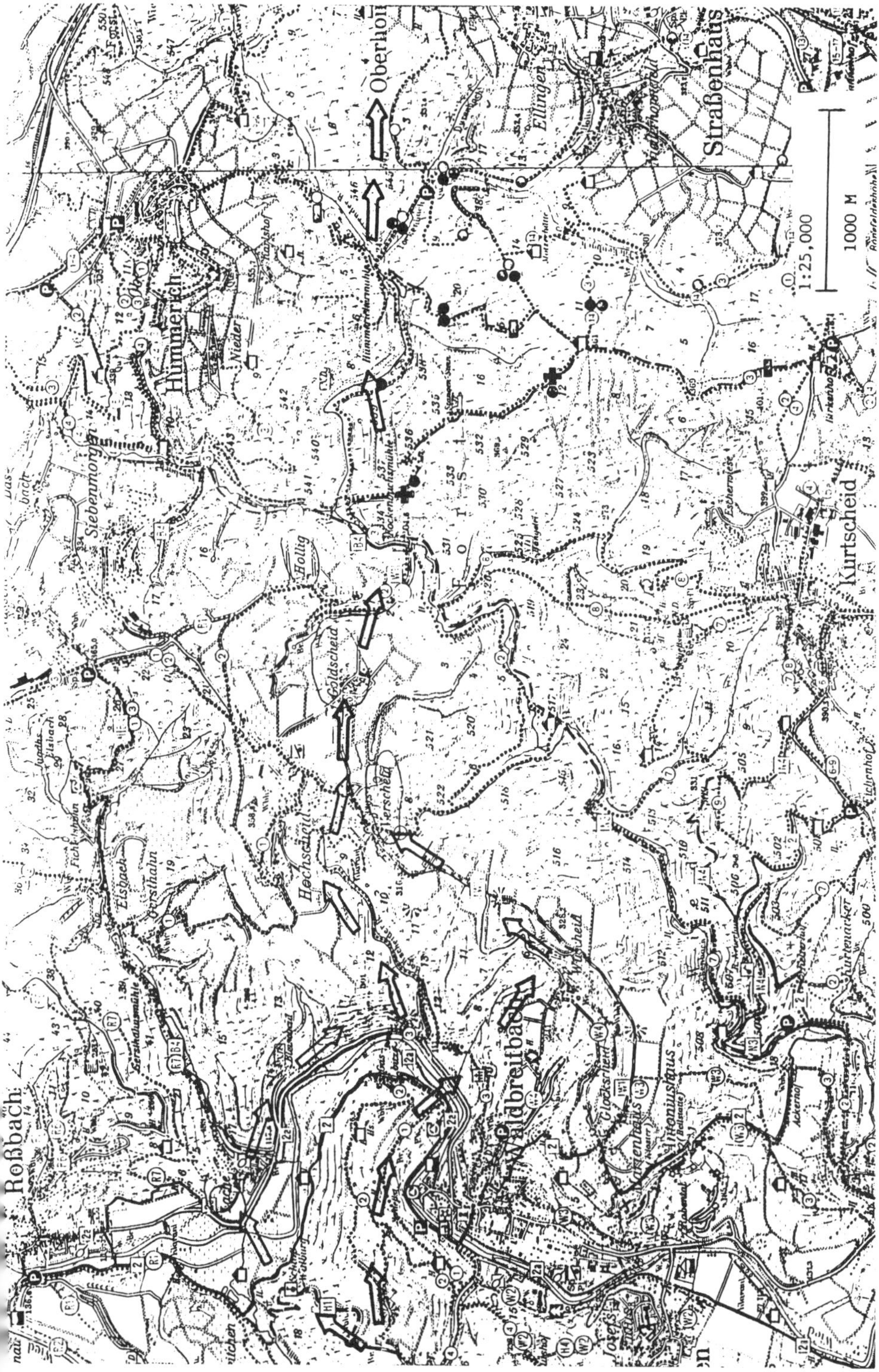
Straßenhaus
Ellingen
Hümmerich
Siebenmorgen
Kurtscheid
Roßbach
Hollig
Goldscheid
1:25,000
1000 M

Brooklyn's Gen. Lauer Attacks Toward Munich and Frankfort

His 99th Division Pushes East From Remagen Bridgehead—Seeks Nazi General Who Used Hospital as Armed Stronghold.

By GAULT MacGOWAN.
Staff Correspondent of THE NEW YORK SUN.
Copyright, 1945. All Rights Reserved.

On the Remagen Bridgehead, Germany, March 23.— Brooklyn-born Major-Gen. Walter E. Lauer's Ninety-ninth Infantry Division—complete with its famous battalion that won a Presidential Citation for holding the northern hinge in the battle of the bulge—kicked off early today in the Brooklyn version of "Drang nach dem osten," or "Drive toward the east," to push the bridgehead forward in the general direction of Frankfort and Munich.

I drove up between the long columns of infantry just before midnight to see them launch the attack, which was planned by Gen. Lauer and his assistant, Brig.-Gen. Hugh Mayberry, who was instructor of Brooklyn's Fourteenth National Guard Regiment from 1926 to 1931. Both men were commissioned in the last war, and both served in the Army of Occupation in the Rhineland, participating in fox-hunts, military exercises and maneuvers in this very Remagen area after the 1918 Armistice.

Although Brooklyn inspiration was responsible for the planning of the attack, the men behind it were from all parts of the Eastern seaboard, including New York, New Jersey, Pennsylvania and West Virginia.

Gen. Lauer was born in Brooklyn — in Macdougal street, he thinks, although he has never been there since his childhood. Mrs. Ernest Scaefer of 161 Franklin avenue, New Rochelle, is his sister, and Alexander Lauer of 85-05 105th street, Richmond Hill, L. I., is his brother.

Use Hospital as Cover.

The Ninety-ninth Division is at present engaged in ferreting out the German general in command of a typical Nazi hospital, standing on a hillside. This sanitarium, which was marked with a large red cross and which our artillery therefore spared, was garrisoned with German troops and our advancing forces were fired on from its windows. The hospital first attracted our attention when a German prisoner who, like the majority of the regular Wermacht, hated his general, volunteered the information that Nazi troops were dug in around the hospital, "contrary to the customs of war."

The Ninety-ninth received other reports that German surgeons were forced to fight in defense of their installations.

The moon shone brightly on the battlefield as our troops forded the river Wied, high above the town of Neuwied, which American forces driving southward entered yesterday. The sights, noises and odors of the battlefield all seemed magnified in the ghostly light.

Jeep in a Shellhole.

Gunflashes and shellbursts illuminated the sky and torchlike flames from a burning village in a valley between the high hills outlined the enemy position when the battle began.

The reek of powder and white phosphorous bursts sullied the pine-scented air, and beside a farm village through which the infantry plodded silently forward you smelled milky aromas. The road was jammed for a time while Negro troops streaming toward the front in big trucks unloaded more ammunition, sweating for the white troops as much as for their own boys in the combat platoons moving forward to support our operations tonight. German 88's were pockmarking the road over which we were advancing. Suddenly our jeep pitched down into a shell hole and we were all thrown out. As we continued forward on foot, an enemy parachute flare, which had earlier lit up the valley, fluttered its silken remnant at our feet, providing a souvenir of my first attack with the Ninety-ninth Division.

and pull each other to make it up the steep incline on the other side."

Lambert Shulz—I Company

"It was not a big river, but it was pitch black and we dog-faced soldiers didn't know how deep it was or what we might be getting into on the other side. It was just bat your ears and go. We stepped into the water and made our way across. Fortunately the water only reached up to about our armpits, up to the chest on some people. That was cold water. This was in March and that water was straight from melted snow somewhere. You could hear the people as they stepped into this cold, cold water. They would gasp, suck in their breath and wish they were somewhere else."

Richard Mills—I Company

By 0635 (March 23) K Company had secured Hochscheid and L Company prepared to attack Verscheid. At 0700 L Company reported they were receiving fire from the Goldscheid area and requested artillery support. They also needed tank and tank destroyer support, but could not contact them. Col. Butler made radio contact with the armor and they were on the move by 0745, following mine detectors. They moved east of Hochscheid to provide support for the infantry. By 0930 L Company had secured Goldscheid, the last of the Battalion's objectives.

"A bazooka round was laid in on one of the houses. The house caught fire and after awhile a woman's screaming made this one of the most devastating experiences I remember. There was no additional firing. Just the dark night lit by the fire of the house and accented with the screaming. (Impossible to forget.)"

Alfred Schnitzer—L Company

A defensive perimeter was set up around the area with one squad and two bazooka teams protecting a 24 anti-tank mine road block at Schule. Casualties had been fairly light and almost 100 prisoners were captured. It was 1730 before the Battalion vehicles were able to cross the river and reach Hochscheid.

"Casualties had been fairly light." After all, the business of war is to kill people and so the military uses euphemisms like this to indicate that less men were killed or wounded in this battle than in other actions. The casualties were not "light" for the men killed or wounded today. The dead were just as dead as if the entire unit had been destroyed and the wounded in just as much pain as if many more had been hit. These men had to cross a river in the dark, under enemy fire, and on the opposite side had to help each other up as the bank was so steep. Every battle is a major battle to those men engaged in it and the casualties are every bit as real in every battle.

"In the darkness of the early morning hours the platoon was climbing up a heavily forested mountainside. We were holding on to each other's clothing and webbing. The branches of the trees were tugging at us. Apparently one of the soldiers somewhere in back of me lost the safety pin of his lapel grenade to a branch. The grenade exploded and killed and wounded several people in back of me.

"Stumbling about on the summit, I slipped over the side and rolled into a tree, injuring my right knee again. The 3rd Battalion medics took me back to their tent. The NCO medic with whom I shared a tent was a kindly soul. He offered me a Purple Heart Medal, which I refused. If I took the medal for this minor injury, my parents would have been notified that I had been 'wounded in action.' My mother would have had a 'heart attack' at the news. Furthermore, it seemed to me that the Purple Heart my father received in World War I for grievous injuries would be demeaned by my acceptance of the decoration for what seemed a very minor injury rather than a combat wound."

Herb Herman—L Company

U.S. Army history: "From 23 March on, First Army was to be prepared to break out to the southeast, the main objective to be

Limburg and the Lohr River valley and link up with Third Army troops once Patton's forces crossed the Rhine. In preparation for the attack, the V Corps was sent into the bridgehead to take over the southern periphery from the 99th Division."

"It was on that bridgehead that I was just exhausted. I was trying to dig a hole up in the rocks and trees. I got down about 3/4 of an inch and I couldn't throw another shovelfull. I just laid down and said, 'Lord. This is it. I'm not throwing another shovelfull. If I'm going to get it, it's going to be here. I'm going to rest, one way or another. I'm going to rest in Your arms or just rest here.' We were getting a barrage with a tremendous number of tree bursts. I just rolled over on my back for a good rest. Shrapnel going everywhere. Didn't care. Could have cared less. I bet you that barrage didn't last another three minutes and I picked up and moved out."

William Blasdel—K Company

Every combat infantryman can understand Blasdel's actions. There comes a time for almost all of them when they just feel they cannot handle any more. Lack of food and sleep combined with great physical exertion leads to bone-deep weariness. Seeing death and destruction all around them continually gets them to a point where the mind refuses to accept any more abuse. Most react like Blasdel and in a short time "pick up and move out" knowing that their comrades are depending on them.

"It didn't take long. Just a little rest and you can go right back at it again. I guess that's the reason young fellows make the best soldiers. They've got a lot to offer in the way of physical strength and endurance and not being smart enough to ask too many questions, I guess."

Richard Mills—I Company

"From March 11 to May 7, 1945, I had the following comforts of life: 2 hot meals, one shower and one change of clothes. It should be noted that my food (when available) consisted of a compressed dry fruit bar (about the size of a Baby Ruth), a chocolate candy bar, a tin of American cheese with bits of tuna embedded in it (about the size of a tuna can) and powdered lemon crystals from a foil envelope that was a little larger than a tea bag. Our common obsession was to sleep in a house overnight."

Herb Herman—L Company

The area east of the Wied River is very hilly with some of the hills 500 to 600 meters high and heavily wooded. The Germans had a number of strong positions in this area, but were surprised by the night attack and consequently were not prepared. The main opposition was from artillery with about 500 rounds being fired at the attacking troops. By now the bridgehead over the Rhine was so firmly established that the enemy could not break it. Supplies and troops had been moved into the area and the plan was to break out of this difficult terrain and assault the German homeland.

"We find that in most cases the riflemen are well in town before the enemy realizes the direction of the attack. Therefore, due to poor communication, enemy artillery is slow in switching their fire. Using heavy machine guns in support, we find that it is better to get into town as soon as possible to avoid enemy artillery fire, which is certain to come in the direction of the attack."

William Bartow—M Company

The attack continued on the 24th along small trails through the hills. Numerous roadblocks had to be cleared and pockets of resistance snuffed out. This was a slow, tedious process with intermittent mortar and artillery fire coming in. This action continued into the last night.

"At daybreak we moved up probably 100 yards or so. There was a ravine there. Straight down in and straight up the other side. We were supposed to get an artillery barrage. In a half hour or so it didn't come so we got orders we're going to move out anyway. We crawled down into that ravine and up out the other side. Just ahead of us there was another steep ravine. Just before we got to it the artillery that was supposed to come in ahead of us came in on us. They were throwing white phosphorous. That's where our first scout got hit. This WP was on his foot and burned three toes and part of his foot off."

Richard Gorby—K Company

At 0001 on the 25th the Battalion resumed the attack proceeding in a column with L Company leading, followed by K and I Companies. After clearing several roadblocks, they reached Hümmerichermühle by 0300. After an artillery preparation, L Company attacked the small town of Ellingen at 0400 and cleared it by 0530 while K Company took the high ground on their left.

"Running up the stairs in a small apartment house, we found a woman cradling in her arms a dying, young, blond German soldier. His entire chest covering had been blown away exposing all his organs. His soft cries for his mother unnerved us so much that we began calling for a medic. Finally, with the house cleared, we left her with her burden."

Herb Herman—L Company

K Company secured the town of Oberhonnefeld and I Company pushed through and took the hamlet of Gierend.

"Another thing I would like to mention is fear. I'm talking about anything from fearful, to scared, to being scared to death. I mean gut-wrenching FEAR. I saw fear do strange things to people. I felt a lot of it myself. In some instances I think it was sort of a catalyst. It made us do things we might not otherwise have done. Acts that were termed by others as bravery. Acts of obvious fear. I know of one instance where a man was evacuated for attacks of appendicitis and when the facts were known, it was just fear. When artillery came in one man would stand up, hug a tree and begin to retch. Fear, to one degree or another, was a constant companion when you were involved in face-to-face combat. In spite of fear, the American soldier was able to perform because of his training. I think we did a commendable job."

Richard Mills—I Company

"Each man had a white rag tied to his shoulder flap and knew that if he heard two knocks on a helmet nearby he had better knock on his helmet three times if he didn't want to get ventilated. Except for flares and gun flashes, the night was black as coal. We went over some of the steepest hills I've ever seen. Machine gun and BAR fire was continuous and artillery kept up on the towns that now were burning.

"We jumped off at night down a narrow little valley following a little wagon road with the whole battalion strung out in single file. It was black as tar and we would move a few hundred yards and stop while the point sprayed everything with BAR's and automatic carbines whenever any resistance was encountered. We looked up at the big wooded hills on each side of the road and knew they were full of enemy. At dawn the battalion was well into enemy lines and our tanks and vehicles would not catch up for several hours. Everywhere the Jerries were coming in to surrender or just hiding in the woods. I and K Companies took two little towns up on the level plain beyond and reported that they had crossed the Autobahn highway. I Company knocked out a Tiger tank that had somehow been bypassed during the night and had come up the valley behind us. Finally our tanks caught up and we moved into towns in full strength and got rid of our POW's and wounded. Went to sleep that night with the sounds of 88's still firing and when I awoke the next morning the sun was shining brightly and the fields as far as we could see were filled with self-propelled guns and armor of the 7th Armored Division. By noon the radio from cub spotter planes reported tanks going through towns thirty miles beyond. We had reached good tank country at last."

Jack Randall—I Company

"Another vivid day. We were attacking with tanks across an open field. The enemy was dropping artillery. Our tanks were firing. I can still see one of our tanks being hit by one of theirs. It was off to my right about 100 yards. I knew it had been hit because it lurched and a puff of smoke went up. All at once the crew dropped out of a trap door in the bottom. I believe they all got out and they scrambled in among us. Then the thing started to blow up inside. Boy, was I glad to see them get out! Those tanks scared the hell out of me. I was always glad I was a foot soldier."

Lambert Shulz—I Company

It was very common for infantrymen to feel sorry for the "poor tankers" in their moving artillery targets. The tankers in turn felt sorry for the "poor infantrymen" who had to move on foot and didn't have the protection of a tank. Even when they all had all the problems they could handle, each was able to feel sorry for someone they felt had things even tougher.

At 1130 men from the 393rd Regiment moved into Niederhonnefeld. At 1830 two squads from K Company moved out to attack Oberraden with friendly artillery placed on the town to help guide them. When the barrage was lifted, the two squads met no resistance as they moved into town followed by the rest of K Company. All positions were secure by 2000. The enemy had again been surprised and the Battalion captured 250 PW's, including seven officers, and a large quantity of war materiél at a cost of one man killed and 16 wounded.

The 3rd Battalion had cut the Autobahn, as had other elements of the 395th farther north, and the Americans now had access to good roads for their armored vehicles. Now a war of movement could be fought to hasten an end to the fighting.

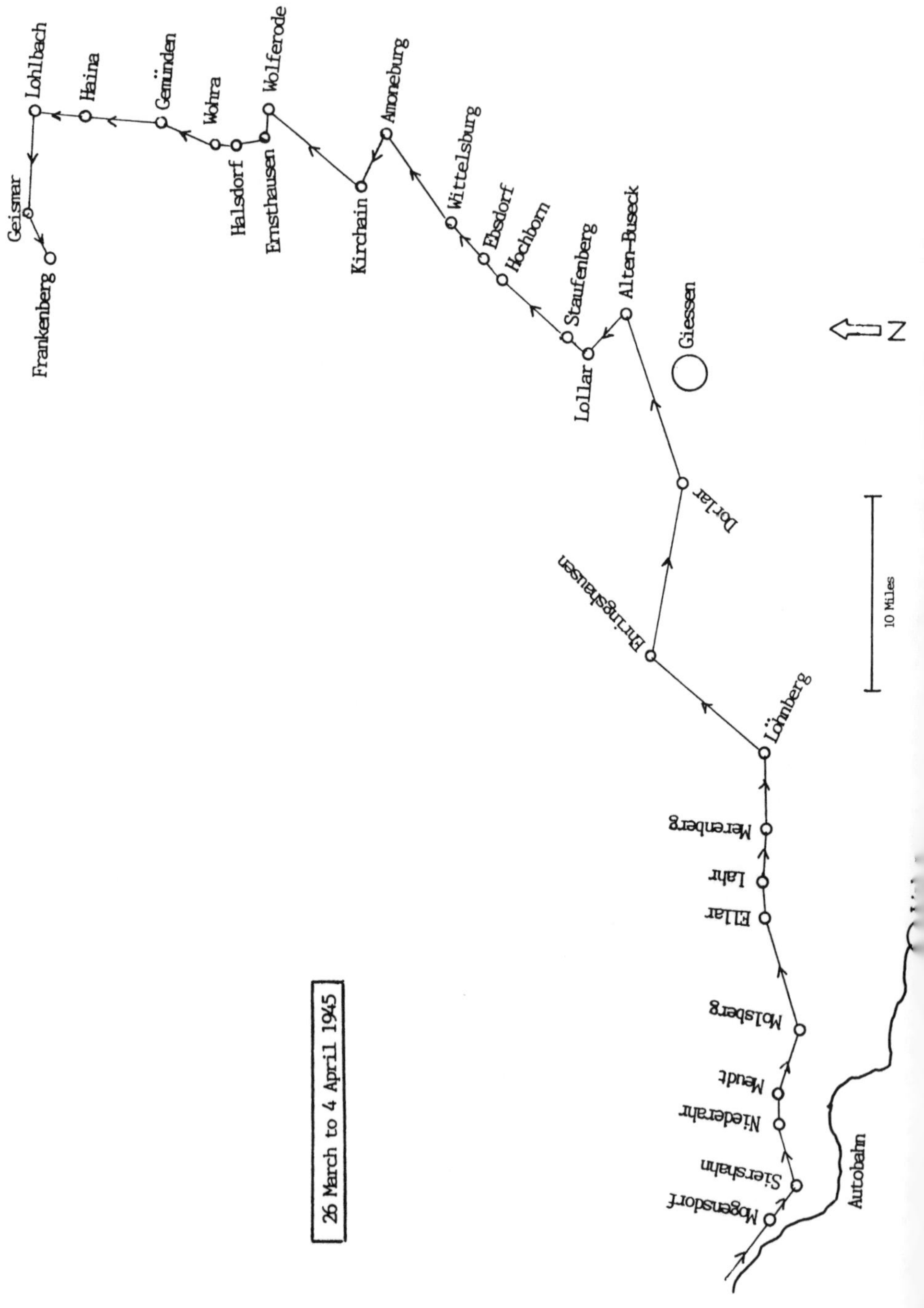
Lohlbach
Haina
Gemünden
Wohra
Wolferode
Halsdorf
Ernsthausen
Amoneburg
Kirchain
Geismar
Frankenberg
Wittelsburg
Ebsdorf
Hochborn
Staufenberg
Alten-Buseck
Lollar
Giessen
N
Dorlar
Ehringshausen
10 Miles
Löhnberg
Merenberg
Lahr
Ellar
Molsberg
Meudt
Niederahr
Siershahn
Mogendorf
Autobahn
26 March to 4 April 1945

The Battalion remained in position on March 26, but on the 27th were loaded on trucks, stripped for action. 7th Armored Division tanks had passed through the 99th and headed east under a full head of steam, racing through town after town in pursuit of the enemy. The Battalion accompanied and followed the tanks for the next four days, mopping up behind them by searching every house, checking wooded areas for enemy troops and making sure that the entire area was secure.

The Battalion left at 0850 on the 27th on trucks through a series of small towns to Meudt, arriving there at 1300. At 1800 they were on the move again, this time by foot to Molsberg. On the 28th the companies moved out separately to clear 18 objectives that had been assigned to the Battalion. All went well and the Battalion reassembled in Merenberg that evening. On the 29th trucks arrived and in seven hours moved the Battalion to Alten-Buseck, where they arrived at 1700. They remained here on the 30th but on the 31st again boarded trucks and moved north to Wolferode and set up defenses there. I Company and the Anti-Tank Platoon stayed in Lollar to guard an Allied PW enclosure.

"The 7th Armored Division passed through the 99th as planned. Our riflemen trotted along behind the tanks to mop up and protect them. We could not keep up so the tanks stopped and picked us up. I chose to straddle the cannon with my feet resting on top of the tank. In this manner I rode through several white-bedsheet-decorated towns screaming at the women peeking out of the windows, 'Heil Hitler; in case we lose.' "

Herb Herman—L Company

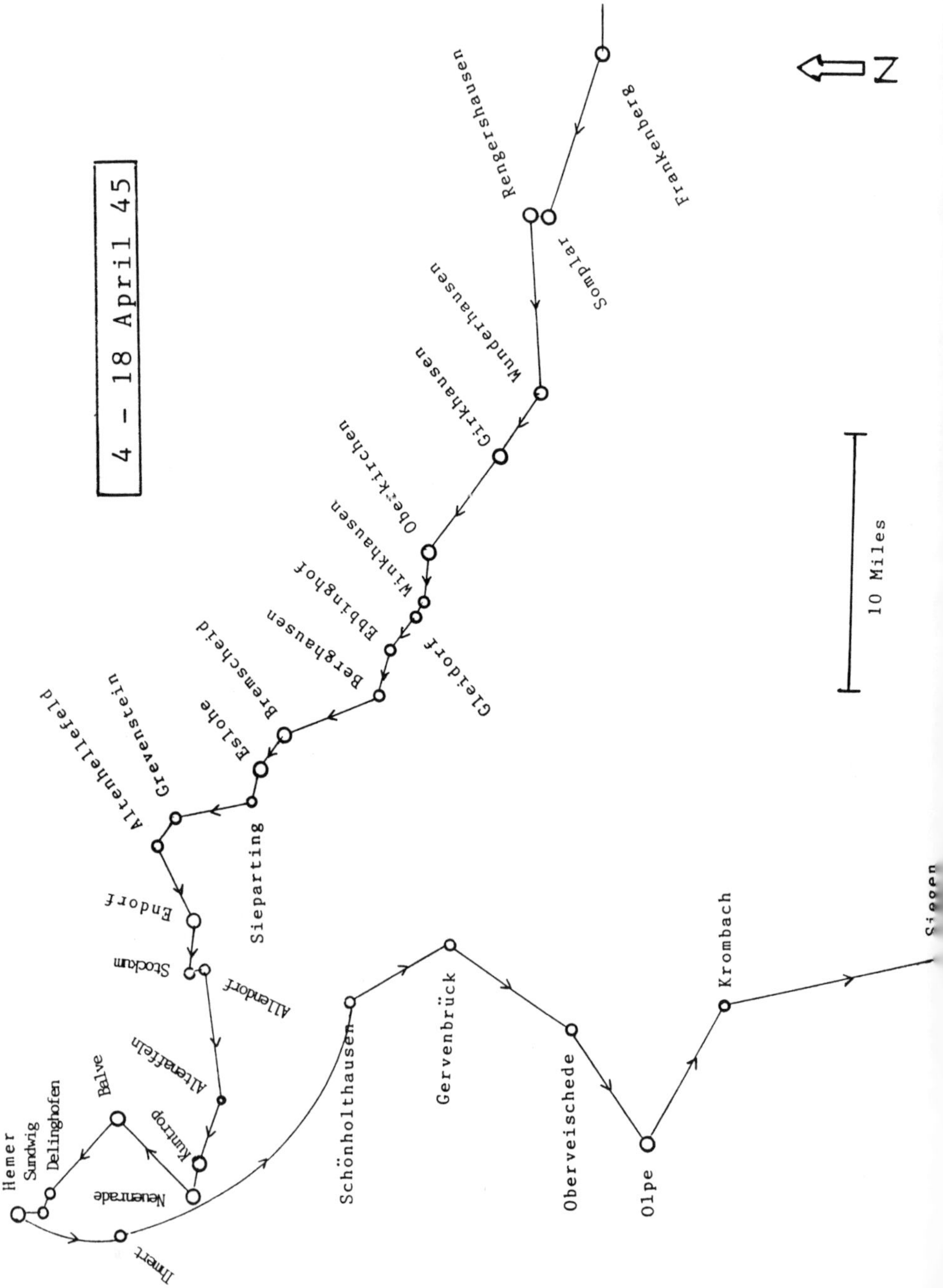
4 - 18 April 45
N
10 Miles
Frankenberg
Rengershausen
Somplar
Wunderhausen
Girkhausen
Oberkirchen
Winkhausen
Ebbinghof
Gleidorf
Berghausen
Bremscheid
Eslohe
Sieparting
Grevenstein
Altenhellefeld
Endorf
Stockum
Allendorf
Altenaffeln
Kuntrop
Neuenrade
Balve
Delinghofen
Sundwig
Hemer
Ihmert
Schönholthausen
Gervenbrück
Oberveischede
Olpe
Krombach

Chapter 8

The Ruhr Pocket

April 1, 1945, dawned clear and sunny. The weather boded well for the Battalion as this was the day that the 3rd Armored Division, coming from the southeast, and the 2nd Armored Division, coming from the northeast, met in the town of Lippstadt and sealed off the area that became known as "The Ruhr Pocket." About 3,000 square miles of rugged, hilly country that the Germans called "Sauerland" was surrounded. This area contained the industrial heart of Germany. In addition, the majority of the German army opposing the Allied Forces was now trapped; seven Corps and 19 Divisions. Original intelligence estimates were that 150,000 troops had been contained, but this estimate turned out to be much too modest as there were actually over 300,000, plus countless slave laborers and prisoners of war in camps throughout the area. This was also Easter Sunday.

> "The word came around that we were going to have Easter Sunday services if anybody wanted to attend. It wasn't a town, really, it wasn't much more than a crossroads. There might have been eight or ten houses and the dinkiest little church. I don't think that little church would hold more than 15 or 18 people. That's where we had the church services. The whole company was there. There wasn't room for everybody in the church so some stood around in the street. The preacher stood in the doorway, the

chaplain, and preached the service. That's one Easter I'll always remember."

Richard Gorby — K Company

On April 2nd and 3rd the Battalion manned their roadblocks, sent out motorized patrols, tested weapons and prepared for the next big push. At 1000 on the 2nd the tank destroyers of C Company, 629th TD Battalion arrived in Wolferode and at 1745 two tanks from C Company, 729th Battalion arrived. These units were added to the perimeter defensive positions. On the 3rd I Company and the Anti-Tank Platoon rejoined the Battalion.

"Everybody took a bath and in this little old town they made underclothes in a factory there, so everybody grabbed some underclothing. I heard about this so I went to the factory to get some underclothes as we'd been wearing these 'long johns' and it was starting to warm up. I wanted to get rid of 'em. All the men's underwear was gone and all that was left was panties. I was going to get rid of this dirty old underwear so I get me some panties, go back and take a bath, throw away my 'long johns' and put these panties on. I'll have you know I had problems for about three or four days until I finally got some GI underwear. Was I glad to see that! It is rather inconvenient without a fly. It was a major convenience that I had just accepted as being, without respect you know. I found out that it's pretty handy to have one of those, especially in your underwear. Anyway, the guys all made fun of me for three or four days. A little humiliation is good for a guy."

William Blasdel — K Company

By this stage of the war the 3rd Battalion had established a reputation as an outstanding fighting force. The 9th Infantry Division and the 7th Armored Division requested use of the 3rd Battalion for an attack to the north and west to get behind German Field Marshal Walter Model, who commanded all the enemy troops in the north end of Germany. As a result of these requests, on April 4th the 3rd Battalion was attached to CCB of the 7th

Armored Division. Heading north and west, the armor/infantry team slashed through town after town, often covering many miles a day. The Germans were disorganized and kept off balance by the continual attacks and were unable to set up solid defensive positions.

"We didn't enjoy that chore (The Ruhr Pocket). I had thought during training in the States, 'Oh boy! For the protection of tanks. Tanks make the difference.' I learned from experience that tanks, rather than helping the infantry, the dog-foot out there on the ground, it works the other way around. The infantry goes ahead of the tanks in a lot of cases and clears the way for them so it's safe for then to proceed. I came to look upon tanks as being noisy attractive targets for whatever kind of weapon the enemy might have. If we were in close proximity to the tanks, or had been riding on them, we were very much exposed to a lot of fire being brought on us. It happened time and time again."

Richard Mills — I Company

At 0950 April 4th the Battalion left Wolferode by truck and arrived in Rengerhausen at 1500. From here they moved on to Oberkirchen where they arrived at 1700. Here the Battalion received orders to attack Winkhausen. Col. Butler wanted to make this a night attack, but there was no moon to shed light. He knew this would make control impossible and the attack was planned for the next morning.

Battalion Headquarters had been set up in a hotel in Oberkirchen. In what was to become a more common experience, they discovered the basement was full of pregnant women. Hitler had encouraged German women of the "proper" background to raise sons for the Fatherland. Hotel basements were large and sturdy and the women gathered there when battle erupted around them. At almost any time at least one of the women was in the pangs of childbirth and wanted help from the Americans. Army medics are not equipped to deliver babies and women had to help each other.

At 0500 on April 5th the Battalion attacked with K Company on the right, L Company on the left and I Company in reserve. By 0700 the attacking companies came under heavy small arms fire. At 1030 two of the attached tanks and one tank destroyer were knocked out by direct fire. At 1100 K and L Companies were held up by heavy small arms fire and direct fire from artillery pieces and were forced to withdraw. The German 88 mm gun was an awesome weapon. Firing a shell almost four inches in diameter at very high velocity, it would penetrate tank armor and was devastating when used in direct fire against infantry. It was so powerful it could be "bore-sighted" for more than a mile. This is what these men were facing. I Company relieved the 2nd Battalion of the 47th Infantry Regiment and set up roadblocks north of Oberkirchen. At 1600 A Company of the 38th Armored Infantry moved north of Oberkirchen to relieve L Company, take over their roadblocks and defend that flank. Orders were to hold for the night. At 1930 the enemy launched a counter-attack against I and A Companies on the north flank, but after two hours of heavy fighting this counter-attack was repulsed. At 2300 orders were received to continue the attack the next morning.

At 0535 on the 6th, the artillery fired a four minute TOT concentration on Winkhausen and ten minutes later K Company attacked. By 0800 they were in the east side of town and at 0845 reported that two machine guns and a tank were firing at them and that they were also receiving heavy mortar fire. At about this same time I Company was ordered forward and almost immediately one of their supporting tanks was knocked out by direct fire from the west side of town.

"The only actual bleeding wound I suffered when a single German tank did us a lot of misery. It seemed that anytime one of these tanks could find as many as four soldiers close enough to constitute a single target, it cut loose with a heavy round on them. I saw the muzzle flash and smoke and hit the ground. The shell hit very close to us. Before I got up again I felt blood trickling down my right cheek. I reached up and felt my helmet and there was a hole through it. One of those shell fragments had penetrated the steel pot, had gone through the bakelite helmet liner, had cut the leather headband as cleanly as any knife could and had then gone into my head. It found a hard head, I guess, because it only went through the scalp and stopped there. There was a little bleeding and a knot came up on my head. I was evacuated for one night and the next day caught up with my unit again, wearing a helmet with a hole through it."

Richard Mills — I Company

L Company was ordered to attack Gleidorf with an infantry company from the 7th Armored Division and a company of tanks. At 0930 they received stiff small arms fire as well as direct fire from 40mm ack-ack guns and were ordered to pull back so that artillery could fire on the buildings containing the enemy. Whomever issued the order did not tell them where to stop and from 500 yards away Col. Butler saw them retreating in disorder. Knowing they had to be stopped, he started across an open field to get to them. As he began his run, a German 88mm fired at him. It missed him and he dropped to the ground. He got his breath and when he got up to run again the 88mm fired again. Again they missed and he dropped to the ground. This run and drop sequence continued all across the field, but finally he reached L Company and got them stopped.

The officers lost control of the accompanying tanks and armored infantry and the men of these units began to drift back in disorder. When they reached the edge of the woods where L Company was digging in, they were surprised to see the 3rd Battalion was setting up defensive positions. One of the armored men asked an L Company rifleman, "What are you doing here?" The L Company private replied, "Col. Butler ordered us to dig in and stay here and we're going to stay." With that, the armored man said, "By God, if you guys can stay, we can too!" With that exchange the retreat stopped, the armored men began to dig in and the area was secure. This was another example of the respect

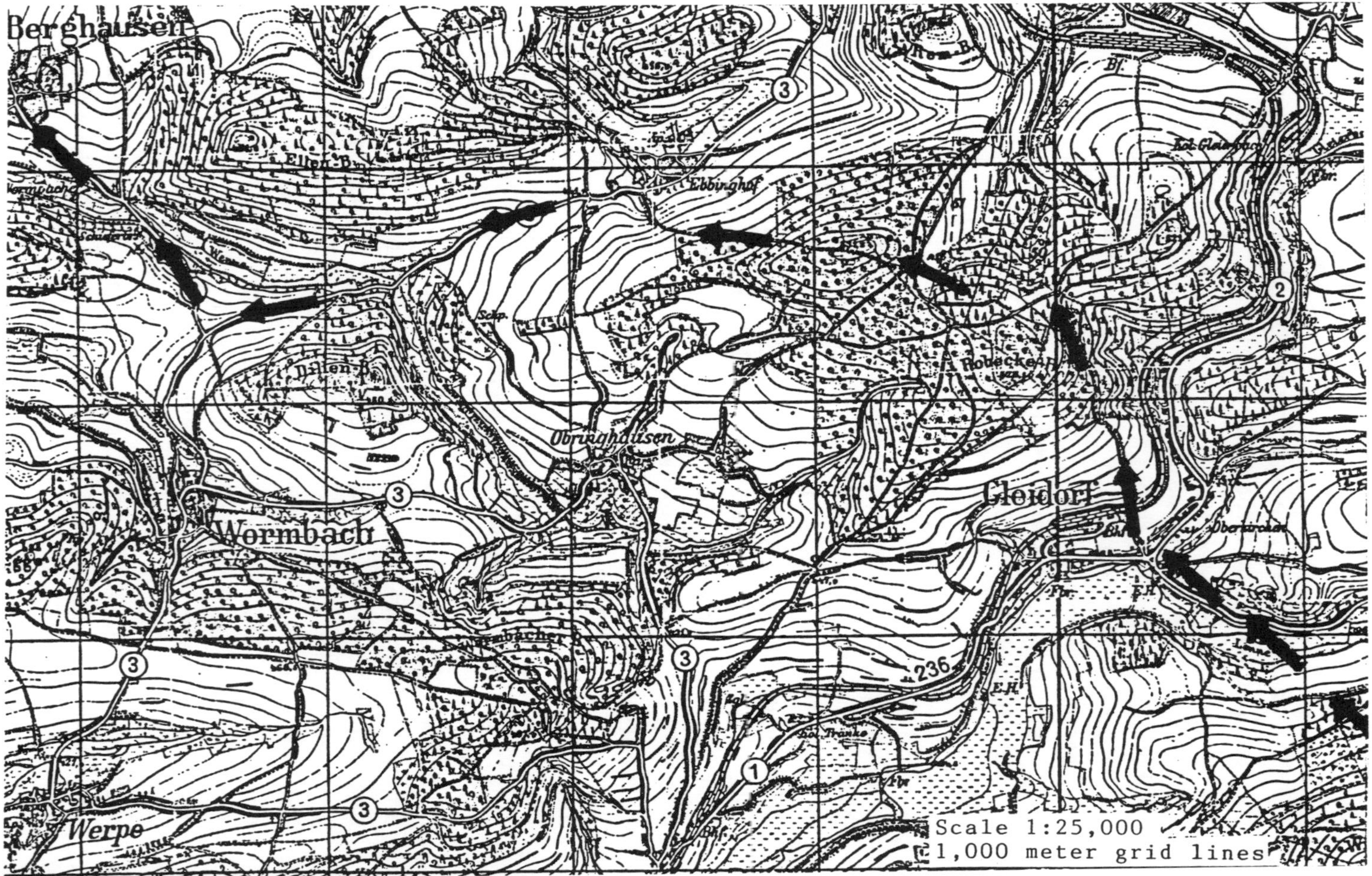
Berghausen
Ebbinghof
Obringhausen
Robecke
Gleidorf
Wormbach
Werpe
Scale 1:25,000
1,000 meter grid lines

and trust that existed in the 3rd Battalion from Col. Butler down to the privates.

At 1630 K Company attacked Gleidorf followed by I Company. By 1930 the town was secure and K Company took up positions in the north side of town and I Company in the west side. Here they prepared for the almost inevitable German counter-attack. The cost had been heavy with a number of men killed and wounded in all three rifle companies. Capt. Paul Price, CO of L Company had been wounded and evacuated as had Capt. Horace Phillips, Jr., the CO of K Company. Lt. Jack Musser, an I Company platoon leader had been killed.

"We came upon what had been the forward units of the 3rd Battalion. Several men had lost their lives. They had been ambushed by Germans. There with them was a medic who was wounded and I asked him, "What's the matter?" He said, 'They shot me.' I said, 'Why would they shoot you with all the red crosses painted on your helmet and on your back and arms?' He said, 'It's meanness, just meanness. After they shot those boys I went to see what I could do for them. The Germans came out and chased me away and finished them off. When I objected they told me to run, to go. I saw that they meant it so I turned to leave and when I did they shot me anyway and left me.' He was shot through the stomach. Bullets had entered his back at about kidney level and gone through his stomach. He was in a pretty bad way. He was a valiant man and I had a lot of respect for him."

Richard Mills — I Company

"Gleidorf was a tough one. K Company got throwed out once and I Company twice before we held. Moving up, we rounded a bend in the road and the fireworks started. The Krauts had a flak gun on the edge of town, trained right on us. When they opened fire, a Mark IV tank also started firing and big mortar fire was coming in. I think a few of us are still carrying around a souvenir from that one. This is where Lt. Musser and Ed Harsh were killed. The Air Force was called in and a P-47 got the tank. We passed there later in the day and the tank was still burning."

Dan Sullivan — I Company

Capt. Mack H. McClendon, I Company CO, was almost lost too. Col. Butler was usually near the center of his battalion when they were attacking, normally within 100 yards of the forward units, so he could keep control. On his way to report to Butler and get his orders, McClendon was hit by sniper fire. The bullet entered his helmet at the rear, circled around his head between the steel helmet and the plastic helmet liner and came out the front, just breaking the skin over his eye. A large band-aid was sufficient to patch the wound. He reported to Butler, got his assignment and returned to his company. In about half an hour he was back and told Col. Butler he had been hit by artillery fire He had looked out from behind a rock just as a German 88mm fired. The round hit his helmet, dented it in about half an inch, knocked it off his head and knocked him to the ground. Between these two incidents, a regimental commander from the 7th Armored, over Butler's objections, had ordered McClendon to send a platoon up a hill, which he had led personally. His first sergeant was killed and several men wounded by the same artillery fire that had dented his helmet. He reported by radio and Butler ordered them to pull back. This is when McClendon had shown up at the Battalion CP the second time. He told Col. Butler that he was at the end of his string. Leaving him there, Butler went to I Company, pulled them back to a protected area and saw that they got some hot food. By the time he got back to his CP, McClendon had calmed down. He returned to I Company.

At 0315 on April 7th the anticipated German counter-attack came with a formidable force of five Tiger tanks from the 130th Panzer Lehr Division and 400 infantrymen from the 1st Battalion, 759th Regiment. Most of K Company was driven back, but two squads from the 1st Platoon stayed in the houses they occupied. The second squad under Sgt. John Martin was in one house and the first squad under Sgt. William Blasdel was in another house directly across the narrow street.

"The incident of this thing was that there were some Germans in this house and there were three Russian laborers. During the night the German man and his wife sneaked out of the house and told the other Germans we were there. The German soldiers came in to capture us and they opened fire on us. The first thing that happened they opened fire with a tank. It was sitting out there about 50 yards from the house, and they opened up with that thing. I was at the top of the stairs because our OP was on the second floor, at a window. The first shot came in about mid-stairs and I was standing at the top of the stairs. Shrapnel cut my clothes and blew a hole in things around there. They fired a couple of more rounds. We bailed out of the OP. The Germans came in to take us then. We opened fire on the ones trying to come in the house. They backed out and went back to the tanks. The tanks opened up and just blew the house away. We didn't have anything to get behind but the furniture. I had six men with me and nobody got a scratch, which was a miracle. There were five or six boys in the house across the narrow street. The Germans captured them, but couldn't get out of the Ruhr Pocket with them. It was too dark to see anything so the Germans bypassed us. They just thought nobody can live in that house. They poured several rounds in and blew away the whole side of the house. This took place about two o'clock in the morning, but you lose track of time. When it finally got light enough to see, we started picking out some targets and shooting. We had a little target practice picking off one or two from the rear, not knowing what happened to the rest of our company. All of a sudden we noticed they were retreating and taking their wounded out so we didn't fire any more and let them remove their wounded.

"Sometimes you ask yourself why you killed some (enemy) and others you didn't. I had the last two retreating Germans in my sights, at about 150 yards, and didn't pull the trigger. The reason, I guess, is that he was helping his wounded buddy.

"Next morning the Lieutenant asked me how many men I had lost. I said, 'None.' He said, 'How many were wounded?' I said, 'None.' Looking at each other in the daylight with all that plaster and dust we looked like ghosts. When you got outside the damage to the house was more apparent. You wondered how the house could stand as they had blown so much of it away with that tank. That was a miraculous thing."

William Blasdel — K Company

Despite being in a house that was destroyed by German tank fire, Sgt. Blasdel did not lose a man. For this heroic action he was awarded the Silver Star and the six men in his squad were each awarded the Bronze Star. These men were: Junior Willis, James Martakos, George Simba, Harry Sandbergen, Richard Gorby and the assistant squad leader, George Snead.

During this same German attack, Lt. Leroy Smith, who had taken command of K Company, took advantage of the darkness and boldly joined a column of German troops just as if he was one of them. He marched down the street with them until he was opposite a house that he knew contained a heavy machine gun. Here he dropped out of the column and ran into the house. He picked up the gun, carried it out and set it up in the center of the street. He commenced firing on the Germans coming toward him and then reversed the gun 180° and fired on those going away from him. Without knowing what had happened to the rest of his company and completely disregarding his personal safety, he swept the street clear of enemy troops.

Sgt. Howard Denhard and another man from M Company had gone into Gleidorf in an effort to find the Battalion CP and to offer 81mm mortar support, if it was needed. They were caught in town by the counter-attack and, with discretion being the better part of valor and to avoid capture, they stayed hidden until they heard the voices of friendly troops that were retaking the town.

By 0500 K Company, less the two squads of the 1st platoon, had been driven from the northern sector of Gleidorf with the loss of one tank.

As they began to lose their infantry protection, the German tanks were afraid to continue their attack and began to withdraw. The situation was chaotic with German and American troops shuffled throughout the town with no clear lines between them. Col. Butler personally led his battalion in an effort to drive the Germans out and retake the town. For the first time he removed his Lt. Colonel's silver leaf from his helmet so as not to draw enemy fire. He and a Lieutenant from his staff dodged into a corner building just as an SS trooper came in from the other side. They met almost chest to chest. All three of them were startled, but the Lieutenant was the quickest to react. He raised his M-1 and emptied it into the German who never knew what hit him as he dropped dead at their feet. In a gesture of disdain, the Lieutenant rolled the dead German over on his back, crossed his hands on his chest and put a flower in his hands as though he was ready to be buried. Word of this spread rapidly and soon there were German bodies all over Gleidorf laying on their backs, with a flower in their crossed hands. The sniper who had shot at Capt. McClendon earlier took a shot at Butler and was killed on the spot.

I and L Companies joined K Company and by 0730 Gleidorf was again secured and the 3rd Battalion was in control of the town. The Battalion CP was moved into town and the men dug in on the high ground to the west and north. They had taken 128 prisoners in addition to the many enemy they had killed and wounded.

"During the battle for Gleidorf we cared for the most casualties ever in our aid station, many from other units and many prisoners. It was here in a farm house in the woods I worked fifty-two consecutive hours at the debridement and surgical patchwork, getting men ready for evacuation. When the last man was shipped, we collapsed.

"As soon as I was able to get myself moving again, I woke Sgt. Stallings and we went out to inspect the trailers and supplies. A 240mm shell hit in the trees above, totaled the trailer and many of the supplies while we only received powder burns of face and neck. Going back into the house, we saw his bed. A long heavy piece of the shell had penetrated the wall of the house, the headboard of the bed, ripped the feather mattress full length and penetrated the foot board. He promised he would never grouch again about me waking him. I'm afraid he didn't keep that vow."

Herbert Orr, M.D. — Battalion Surgeon

In many ways the battle at Gleidorf was more severe than the battle at Höfen for which the Battalion received a Presidential Unit Citation. They suffered more casualties here and again defeated superior forces. Because of the attrition they had suffered, the Battalion was under strength and more was required of each man. Had they not been the battle-hardened, close, cohesive unit they were, they would not have been successful.

It is amazing that the Battalion maintained the same high standards of combat efficiency they had first displayed on December 16. Despite the continuing turnover of officers and men, the unit never faltered and continued to be an effective fighting force until the war ended. The only constants were the Battalion Commander and some key non-coms.

"We had been short of officers, I guess ever since Höfen. The non-coms were a pretty good group of guys. The men had confidence in the ability of their non-coms. We had a number of dangerous and difficult situations and I finally boiled it down to, 'What does the Colonel say? If it's from the Colonel, we'll do it.' The men never questioned the wisdom of Col. Butler and his tactics and what he planned to do."

William Blasdel — K Company

"After that day, when we took stock of who had been evacuated and who was still with us, we found that again I Company and the 3rd Battalion in general had lost a bunch of people. Our numbers had again been reduced drastically."

Richard Mills — I Company

"The first platoon of I Company was ordered to clear out a section of woods near Gleidorf. We came upon a supply dump, hidden in the woods and guarded by one lone Kraut, who gladly gave up. As I was rooting through the supplies I came upon several cases of Norway sardines. Right away the Kraut guard started yelling, 'Nicht gut! Machen ze krunk.' Naturally we told him to get the hell out of the way. We weren't about to pass up this treat. We ate our fill and later we all had the worst case of GI's in military history. When I was back in France, I was talking to a PW who had been in that area. He remembered that supply dump and those sardines. The Norwegian people had put a strong laxative in sardines packed for the Krauts. The first platoon got it instead.

"The little Kraut guard I mentioned stood by and watched as we destroyed rifles, etc. I was down to the last rifle and was ready to smash it against a tree when he tapped me on the shoulder and gestured for me to give him the rifle. Since the bolt was out, I gave it to him to see what he was going to do. He stood the rifle against a tree, spit on his hands, picked up the rifle and smashed it to bits. He then turned to me and said the war is over for him. He thanked us for sparing his life and said we would not have to wait long to enjoy what he had just done. He said Hitler and Deutschland were 'kaput.' "

Dan Sullivan — I Company

"I do remember that we were going night and day in the Ruhr Pocket battle. We would probably go to about ten or twelve o'clock at night. Then we would take our turns standing guard, which would amount to a couple of hours. Then we'd crank up and go again about 5 o'clock in the morning so we were getting by with only a few hours of sleep a day for a period of two weeks. For the most part we had very little sleep."

William Blasdel — K Company

At 0500 on the 8th the Battalion attacked with K Company on the right, I Company on the left and L Company in reserve. The woods north of Gleidorf had to be cleared so that the armor could get into position to fire on Friedberg. By 0830 the east side of the wooded area had been cleared and three hours later the west side was also clear. At 1645 an armored task force moved through the Battalion and captured Ebbinghof. There was no doubt by this time that the Germans had lost the war, but with their backs against the wall they fought desperately and American casualties continued to mount.

Early on April 9th the 3rd Battalion was detached from CCB of the 7th Armored Division and attached to CCR. At 1700 that afternoon I Company was attached to Task Force Brown. The rest of the Battalion went to Berghausen by truck, arriving at 1840. K and L Companies cleared the high ground north and west of Berghausen and assembled at 2300 in Heiminghausen.

The Battalion, minus I Company, spent much of the 10th on trucks, arriving at their assembly area at 1730. L Company moved out northwest along a creek toward Bremscheid, mopping up after an armored attack. K Company followed them. L Company received fire from Eslohe. Sensing that they were in trouble, Col. Butler leaped on one of the accompanying tanks and personally manned a machine gun to support his company. This encouraged the tanks and their armored infantry to join in the fight and the town was soon cleared. L Company then occupied the high ground to the north and west.

On April 11th the 3rd Battalion freed the men of the second squad of K Company's first platoon who had been captured in Gleidorf, as well as their captors. These men said they had had very little to eat as their captors moved them back and forth across the area, trying to escape from the Ruhr Pocket. They (the Germans) could not find an escape route so they finally surrendered and were taken prisoner themselves. In questioning the Americans, the German interrogating officer had discovered that these men were from the 3rd Battalion, 395th Infantry. On learning this, the German said that they called this battalion "The Nighthawks" because of their proficiency and effectiveness at night fighting. The 3rd Battalion had established a reputation with the Germans as well as with the Americans.

Also on the 11th the Battalion CP was established in Eslohe. L and K Companies mopped up the town of Sieperting. One platoon of K Company stayed to guard roadblocks west of town and the rest of the Battalion boarded trucks at 1130 for a two hour trip to an assembly area near Mathmecke. At 1710 I Company reverted to Battalion control and at 1900 K Company left with an armored task force of CCA.

April 12th was a day of continuous action. At 0600 the Battalion, less K Company, boarded trucks and with a battalion of medium tanks from Task Force Brown, moved to Endorf through a series of small towns. Their mission was to cut behind the Germans and they caught a whole Corps of Germans trying to escape. There were infantry, artillery, tanks and many other vehicles in the Corps train and the Battalion ran into the back of this group. The Battalion's lead tank opened up with all their weapons and continued to fire at the retreating Germans until they ran out of ammunition. Then another tank moved into position and continued firing until he too ran out of ammunition. This continued until the enemy had received too much punishment and they capitulated. By the time they had reached Küntrop the Battalion had destroyed innumerable guns, tanks, trucks, half-tracks and horse drawn vehicles. Enemy installations were overrun, including regimental CP's and quartermaster vehicles and supplies. Thousands of prisoners were taken, including many high ranking officers. The 3rd Battalion had two prisoner of war pools out in a field with 2,500 to 3,000 Germans in each field. Not having enough men to really guard such a large number of prisoners, Col. Butler had some tanks line up around the fields facing the prisoners and through loud speakers told them to sit still. Either of these pools could have overwhelmed the Americans had they made a concerted effort. When a nose count was finally made, there were 7,000 prisoners. The Battalion had also released some American PW's, including some of the I Company men who had been captured on December 16 in Höfen. L Company established defensive positions and roadblocks west of Neuenrade while I Company guarded prisoners.

> "The PW's started pouring in there. I was separating them. One of the things that pissed me off was that many had GI shoes on. I made them take 'em off and walk down the damn road with no shoes on. I was separating the officers, non-commissioned officers and the soldaten, because I didn't want them to be together. I also made them take everything out of their pockets. Some still had guns on them, some still had knives. I even made them fork over pen knives and pocket knives. I had a stack two and a half to three feet tall just of knives and other things they had on 'em."
>
> William Bartow—M Company

> "There just seemed like the whole German population was coming in to surrender. They came up that road. Soldiers marching four abreast. They had throwed their guns away and everything. A lot of them even throwed their uniforms away. This was the first time I had seen for real the leather pants the people wore down in Bavaria, Austria and Switzerland. I seen pictures of them, but never like them soldiers dressed in their little leather short pants coming in to surrender. They were singin' and laughin'. They were happy as could be. You'd never know they were a defeated army."
>
> Richard Gorby—K Company

On April 13 the 3rd Battalion was attached to CCA, 7th Armored Division. By truck they moved to Balve via Küntrop and

Langenholthausen. K Company returned from their detached service. With L Company in the lead, the Battalion reached a position in the woods on the high ground south of Deilinghofen and Sundwig where they dug in for the night. Tanks and tank destroyers of the task force moved into position and placed direct fire on the road from Deilinghausen and scored hits on a half-track towing a 105mm howitzer and three command vehicles.

At daybreak the next morning (April 14) the Battalion moved in and occupied the town of Sundwig against direct artillery fire as well as mortar and small arms fire. Here the Battalion was attached to the 394th Infantry Regiment.

"When we got to the town of Hemer we were told to hold up just outside of town and to cease fire so negotiations could be completed for surrender and declaration of the town as an open city. Sitting on a main highway just outside of town, we noticed a Gasthaus and Bierstube down the road. Several of us walked to the Bierstube, which was full of German soldiers, and ordered three beers. Nobody bothered us. When I tried to pay with occupation currency, the bartender told me he could not take it. I told him to hold it until tomorrow or the day after and it would be good, so he took it."

George Prager—L Company

At 2030 the Battalion moved into the open town of Hemer. Their mission was to guard the 23,000 Allied PW's in a large open field on a hill above the town. This prison camp was a real horror. It was as bad as the infamous Andersonville of our Civil War. A large open field, surrounded with concertina barbed wire was filled with thousands of starving men. Open slit trenches for waste disposal, little shelter, contaminated water. Most of the prisoners were Russian or Polish, but there were some Americans and other Allied troops. The Battalion was also charged with occupying several German hospitals. L and M Companies took charge of the Allied PW camp while I and K Companies sent out motorized patrols to police all the Allied prisoners and displaced persons. All of these prisoners were starving and difficult to control.

A large group of Russian prisoners had left the camp in search of food. There was some looting and raping but food was their main interest. They had found some grain cars on rail sidings and had broken into them and were stuffing raw grain into their mouths in their desperation. Knowing that this could kill them, Col. Butler was determined to get them back to the camp where they could be properly fed and treated. I Company had just eaten so Butler had some I Company cooks load used cooking utensils in a jeep which drove slowly past the prisoners. The smell of food from these pots and pans attracted their attention and the jeep slowly drove back to the enclosure with a line of prisoners following it a la Pied Piper. At the camp they were fed properly and the difficult task of repatriation began.

"Some of the American prisoners hitched a horse to a wagon and drove to the rail siding and loaded it with grain which they took back to the camp. They killed the horse and were going to cook the horse and grain together. The prisoners were so desperate for food, they tore at the innards and stuffed the still steaming intestines into their mouths. That was the awfullest thing I've ever seen in my life."

William Bartow—M Company

"I saw three prisoners eating the eyes off the dead horses. It was the only meat left on the cadavers. I think that's the worst sight I've ever seen."

Edward Zioncheck—M Company

"Big PW camp captured. Gates opened and many prisoners went into town. Former guards were captured and hung from lamp posts and many German women were raped. Our patrols had to round up everyone we could find and put them under guard again as all required a special diet due to near starvation. We heard stories of the German guards putting wild dogs in cells with Russian PW's who killed the dogs and ate them."

Jack Randall—I Company

U.S. Army history—"On 15 April the commander and all that remained of the once mighty Panzer Lehr Division surrendered to the 99th Division."

"Our unit overran a Slav POW camp (Stalag VI A). It was an open field as far as the eye could see, with open slit trenches for waste disposal. The field was surrounded by barbed wire and wooden guard towers. The survivors were living skeletons. We were ordered to stay there overnight to keep the survivors in the prison camp away from the Germans in the town. Our cooks showed up and dished us out a hot meal.

"The starving POW's escaped their cage and ended up in the local gardens eating raw potatoes. Apparently food and medical help had not arrived. A few came over to us as food was being slopped in our mess kits. One of our squad got so upset he spilled the mess kit on the ground. The POW's threw themselves on the ground and fought to scoop up the food with their hands. I stifled the impulse to hand one of them my mess kit and ate the slop. It was my first hot meal in over a month. Nevertheless, a sense of guilt remains to this day."

Herb Herman—L Company

"I opened a C ration can and began eating. One of the prisoners came over, put his back to a tree and slid down to the base of the tree. He was watching me eat with that starved look. I couldn't eat any more. I had to give him the ration. I started to hand it over. He shuffled his feet. He didn't have the strength to lift his feet, he shuffled 'em. I gave him this partially opened can. He didn't have the strength to turn the key to open it. I opened up the can and he gobbled the food down. He got convulsions and died. It was too rich for him."

Edward Zioncheck—M Company

"We began caring for the prison camp problems. The starving, emaciated, lousy men who had to be handled so carefully not to stress them more. The worst thing was for some friendly GI to give up a D bar (500 calories of concentrated food—chocolate, fat and sugar). This would too often be the final insult to the damaged, starving intestines of the poor man."

Herbert Orr, MD—Battalion Surgeon

This was the effective end of the fighting in the Ruhr Pocket. Field Marshal Model took his own life as he felt no Field Marshal should ever be taken prisoner. The German army was destroyed as an effective fighting force, but there were still isolated areas of resistance that had to be subdued. There was also the persistent rumor of a "National Redoubt" in the Bavarian mountains near Berchtesgaden. With this battle over, the 99th prepared to move southeast to join with the Third Army and clear up that area.

The Commanding General of the 7th Armored Division, Major General R. W. Hasbrouck, said, "I wish to express my appreciation for the fine service rendered by the 3rd Battalion, 395th Infantry while attached to this division during the reduction of the Ruhr Pocket. They assisted materially in the success of the operation. Their capture of GLEIDORF and subsequent repulse of a determined counter-attack made at night to recapture the town is deserving of high praise.

"Please accept my thanks for the loan of such a fine unit and convey to its officers and men my appreciation and that of my division for the excellent work done by them."

Butler's Battlin' Blue Bastards

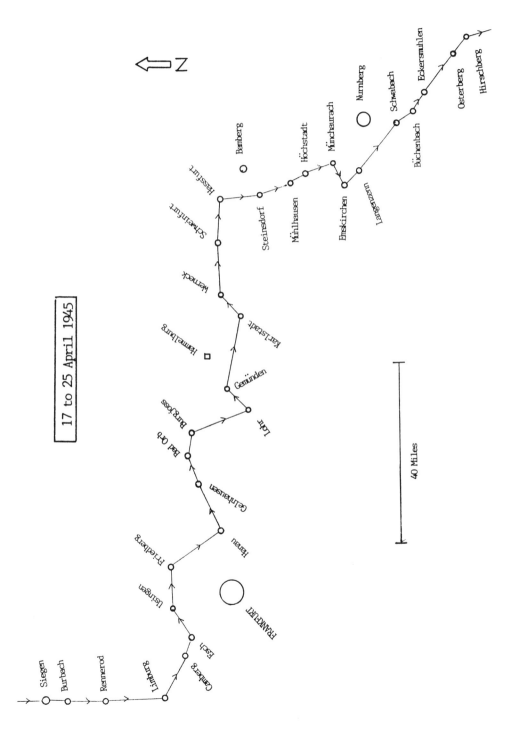

17 to 25 April 1945

CHAPTER 9

To the Third Army

With the Ruhr Pocket effectively sealed off and the German surrender, organized resistance here was at an end. Police and administrative duties remained, but these did not really need combat troops. The 3rd Battalion, as well as the rest of the 99th Division, spent a day or so resting, cleaning weapons and reorganizing. At 1000 on April 16th the Battalion was relieved by the Reconnaisance Troops of the 629th TD Battalion and reverted to 395th Infantry control. On the 17th the Battalion stayed in Hemer, but were ordered to be ready to move.

At 2000 on the 17th the Battalion left Hemer by truck for Steinsdorf where they arrived by 2100 on the 18th of April. The whole trip was about 300 miles and was made with organic transportation. Since the entire Division was involved in the move, there were not enough vehicles for all the men to ride at once so this was a shuttle move. The trucks would carry men some distance, let them off and return to pick up more men. Each group would march until it was time for the trucks to pick them up again. The 786th Tank Battalion and the 629th TD Battalion were attached to the 99th so they drove their own vehicles and also carried infantrymen with them. As many as 48 infantrymen would get on one tank so they would not have to march. A trip this long and with this many men put terrific wear and tear on the vehicles and it is a credit to the maintenance men that they were able to move this far, this fast and keep all those vehicles in service.

"Our platoon was taken out of the line and driven back for a rest. It was a drizzling cold day that found our platoon standing in single file waiting in front of a pyramidal tent housing many showers. As we stood there in a state of miserable exhaustion, a jeep rode up at our backs. In our state of mind no one was curious enough to turn around. A voice barked out requesting the presence of the senior NCO. With a little more encouragement, a Corporal responded. General Patton, standing up in his jeep, delivered a short lecture on military etiquette. Sensing our lack of interest, he permitted the Corporal to tell him that we had just been relieved from combat for a rest. Patton cooled down and after a few more words on regulations in this man's army, he left us to revel in our misery. Eventually we got our showers, new clothes, an extra pair of socks and some food. I can't recall sleeping there overnight. Shortly we were on trucks again going back to our unit. So much for our period of rest and relaxation. It was the only time we were officially out of combat and had any kind of rest."

Herb Herman—L Company

The rifle companies were quartered in buildings in Steinsdorf and M Company in Ndr. Dorf. Here they spent several days resting, repairing equipment and preparing for the next action. While the German army had essentially been put out of business, there were still some units in southeast Germany that were determined to carry on the fight. There was no longer any overall command structure in the German army and local commanders made their own decisions. The Battalion officers attended a demonstration of amphibious river crossings to prepare them for the possible necessary crossing of the rivers ahead of them.

During their successful actions in the Ruhr Pocket, the Division and the Battalion had commandeered some German vehicles and put American markings on them. However, they were now attached to the U.S. Third Army, General George S. Patton Commanding, and General Patton was a stickler for military regulations and all non-issue equipment was ordered to be disposed of. In addition, because it was "Regulation," the riflemen were again ordered to carry their much-despised gas masks. The men felt the gas masks served no useful purpose, were bulky and uncomfortable to carry, and just added to the normal heavy burden they carried.

All through their previous combat actions men had been wounded and evacuated. Many of these men were so severely injured that the war was over for them, but many also had relatively light injuries that healed quickly. These men were once again declared fit for combat and returned to their units. The return trip was not always smooth.

> "There I sat, the slight wounds healed, fit for action, and my buddies off somewhere fighting a war. An extremely frustrating experience. I tried to think of ways to go AWOL from the hospital but had no idea where the 99th was or how to get there.
>
> "Finally we moved again, to a Third Army Replacement Center. Signs reading, 'UNIFORM VIOLATIONS WILL BE PUNISHED BY SUMMARY COURT' were everywhere. My introduction to the Third Army did not inspire any friendly feelings for its commander.
>
> "Next stop was the 99th Replacement Depot. The same old paperwork started over again. I was lucky enough to spot our company mail clerk so I threw my stuff in his jeep and said goodbye to the army replacement system. It is my sincere hope that they revamped this system for later wars. As it was, there were thousands of good trained men who were badly needed at the front, but just sat mouldering for weeks in the stupid system. Maybe not all were as anxious to get back to their outfits as I was, but I do know there were a good many."
>
> Homer Kissinger—M Company

On April 22nd the Battalion moved another 60 miles by truck to an assembly area near Buchenbach. Their mission, as regimental reserve, was to reconnoiter routes of attack behind the attacking battalions. At this time Company C of the 629th TD Battalion and the 3rd Platoon, Company C of the 786th Tank Battalion were attached to the 3rd Battalion. At 1800 on the 23rd they marched to an assembly area in the woods near Eckersmühlen, arriving at 2145. On the 24th the Battalion moved on foot to Weinsfeld, leaving at 1230 and arriving at 1500. At 1700 they were again on the move and arrived at Osterberg at 2230, where they bivouacked in the woods.

At 0200 Col. Butler returned with orders for the Battalion to move to the Altmühl River. Starting at 0700 on April 25th the Battalion made a truck shuttle march and by 1300 were all assembled in the vicinity of Hirschberg, a little more than 1,000 yards from the Altmühl. Movement was over and the fighting was to resume.

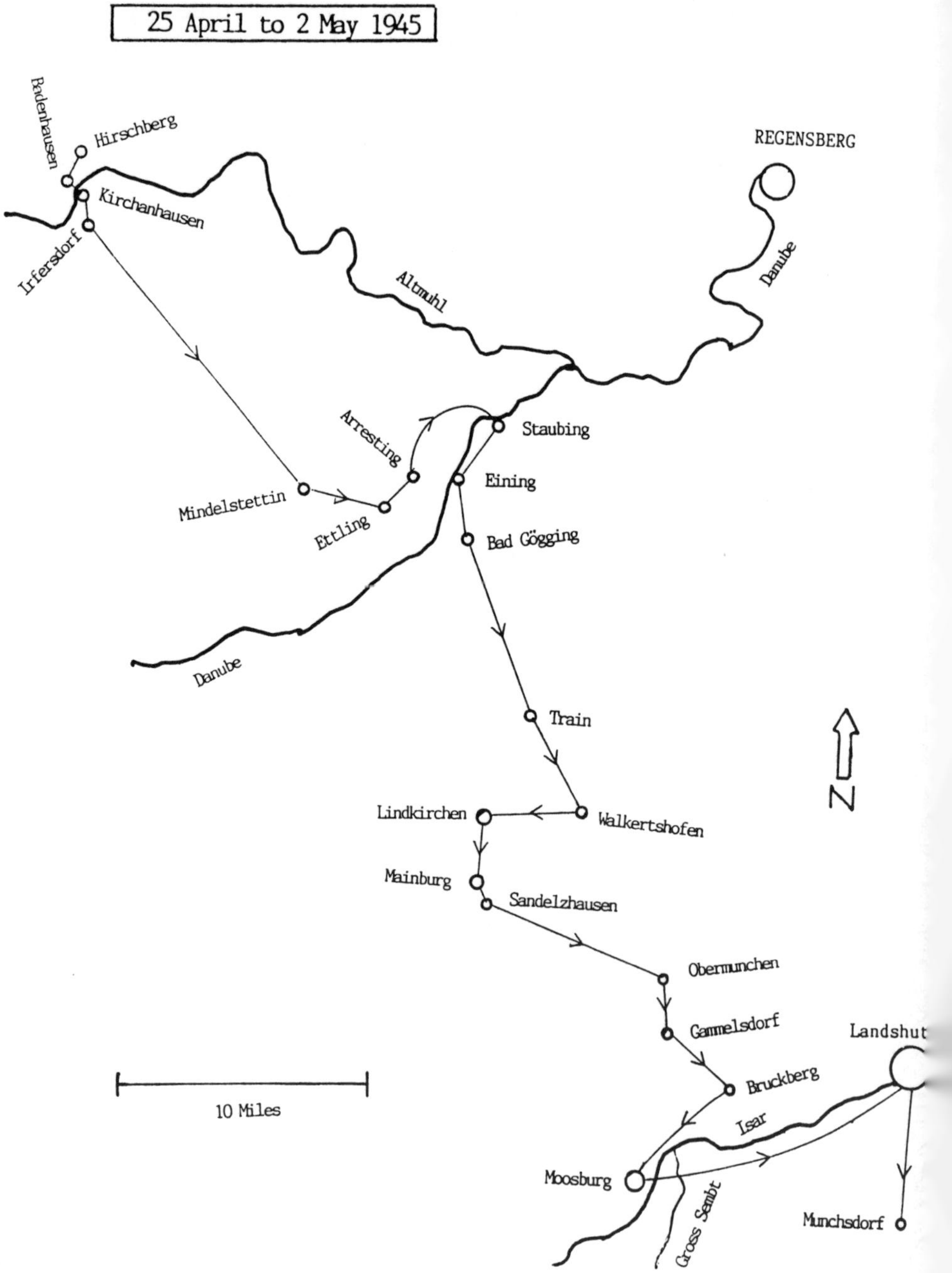
25 April to 2 May 1945
Redenhausen
Hirschberg
Kirchanhausen
Irfersdorf
Altmuhl
REGENSBERG
Danube
Arresting
Staubing
Eining
Mindelstettin
Ertling
Bad Gögging
Danube
Train
Lindkirchen
Walkertshofen
Mainburg
Sandelzhausen
Obermunchen
Gammelsdorf
Landshut
Bruckberg
Isar
10 Miles
Moosburg
Gross Sembt
Munchsdorf

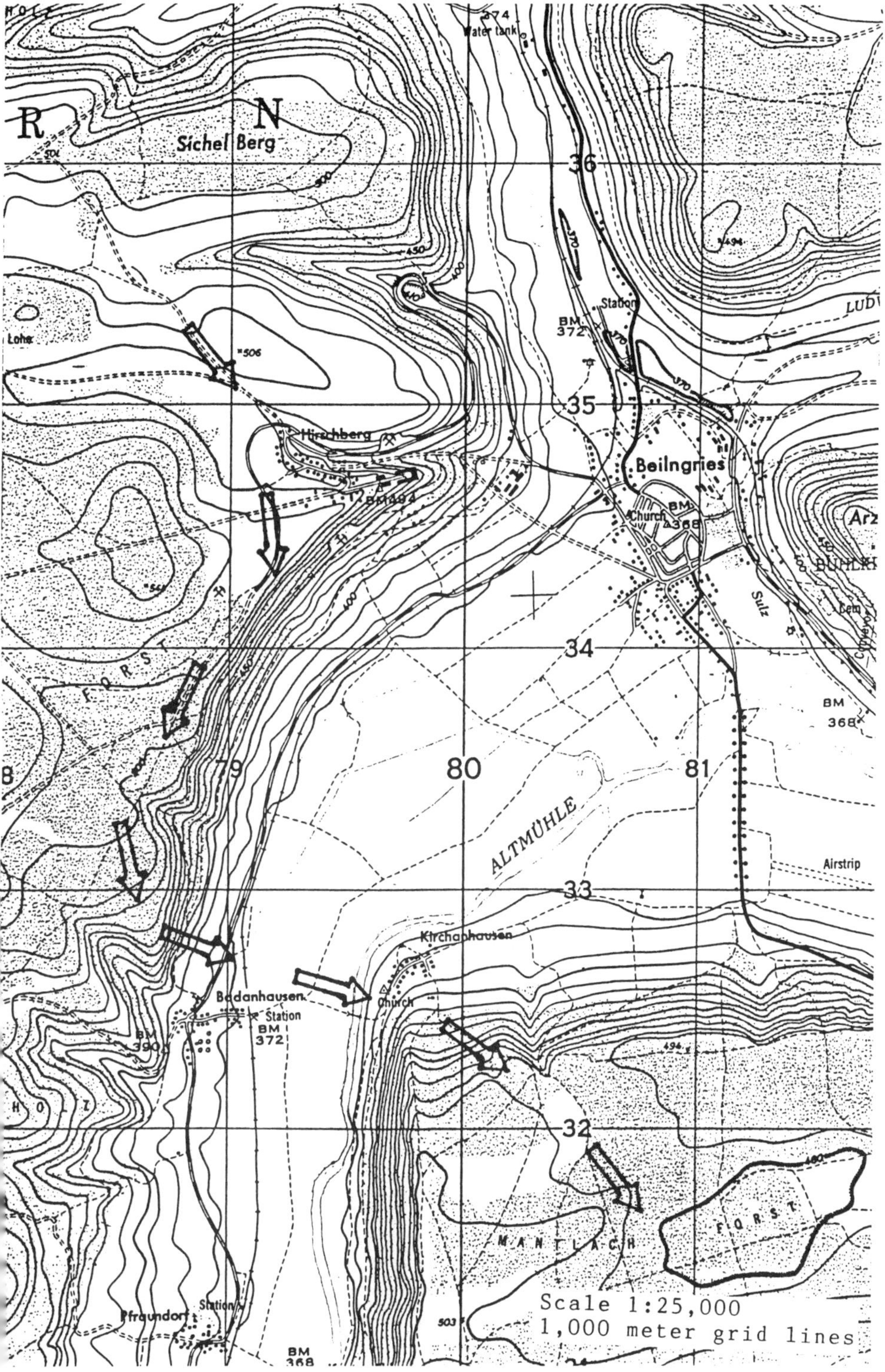

R
N
Sichel Berg
Lohe
Hirschberg
Beilngries
Church
Station
BM 372
36
35
34
33
32
79
80
81
ALTMÜHLE
Sulz
Airstrip
BM 368
Kirchanhausen
Bodanhausen
Station
BM 372
BM 390
Church
MANTLACH
FORST
Pfraundorf
Station
BM 368
Water tank

Scale 1:25,000
1,000 meter grid lines

Chapter 10

The Altmühl, Danube and Isar Rivers

At 1730 on April 25th the Battalion jumped off on their attack across the Altmühl River in the vicinity of Kirchanhausen. In prior attempts to cross, a tank battalion had been destroyed, an armored infantry battalion had been chewed up and an engineering battalion reduced to 16 men. Col. Butler requested permission to make a night attack, but was ordered to cross at once.

The route of the attack was down an almost vertical limestone escarpment, about 300 feet high, to the flat, open river valley. From the bottom of the hill it was over 500 yards to the river across open fields. Once across the river, it was another 100 yards to the village of Kirchanhausen and the hill on the far side of the valley. The river itself was wide, chest deep and flowing swiftly. Although there were few enemy infantry, the entire area was well covered by German artillery, mortars and machine guns. The enemy forward observers had very good visual coverage of the area. A formidable obstacle indeed!

The attack was made with I Company on the left, L Company in the center and K Company on the right. All companies were spread out in a long line and all moved together. M Company set up their mortars and heavy machine guns on the forward slope of the hill to provide covering fire.

The command group of about 35 men moved right behind the attacking companies. His radio man was exhausted so Col. Butler put the SCR-300 radio on his back and started down a small road. German forward observers apparently saw them and artillery explosions started walking up the road toward them. They took cover off the road and the artillery went by them with no casualties. Reaching the bottom of the hill, this group took cover behind a barn and again were spotted by German observers. Thirty rounds hit within a 30 yard radius, including tree bursts, and the only injury was one man being hit by a log that had been jarred loose and rolled down the hill.

The attacking companies were assaulted by enemy fire as they ran across the open area and struggled across the river. Had they not all moved at the same time as fast as possible, casualties would have been much heavier than the 23 men who were killed or wounded.

There was a church in Kirchanhausen and, knowing that church steeples were a preferred location for forward observers, the mortars picked this as a primary target. Setting his gun just by estimating the range and direction, one gunner put his first round right into the steeple. The mortars were able to put very heavy fire on the town as they had found a truckload of mortar ammunition that had been abandoned by the previous attackers when they had been driven off.

The heavy machine guns fired across the valley over the heads of the attacking riflemen and set buildings on fire in Kirchanhausen with tracer rounds. When ordered to move forward, they could see that they would have to cross a small bridge as the riflemen were having great difficulty crossing the river just carrying rifles. Some riflemen who were crossing the bridge were under very heavy fire.

"We was spread out. I was scared. The only thing I could think to do was to present the section (heavy machine gun) out there as a target and when they shift their fire to us, let them guys cross the river below us. They shifted fire and it worked. I told the guys, 'When they start shooting artillery on us, every man for himself as we go across the river.' We all took off and went down across the bridge."

William Bartow—M Company

"I started crossing that field and I heard these rounds come in, everyone of which was going to go into my hip pocket. Finally I heard one come in close and hit the ground and it went off. The next thing I remember is the mortar platoon sergeant saying, 'Come on. Let's get up and go.' After I got across the bridge and into the town I looked at my helmet and I had a nice crease in there. It cut the netting on my helmet and knocked me out and I didn't know what it was."

Edward Zioncheck—M Company

Ordered to continue the attack in the dark uphill into the Montach Forest, the Battalion was held up by heavy machine gun fire, but the mortars soon stopped this. When the area was cleared the Battalion CP was set up in Badanhausen. I Company was ordered into Irfersdorf and were in position there by 2330.

On April 26 the Battalion assembled and, with K Company motorized, moved out for an attack across the Danube River, about 50 kilometers southeast. At 2130 the Battalion CP was established at Ettling. K Company, with support from M Company, set up a defense line here while I and L Companies were in Mindelstetten.

"Somewhere along the line, our group captured a horse drawn pay train with a large supply of wine and brandy. My share was two bottles of French champagne and all the mark notes I could stuff in my pockets. Straggling down the road, swigging away, a plane strafed us. I lost the wine jumping into a ditch and then my stomach contents, leaving me a very woozy first-time drunk."

Herb Herman—L Company

The next day, April 27, K Company again boarded tanks and tank destroyers as their original mission was to cross a bridge in

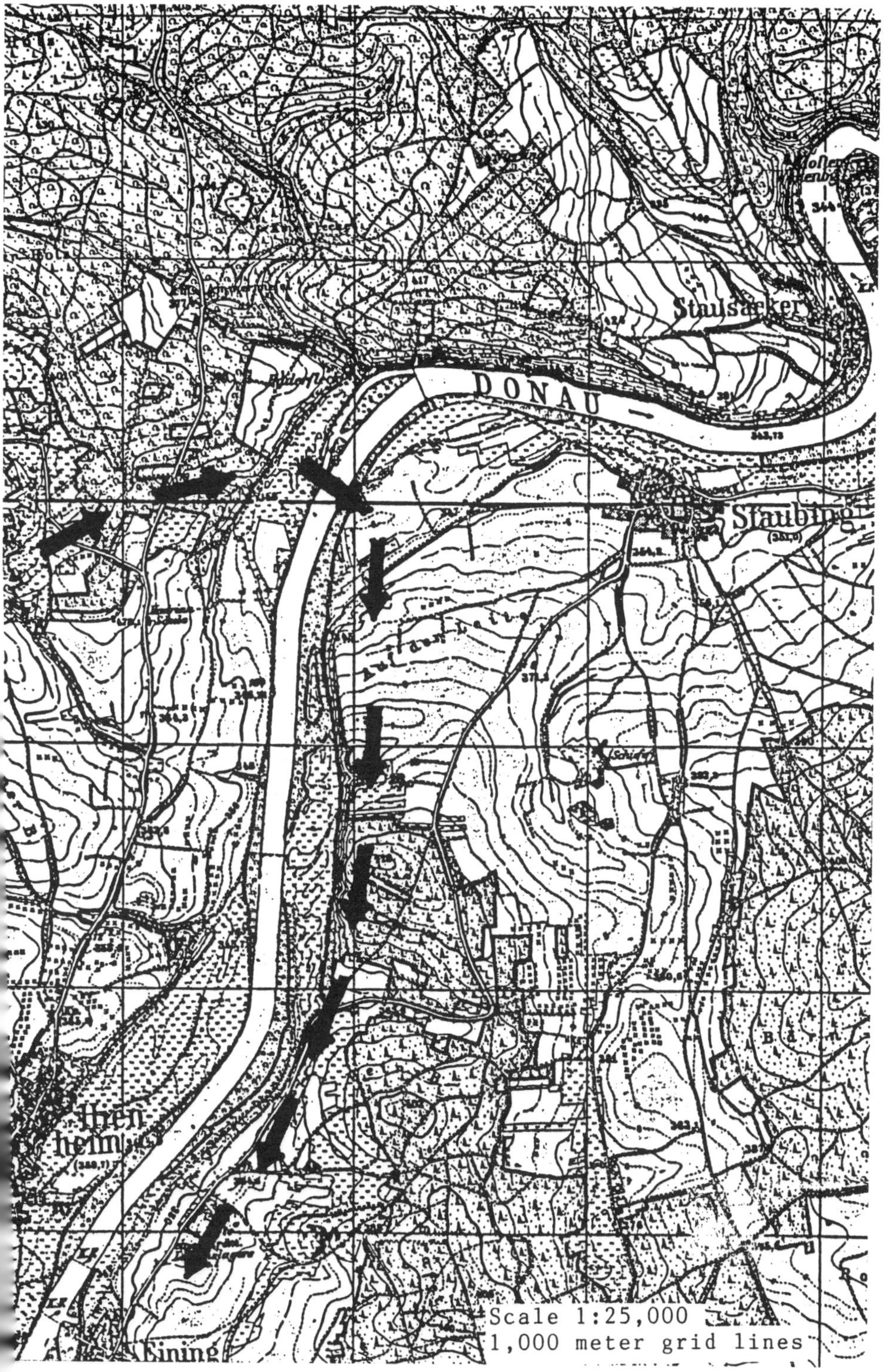

DONAU
Staubing
Staußacker
Ihrenheim
Eining
Scale 1:25,000
1,000 meter grid lines

the 395th regimental area near Arresting while the rest of the Battalion crossed on foot bridges. The entire Battalion was then to attack the enemy from the flank. F Company of the 395th Regiment crossed the Danube in assault boats, but were pinned down on the south bank by extremely heavy small arms and artillery fire and were unable to advance as planned. The enemy directed heavy mortar, artillery and direct anti-aircraft fire on the north bank so supporting troops were unable to cross and help the men on the south bank. Because of this hold up, the 3rd Battalion moved to the vicinity of Staubing in the 393rd sector. K Company had dismounted and joined the rest of the Battalion. The first elements of the Battalion crossed the Danube on amphibious trucks (DUKW's) at 1930 and by 2010 the entire Battalion was on the south side of the river. They encountered no opposition as they crossed. Scrambling down the river bank to board the DUKW's and up the opposite bank was difficult because of the water and mud. Col. Butler slipped and fell and found out later that he had fractured a couple of ribs.

> "When I Company reached the Danube, the engineers had a pontoon bridge across it. It was here that we got a look at General George Patton, who was checking his tanks as they crossed the bridge. He also got a look at Company I. He gave a pretty good stare and I don't think he approved of our looks."
>
> Dan Sullivan—I Company

> "At the Danube crossing I became quite upset and unforgiving because General Patton, standing there with his famous pearl-handled revolvers, would not allow us to infiltrate our medical vehicles among the tanks to catch up with our infantry, already too far ahead."
>
> Herbert Orr, MD—Battalion Surgeon

The 3rd Battalion's first objective was the town of Bad Gögging. During the river crossing, it had started to rain. To make things still more difficult, the south bank was wet and marshy until the men reached the high cliffs on the far side of the river valley.

"It seemed we were going through a swamp. I didn't think there was any dry land, just swamp is what it was. It turned cold. I got wet wading them swamps and about half froze. We kept going all night then. Once in awhile machine guns would open up, a burp gun would rattle. We didn't stop. We just kept going. I really don't know how much ground we covered that night. In the morning then, it was fog and we were coming up out of that swamp. We were going uphill. We didn't even stop. We didn't even hit the ground. Just kept walking. Since then I've often thought that if I was a German up there, looked down on that swamp and see these crazy buggers coming up out of that swamp like men out of the past, it would have been enough to scare you. But that's what we did."

Richard Gorby—K Company

Reaching the cliffs on the south side, the Battalion moved in a double column along ledges. The order of march was K Company, I Company, Headquarters Company and L Company. Darkness had fallen and just over a mile from the river K Company encountered an undetermined number of infantry supported by dug-in machine guns. K Company was pinned down, but they did manage to get their machine guns in action. I Company supported them with mortar fire and also sent one platoon into the woods to the enemy's left to out flank them. Two of the enemy were killed, one captured and the rest withdrew.

At 0145 on the 28th the original march order was resumed as the Battalion headed for Bad Gögging via Eining and reached Eining without encountering any opposition. As they pushed on and reached Heiligenstadt they were fired on by three German tanks withdrawing east of Unter Ulmin. Two men were killed and ten wounded in addition to an unknown number of German civilians.

"The last house there beside me, that would be the side away from where we were coming in, all the women and kids had got in that building. Them German tanks opened fire on that house and they just demolished all the women and kids."

Richard Gorby—K Company

Reports were that this area was defended by the SS Division Niebedungen and this is indicative of the mind-set of SS troops. They knew the house contained German women and children and also knew that the war was practically over and yet felt it necessary to demonstrate their reputation for brutality.

Moving from Heiligenstadt toward Unter Ulmin the troops heard vehicles moving west toward Neustadt so they moved to the side of the road and surrounded them when they appeared. Three enemy transports and 40 men were captured. Moving into Unter Ulmin another 34 enemy were captured without opposition. By 0500 Bad Gögging was secured. The men moved into buildings here and rested until they resumed the attack at 1300. Their objective was the town of Forsternbach. K Company was in the lead followed by I, L and HQ Companies. Nearing the town K Company received small arms and machine gun fire from a high knoll on the east side of town. The company 60mm mortars and supporting artillery opened fire on this knoll and also on the east end of town. The armor supporting the Battalion had all bogged down, with the exception of one tank. The artillery and mortar fire quickly collapsed the opposition and the town was secured. One hundred and forty-nine prisoners were captured.

At 0700 on the 29th the Battalion moved out on foot to continue their southward advance. No resistance was encountered and they arrived in Train at 1330 where they stopped to rest. It proved to be a short rest as they moved out again at 1400 with L Company in the lead.

"Walking through a town, I was surprised to see a bakery with bread piled up in the window. The desire for a real piece of bread overcame me and I stepped out of line and entered the store. I requested a loaf of bread in my best

Yiddish, while flashing a ten mark note. The baker informed me that I needed a ration book for a loaf. Apparently this kind of obtuseness was a common trait among Germans. However, my time was too limited to discuss morals, ethics and guilt. I slipped the safety off my M-1 rifle and repeated my request while tossing the ten mark note on the counter. The baker pushed a loaf across the counter along with a fistfull of crumpled mark notes and some pfennig coins. Unfortunately the loaf was 'ersatz' (sawdust and some grain) and not up to my expectations."

Herb Herman—L Company

By 1700 they were in Walkertshofen. Here the Battalion transportation caught up with the foot troops and they made a shuttle move to Bruckberg. The first elements arrived here at 2100 and the last units from K Company arrived at 0300 on the morning of the 30th. At 1600 that evening the Battalion moved to Moosburg on the Isar River.

"After the Danube River crossing, we were involved in something that was really a joy. Our unit was privileged to open up a slave labor camp in the area of Regensburg. We opened the gates, which we found immediately was a bad mistake as those people went on a looting rampage, a vengeance campaign which we had to stop. We had to gather them back up and put them back inside to provide them with medical attention, rations and to protect the German population against them. The tables had turned. We knew we had made a lot of people happy by starting the process that would change them from being slave laborers back to being Russian, Italian, Romanian, etc. citizens. It was something to be there. I remember very vividly one man who mounted a stump that was 2 feet across and about 2 feet high. That was his stage from which he sang 'O Sole Mio!' in the most beautiful baritone I had heard in a long time. It was a joy to see so much joy.

"We then came to an American prisoner camp. That was a great thing. Air Force, infantry. I think we liberated some of our own people there, some of our own 99'ers. We did liberate a cousin of a girl back home who later became my wife. That was sort of a fitting end to the war for us, to liberate some of our own people; take back some of those who had been taken from us. It was a good feeling."

Richard Mills—I Company

"At Moosburg we liberated a bunch of our own POW's (Stalag VII A). We were passing our K rations to them as we went by and they looked like a pretty happy bunch. I also ran across an old school mate behind that fence."

Dan Sullivan—I Company

It was here that the Battalion lost its leader and driving force. Going upstairs to report to the Regimental Commander, Col. Butler passed out. Completely exhausted, both physically and emotionally, Butler was ordered to the 99th Division hospital by the Division Surgeon for a complete rest. In addition to the burden of command, the lack of sleep and proper food, the constant danger in six months of virtually constant combat had taken its toll. He had lost 35 pounds; he had been the target of snipers numerous times; 7 times the windshield on his command jeep had been shot out; he had narrowly escaped machine gun fire many times; he had been the target of direct fire from an 88mm gun; he had been wounded and he had seen many of his men killed and wounded. His body and mind had taken far more abuse than most humans could stand. The war was near its end and it was time for someone else to pick up the burden.

It was at Moosburg that the Battalion also lost their Battalion Surgeon, Major Herbert S. Orr, who also finally needed hospitalization for the battering his body had taken during the months of combat.

At 2000 the Battalion crossed the Isar River on a dam that was intact and headed northeast behind the 2nd Battalion. They crossed the Gross Sembt River. The 2nd Battalion was in contact with the enemy and was receiving small arms and mortar fire. At 0145 the 2nd Battalion pulled back and artillery fired a concentration on the enemy strong points. At 0300 the 3rd Battalion passed through the 2nd Battalion and met little resistance. By 0530 they had reached Hofham and were ordered to secure and hold the area.

On May 1, 1945, Lt. Col. Oliver W. Hartwell assumed command of the 3rd Battalion—395th Infantry. At 1400 May 1st the 3rd Battalion was attached to the 393rd Regiment and ordered to screen the area south of the Isar River between Hofham and Achdorf as well as the high ground overlooking the river and the railroad bridge at Achdorf. After much difficulty in crossing the Isar because of all the blown bridges, the armored units attached to the Battalion joined them for this operation. I and L Companies moved along the high ground along the river while K Company and the attached armored units moved on a parallel road. Word was received that the 393rd Regiment had crossed the Isar at Achdorf and, meeting no resistance, had moved on to Landshut. The Battalion was ordered to proceed to an assembly area near Seepoint. The 394th Regiment passed through this area and the 3rd Battalion reverted to control of the 395th Regiment, which was in Division reserve.

At 1130 on May 2nd the 99th Division received orders to "Halt in place," assemble and await orders. The fighting was over at last.

At 0141 on May 7, 1945, Colonel General Alfred Jodl, in the name of the German High Command, signed an unconditional surrender document.

Chapter 11

Aftermath

The shooting had stopped and death was no longer a constant companion. No one appreciates the cessation of war more than the men who have to fight it. Only they know what war is really like.

> "The next morning the war's over. Everybody was very happy. I remember our squad all got together. We set up there, sang a couple of hymns 'cuz we were all so glad to be alive, I guess. That just about takes care of everything, I think."
>
> Richard Gorby—K Company

> "I'd like to give a little personal testimony about the protection of the Lord. I really feel that the Lord put an umbrella over me that protected me through all of this. Sniper fire, the tank that shot the house up and all of this and the phosphorous. Lots of times we escaped without a scratch. I give God all the credit for His protection in all of this. By His mercy and grace I walked out of that thing without a scratch. I want to give Him, the Lord, thanks for bringing me back in one piece."
>
> William Blasdel—K Company

"When combat ended in Europe, there were two of us from the original squad of 12. Neither of us got a scratch, even from a C ration tin. The other guy was Jack Wills."

Hugh Ferris—Headquarters Company

"My main memory of combat was that there were only two ways out. Wounded or dead. You simply existed as best you could and hoped against hope that your ultimate wound would be minor. The end of the war was never visible to the imagination of an infantryman. It looked like it would last forever."

Robert Parks—K Company

"There was one stretch of 83 days and another of 67 days that made up our active participation in the shooting war in Europe. It doesn't sound like a lot of time. It actually wasn't compared to other units who had been committed for months and months before we were, but each of those periods of commitment as infantry into a shooting war seemed like a lifetime to us. The people around you were there today and gone tomorrow. You kinda start counting up. When it's all done you notice that there are only two of you who lasted from the beginning to the end out of a beginning number of 46. That makes you think too."

Richard Mills—I Company

Even though the fighting had stopped, there was a lot of work to be done by the men of the 3rd Battalion. The entire country of Germany was a shambles and had to be put back in working order.

Literally millions of people of many nationalities had to be cared for and returned to their homes. Many thousands of POW's the Germans had held had to be identified, have their medical needs attended to and returned. The army troops were ordered to find and arrest German war criminals for trial. The phone system had ceased to exist and water systems had to be restored to working order. Civil administrative organizations had broken down and had to be reestablished. Saboteurs and potential diehard fanatics had to be identified and put under guard. Roads and railroads had to be put back in working order. Because of the bombings and heavy fighting in many places, there were practically no houses or buildings that were habitable. All of these things, and more, had to be put right and the army was the only organized force able to do them.

Third Battalion Headquarters was moved to Hammelburg and the individual companies in the surrounding area. I Company moved to Bad Brückenau. Lt. Col. Butler had returned from the hospital and had resumed command of the Battalion.

"The company stayed in an old hotel on the side of a mountain. There was an olympic-sized swimming pool in town and three good gasthauses. There were mineral springs in the area and many bath houses. When we were moving through towns we only saw the very young and the very old. Now everyone was showing. All these goodies now, but NO FRATERNIZATION. Our duties now were to set up roadblocks and check POW's returning to their houses.

"About 10 kilometers out of town was an ammo dump we were to guard. There were a lot of explosions going on out there that nobody knew anything about. Right next to the dump was a DP camp with thousands of Russian, Czech, Polish and Ukranian women."

Dan Sullivan—I Company

Numerous roadblocks were established so that the credentials of all people passing could be checked as a part of the sorting out process. Many of the German civilians, displaced persons and former prisoners were grateful and helpful, but many were surly and angry and tried to disrupt the transition back to "normal" life. Because of the political situations in their home countries, many of the ex-prisoners and displaced persons strongly resisted any attempt to ship them back to their native lands. Several women claimed they had been raped by men of the 3rd Battalion, but all of these cases were disproved.

> "While we were there, a German woman showed up and claimed she had been raped within the past hour. Col. Butler told our medical officer to examine her and see if it was so. He took me with him as a witness and interpreter. On finishing his examination, he informed the Col. that she had indeed had intercourse. The Col. got mad and ordered everybody including clerks, cooks, drivers, HQ personnel, whoever was there, to stand inspection. Everybody was lined up in a hollow square, facing each other. He then told me to take this woman between the rows of two's and let her look at every man. She and I walked through the ranks and, upon finishing our inspection, Col. Butler had me ask her if she had spotted the rapist. She told me, 'Yes,' and pointed right at me! The Col. blew a fuse and told the MP's to throw the witch out. It seems that at the time of the alleged rape I had been with the Col. and he was my best alibi and witness to my innocence that I could ever have had."
>
> George Prager—L Company

When a war ends there is a lot of military equipment still around. Just outside Bad Brückenau there were more than 20 railroad cars on a siding, most filled with ammunition and high explosives. Men from the 3rd Battalion were detailed to guard this so that it would not fall into the wrong hands before proper disposition could be made. There was water running in the ditch next to the railroad grade and to relieve their boredom, some of the men would throw things in the water and shoot at them as they flowed along. It must be remembered that these men were combat veterans who felt very much at home with firearms and explosives. In shooting under the train at objects in the water, one of the men got a little careless and fired too high, hitting a rail car. An M-1 round into a carload of explosives produced the result you would expect. With a series of roars and blasts the entire train exploded in a huge fireball. The noise could be heard for miles.

Far better than a 4th of July celebration. For several days court martial proceedings were considered against the guards, who had visions of many years in prison, but no formal charges were ever filed.

With the war over, the men were concerned about what would happen to them next. They were citizen-soldiers and anxious to return home, now that the fighting had stopped. The war against Japan was not over and many felt they would be transferred to the Pacific theatre. In the event, this did not happen. Finally the army announced that a number of divisions would be returned to the United States for demobilization. The 99th was one of these divisions. At the same time, a point system (adjusted service rating) was established to select the individuals that would go home. Each man received 5 points for each major campaign, wife, wound, child, age, etc. and 85 points were needed for this first selection. Units that had been in combat longer than the 99th had more "high point" men so they were transferred to the 99th while the lower point men of the 99th were transferred to divisions that would remain in Germany as an Army of Occupation. On September 24, 1945, the 99th Division landed at Norfolk, Virginia, and Camp Miles Standish, Massachusetts, and was inactivated 27 September 1945.

Men of the 3rd Battalion performed a number of occupation duties in their new units and were sent home in groups and as individuals over the next several months. Almost all of them were sent home by the end of 1945.

> "There was a case or two that I know of where a fellow was wounded, he recovered, was commited to combat a second time, wounded again and evacuated back to the U.S. and was finally discharged in time to take advantage of the first vote for which he was eligible at the age of 21. There were fellows who went to war, got a pretty good chunk of it under their belt and returned home by the time they were legally mature."
>
> Richard Mills—I Company

Epilogue

When the shooting stopped only a handful of the men who had sailed so bravely out of Boston Harbor in October 1944 were still "Present and Accounted For." Even some of them had been wounded at least once. Many men of the Battalion lay in military cemeteries in Europe, such as Henri-Chapelle and Netherlands American Military Cemetery. Some had been returned home to be buried in military and civilian cemeteries in the U.S.

Numerous others returned home with grievous mental or physical injuries that would last until death. Even with the war ended, men still were killed and injured in such mundane things as traffic accidents.

"Man is an amazing piece of equipment. I firmly believe that a conditioned man can probably outperform any animal in the world in endurance and tolerance. I found that man can take a tremendous amount of punishment and endure, but it's amazing at times how little it takes to kill a man. He's so delicate; life is so fragile. At other times it seems a man can be nearly cut in half and survive."

William Blasdel—K Company

A few of the men stayed in the army and had military careers. Many served, as Regulars or Reservists, in the Korean "Police Action" and a lesser number also served in Vietnam. These men of honor must never be forgotten. They gave their all so that we could continue to live in peace and tranquillity.

"I started out with the 99th Division December 1942 in Camp Van Dorn, Mississippi, and, by God's grace, went all the way through. I have been forever grateful for my good mind, strong body and soul. And for those that didn't make it, may there always be a moment of silence."

William Bartow—M Company

"My time with I Company had to be the biggest adventure of my life. We can be thankful we had men like Captain Burgin and Colonel Butler. They still have the respect of all the men I have talked to."

Dan Sullivan—I Company

"The morale of the men was amazing. I want to say this about those guys I was with in the army. When we went overseas most of the men were expert riflemen. That accounted for quite a little for their being able to withstand and make good soldiers. Another thing I noticed about those guys—most of them were from pretty good family backgrounds and had a fear of the Lord in their hearts. I found out that the thing that gives a man his spirit—these men had fear, but they had a facility in that they had clear thinking minds and they had faith in the Lord. I believe that sustained them a great deal."

William Blasdel—K Company

"As I look back on that period and conjure up all the events that I can remember, they wouldn't fill more than a couple weeks time. I was on the front for months but most of the time is lost in memory. Like a lot of combat soldiers, the return to civilian life was both a blessed relief and a trying time. I talk very little about the war as a person who was not in combat can neither understand or empathize with my feelings."

Robert Parks—K Company

"I would not want to go back, but I made a lot of friends whom I still hold dear. Once a year we get together for a reunion. I still receive a Christmas card from a family I stayed with in Belgium during a break. I realize that many of the things we did were wrong, but no one, unless you saw how mean those people were—the little children and the old people machine gunned and burned to death—can judge us. I have no regrets, just sad memories."

Warren Wilson—I Company

"This is like a free-swinging Rorschach test without ink blots. My memory will not allow me to get into greater bad detail. Would probably require psychological help to do it. I don't want to remember better than that."

Alfred Schnitzer—L Company

As time passed, these men became fathers and grandfathers. Some achieved great success in their chosen fields and many lived their lives on a more modest scale. Regardless of their achievements they have always had a common bond of their service together in the 3rd Battalion and each of them is proud to say, "I was one of Butler's men. I fought with Danube Blue."

BIBLIOGRAPHY

Arrington, Grady P. (c1959). *Infantryman at the Front*. New York: Vantage Press.

Cole, Hugh M. *The Ardennes: Battle of the Bulge*. Washington, D.C.: Office of the Chief of Military History.

Eisenhower, John S. D. (c1969). *The Bitter Woods*. Nashville, TN: The Battery Press.

Elstob, Peter (c1971). *Hitler's Last Offensive*. New York: The Macmillan Co.

Lauer, MG Walter E. (c1951). *Battle Babies—The Story of the 99th Infantry Division in World War II*. Indiana, PA: A.G. Halldin Publishing Co.

MacDonald, Charles B. (c 1985). *A Time For Trumpets*. New York: William Morrow & Co.

MacDonald, Charles B. *The Last Offensive*. Washington, D.C.: Center of Military History, U.S. Army.

Niedermayer, Walter (c1990). *Into the Deep Misty Woods of the Ardennes*. Indiana, PA: A.G. Halldin Publishing Co.

Parker, Danny S. (c 1991). *Battle of the Bulge*. Philadelphia: Combined Books.

Ryan, Cornelius (c 1966). *The Last Battle*. New York: Simon and Schuster.

Toland, John (c 1959). *Battle, The Story of the Bulge*. New York: Random House.

History of the Seventh Armored Division. (c 1982). Dallas: Taylor Publishing Co.

Eight Stars to Victory. (c 1948). *History of the 9th Inf. Div.* The Ninth Infantry Division Assn.

S-3 Journal. 3rd Battalion, 395th Infantry. 15 September 1944-4 May 1945.

U.S. Army. History of the 395th Infantry Regiment. 1 January 1944-31 March 1945 and 1 May 1945-31 August 1945.

395th Infantry After/After Action Reports. 9 November 1944-11 May 1945.

APPENDIX

Lt. Col. McClernand Butler—1945

BIOGRAPHY

Lt. Colonel McClernand Butler

Lieutenant Colonel McClernand Butler was born in Springfield, Illinois on July 10, 1910, into a family with a long military background. His great grandfather, General John Alexander McClernand, raised a corps of infantry at the request of President Lincoln and commanded this corps in the Civil War. His uncle, General Edward J. McClernand, was a West Point graduate and was awarded the Congressional Medal of Honor during the Indian Wars. His father was a Major in the Illinois National Guard.

At the urging of his father, who was Company Commander of the local National Guard company, Butler joined the Illinois National Guard in 1926 when he was 16 years old.

From 1930 to 1933 Butler attended West Point. A member of the boxing team, Butler set a school record on the rifle range and tied the school record on the pistol range. However, French was his downfall and he left West Point before graduating.

On 2 July 1933 he was commissioned a 2nd Lieutenant in the Illinois National Guard. He entered Federal service on 5 March 1941 as a 2nd Lieutenant. His promotions were as follows:

5 March 1941	2nd Lieutenant
22 March 1941	1st Lieutenant
23 May 1942	Captain
30 January 1943	Major
21 March 1944	Lieutenant Colonel

Lieutenant Colonel Butler was a member of the original cadre when the 99th Infantry Division was formed at Camp Van Dorn, Mississippi, and was assigned as S-3 of the 395th Regiment. Shortly after returning from the Command and General Staff School at Fort Leavenworth, Kansas, Butler was appointed Commanding Officer of the 3rd Battalion, 395th Infantry Regiment. At the end of the war in Europe, he was appointed Regimental Executive Officer of the 393rd Infantry Regiment on 22 May 1945. On 17 July 1945 he was appointed Regimental Commander of the 394th Infantry Regiment and remained in this assignment until the regiment was returned to the United States. He was separated from the service on 14 January 1946.

With a close friend, Colonel G. B. Lahey, he helped form the 123rd Infantry Regiment, Illinois National Guard, 44th Infantry Division. This division was mobilized in 1952 because of the war in Korea and Butler received his orders for the Far East. He was originally assigned as a Battalion Commander in the 7th Infantry Division and later was assigned to the division staff.

Lieutenant Colonel Butler has served in the National Guard and the Army Reserve for 34 years, 11 of which were in Federal service.

His decorations and awards include; American Defense Medal; American Theater Medal; European, African, Middle East Medal; Army Occupation Medal (Germany); Combat Infantryman's Badge; Silver Star; Distinguished Unit Citation; Purple Heart; Bronze Star Medal; Oak Leaf Cluster, French Croix de Guerre; Belgium Ordre de la Couronne; Belgium Fourragere; and World War II Victory Medal.

Colonel Butler had attended the Battalion Commander and Staff Officer School; Division Officers School; and the Command and General Staff School.

In civilian life Colonel Butler was an office manager for the Illinois Bell Telephone Company in Ottawa, Illinois. He is now retired and lives in Ottawa with his wife, Madge. They have one daughter, Susan.

3rd Battalion - 395th Infantry - 99th Division   16 December 1944

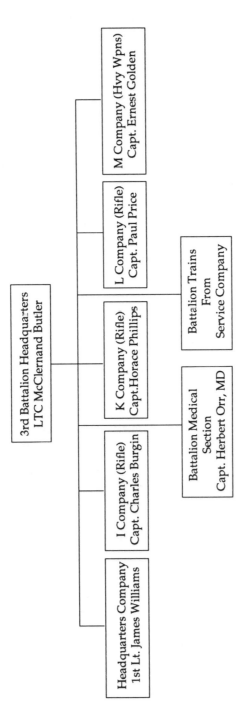

Battalion – 836 Officers and men
Rifle Company – 193 Officers and men
   3 Rifle platoons – 3 squads per platoon
   1 Weapons platoon – light machine guns and 60mm mortars
Weapons Company (M) – 166 Officers and men
   8 Heavy machine guns and 6 81mm mortars

DISTINGUISHED SERVICE CROSS

Private First Class *Richard D. Mills*, 38553332, 395th Infantry Regiment, United States Army. For extraordinary heroism in action against the enemy on 18 December 1944, in Germany. When the enemy launched a furious attack against his unit's position and penetrated the main line of resistance, Private First Class Mills opened fire with his automatic rifle, killing many of the enemy and wounding others. Time and again he turned back their repeated fanatic attempts to pass his position. On the final attack, Private First Class Mills' weapon jammed. With utter disregard for his personal safety, he left his foxhole, and standing in the open, hurled grenades dispersing the hostile attack. By his superb personal courage and unhesitating action, Private First Class Mills contributed materially to the stemming of the German drive and protecting of his battalion's communication lines. Entered military service from Texas, Hq 1st U.S. Army, Courtney H. Hodges, Lt. Gen. Commanding.

DISTINGUISHED SERVICE CROSS

Sergeant *Thornton E. Piersall*, 18147913, 395th Infantry, United States Army, for extraordinary heroism against the enemy on 18 December 1944, in Germany. When a strong German force threatened to sever a vital supply route to his company's defensive area, Sergeant Piersall, occupying a position in the path of the assault, held his ground. Wave after wave of hostile troops attacked him but he repulsed each attack by his intense fire. In desperation, the enemy brought up a machine gun and a rocket gun in an attempt to eliminate this threat to their advance. With his ammunition supply exhausted, Sergeant Piersall, with complete disregard for his life, courageously crawled from his emplacement, secured a grenade launcher and grenades from enemy dead in front of him and returned to his position. Taking careful aim, he fired two rounds with devastating accuracy, knocking out both the machine gun and the rocket gun. The heroic actions and exemplary bravery displayed by Sergeant Piersall prevented a heavy penetration into his company's area and reflected the highest traditions of the Armed Forces. Entered military service from Oklahoma. Per par 2, GO no. 21, Hq 1st U.S. Army, Courtney H. Hodges, Lt. Gen. Commanding.

Headquarters Third Battalion
395th Infantry
APO 149 U.S. Army

Subject:

TO: All members Third Battalion, 395th Infantry

It gives me a great deal of pleasure and fills me with pride to have had the honor of commanding a unit that has established the reputation for itself that you members of the Third Battalion, 395th Inf. have done. The battalion Staff has collected the following facts, which show our accomplishments while in combat in the ETO. I believe you will find this record is one to be proud of, and if not the best, will rank high against any other Unit's record in the army under the same combat period of time.

I. Battalion First in the Division

   A. First on line in the ETO, vicinity of Höfen, Germany, 9 Nov. '44
   B. First Presidential Unit Citation
   C. First men awarded the Distinguished Service Cross
   D. First across the famous Erft Canal, second water barrier in the First Army's dash to the Rhine.
   E. Life Magazine's 16 April '45 article, "The Victory of the Rhine," by Charles Christian Wertenbaker, in this connection reads in part, "On March 1st, Lightening Joe Collins sent his 99th Division from far to the rear, across the Roer and the Erft and through the Third Armored Division to attack the corps objective. By March 5th it had cleared the west bank of the Rhine." The Third Battalion, 395th Inf., was attached to the Third Armored Division in expanding the bridgehead at the Erft.
   F. Battalion captured the first town of the Division by the capture of Bergheim and Kenten, east of the Erft Canal, on the 1st of March '45.
   G. Battalion was the first and only battalion in the division attached to an Armored Division, working with all three Combat Commands of the 7th Armored Division from 4 April '45 to 17 April '45 and being attached to the Third Division (Armored) crossing the Erft Canal.
   H. Third Battalion, 395th Infantry was the first in the division to reach the West bank of the Rhine River.

II. First in the Regiment

   A. Third Battalion led the regiment in the crossing of the Rhine at the now famous, but "Kaput," Remagen Bridge.
   B. Third Battalion led the regiment in the assault crossing of the Altmuhl River.
   C. Third Battalion combat soldiers hold the only two Distinguished Service Crosses awarded to members of the 395th Inf. Reg. (Thornton Piersall & Dick Mills)

III. Achievements

   A. The battalion has 182 days in combat or operations in the ETO, approximately 150 days being front line contact with the enemy. From 9 Nov. '44 to 9 May '45 in six months or 180 days, bring the above total of 182 days an outstanding figure for operations in the ETO.
   B. The battalion capture by official count 53 towns or populated places in addition, unofficially, battalion troops in extremely rapid advances were first in Allerheiligen and Ner Ronnefeid, raising the count to 55.
   C. In addition to the above count of 55, 13 towns were screened and cleared of the enemy after passage of an Armored task force.
   D. In operations with its own division, the battalion captured 1998 PW's and on the 13th of April '45, while attached to the 7th Armored Division, working with a task force of that unit, an estimated 5000 PW's were captured.
   E. In addition to the approximately 7000 PW's just named, Third Battalion, 395th Inf. aided substantially by the capture of Sundwig, Germany and Hemer, Germany in the release of 24,000 Allied PW's at Hemer, and also the capture of 28,000 PW's, by the 395th Infantry. This vast number of PW's taken by the 395th Infantry included eight Generals and one Admiral.
   F. The Third Battalion, 395th Inf., made the initial enlargement of the Erft Canal and liquidated opposition at the actual bridge site at Bergheim, Germany which the Third Armored Division used at its spring board for its dash to Cologne.
   G. While the Third Battalion was attached to the 7th Armored Division, it played a major roll in fighting the armor loose in the crushing of the Ruhr Pocket. During the attachment, the Third Battalion fought with all three combat commands of the 7th Armored Division, and repulsed a German Division's counter-attack at Gleidorf, which so disorganized the enemy, that no

effective resistance was encountered until the final surrender of the enemy in the Ruhr Pocket.

H. The Third Battalion engaged in the extremely difficult fighting in enlarging the Remagen Bridgehead over difficult terrain, and started a one night attack with a penetration so deep and was so silent as to capture an enemy Regimental Command Post intact. This enemy CP felt so secure in the rear, that no local security was in evidence. This night attack and other operations contributed largely to the demoralization of the enemy in that sector, and the 7th Armored Division was able to break loose to the South along the Autobahn.

IV. Commendations:

Commendations were received by the battalion from Colonel George W. Smythe, Commanding Officer of the 47th Infantry Regiment, and Major General R. W. Hasbrouch, Commanding General of the 7th Armored Division. These commendations were as follows:

A. Headquarters 47th Infantry Regiment:

The 47th Combat Team was alerted and moved to the Monschau-Höfen Kalterherberg line on 17 December 1944, at which time the 3rd Battalion 395th Infantry, was attached to the Regimental Combat Team.

Throughout the entire period of this attachment, from 18 December '44 to 1300 30 Jan. '45., the combat efficiency of the 3rd Battalion of the 395th Infantry was outstandingly apparent. On 18 Dec. '44, at a critical point in the enemy counteroffensive, this battalion withstood the shock of a strong enemy attack and threw them back with heavy losses. The courage and steadfastness of this unit in holding the vital Höfen-Alzen area during a period in which our lines were fluid, is highly commendable. After the line had been solidified, the 3rd Battalion, 395th Infantry, continued to hold the Höfen-Alzen area and constantly harassed the enemy with patrol action, taking a number of prisoners. During this period the battalion was under continuous heavy enemy artillery and mortar fire.

The superior combat efficiency of the battalion, its excellent staff work and its cheerful attitude of cooperation with the 47th Reinforced Combat Team is deserving of high Commendation.

B. Headquarters 7th Armored Division:

I wish to express my appreciation for the fine service rendered by the 3rd Battalion, 395th Infantry while attached to this division during the reduction of the Ruhr Pocket. They assisted materially in the success of the operation. Their capture of Gleidorf and subsequent repulses of a determined counter-attack made at night to recapture the town is deserving of high praise.

Please accept my thanks for the loan of such a fine unit and convey to its officers and men my appreciation and that of my division for the excellent work done by them.

C. The 99th Infantry Division G-2 REPORT 128 contained the following information on the outstanding work of the battalion in Höfen, Germany:

The incident in Höfen which led to the capture of his entire company was not the first unpleasant encounter that Lt. Bemener, CO. of the 2nd Co. 753 VG Regt, had had with the 99th Div. The 3rd Bn. 395th Infantry, which was recently awarded the Presidential citation for its action at Höfen, will be interested in the following statement made by Lt. Bemener. He was commander of the 5th German Company 753 VG Regt, at the beginning of the Ardennes Offensive, and, as such, part of the II Bn, which had the mission of attacking and taking Höfen, S. of Monschau. The 5th Co. was to attack our strong-point on the night of 18-19 of Dec. '44 at its northern approaches. Although the approaching German soldiers were a perfect target, our troops allowed them to advance to within 10 feet of our defensive position. A sudden burst of rifle, MG, and mortar fire, nearly eliminated the PW's company, and only a very few were able to get away, leaving their dead and wounded behind.

At the conclusion of the interrogation, when Lt. Bemener was ready to leave, he turned to ask casually if the interrogator knew what American unit had held Höfen, he added, "They must have been one of your best formations." When asked what reason he had for this opinion, he answered, "Two reasons: one, *coldbloodedness;* two, *efficiency.*

V. Summary

In conclusion it should be noted that the fighting spirit and excellent work you as members of the Third Battalion, 395th Infantry have demonstrated, gained the immediate respect of veteran organizations wherever and whenever we came in contact with them, and the reputation we have as a result in the ETO, is one to be proud of and jealously guarded.

As for my own personal feelings, I am proud to have the honor and privilege of being a member of this unit.

McCLERNAND BUTLER
Lt. Col., Infantry
Commanding

LOCATIONS OF 3RD BATTALION CP'S

LaFeuillie, France, 4 Nov 44

Aubel, Belgium, 5 Nov 44

Kalterherberg, Germany, 9 Nov 44

Höfen, Germany, 10 Nov 44

Kalterherberg, Germany, 30 Jan 45

Rocherath, Belgium, 4 Feb 45

Hollerath, Germany, 6 Feb 45

Hellenthal, Germany, 8 Feb 45

Krinkelt, Belgium, 11 Feb 45

Moderscheid, Belgium, 12 Feb 45

La Minerie, Belgium, 20 Feb 45

Stolberg, Germany, 27 Feb 45

Elsdorf, Germany, 28 Feb 45

Bergheim, Germany, 1 Mar 45

Oekoven, Germany, 4 Mar 45

Kuckhof, Germany, 5 Mar 45

Meckenheim, Germany, 9 Mar 45

Ringen, Germany, 10 Mar 45

Bruchhausen, Germany, 11 Mar 45

Ronigerhof, Germany, 14 Mar 45

Sprietchen, Germany, 23 Mar 45

Hochscheid, Germany, 24 Mar 45

Hümmericher, Germany, 25 Mar 45

Ober Honnefeld, Germany, 26 Mar 45

Meudt, Germany, 27 Mar 45

Merenberg, Germany, 28 Mar 45

Alten-Buseck, Germany, 29 Mar 45

Lollar, Germany, 31 Mar 45

Wolferode, Germany, 2 Apr 45

Oberkirchen, Germany, 4 Apr 45

Winkhausen, Germany, 6 Apr 45

Gleidorf, Germany, 8 Apr 45

Berghausen, Germany, 9 Apr 45

Menkhausen, Germany, 10 Apr 45

Küntrop, Germany, 12 Apr 45

Balve, Germany, 13 Apr 45

Hemer, Germany, 15 Apr 45

Steinsdorf, Germany 18 Apr 45

Buchenbach, Germany, 22 Apr 45

Weinsfeld, Germany, 24 Apr 45

Hirschberg, Germany, 25 Apr 45

Pirkenbrunn, Germany, 27 Apr 45

Bad Gögging, Germany, 28 Apr 45

Bruckberg, Germany, 29 Apr 45

Moosburg, Germany, 30 Apr 45

Landshut, Germany, 1 May 45

Kupmuhlde, Germany, 3 May 45

Hammelburg, Germany, 9 May 45

COMMANDING OFFICERS

3rd Battalion

1 Jan 44	Lt. Col. James S. Gallagher	0174034
1 Feb 44	Maj. McClernand Butler	0373122
1 Mar 44	Lt. Col. McClernand Butler	0373122
1 May 45	Lt. Col. Oliver W Hartwell	0323150

HQ Company

1 Jan 44	1st Lt. Ernest F. Golden	0423107
1 Feb 44	1st Lt. James W. Williams	01296307
1 Jan 45	Capt. James W. Williams	01296307
5-31 Jul 45	1st Lt. John A. Walker	0885776

I Company

1 Jan 44	1st Lt. Benjamin L. Wesson	0403567
1 Feb 44	2nd Lt. Victor E. Madura	01299916
20 Mar 44	Capt. Charles B. Burgin	01296166
5 Mar 45	1st Lt. Gene S. Stalcup	01317207
31 Mar 45	Capt. Mack H. McClendon, Jr.	0387294
1-16 Jul 45	1st Lt. Paul E. Wells	01291553
17-31 Jul 45	Capt. Houston D. Smith, Jr.	0467095

K Company

1 Jan 44	1st Lt. Robert H. Boyden	0390174
1 Feb 44	Capt. Keith P. Fabianich	024151
25 Nov-7 Apr 45	Capt. Horace B. Phillips, II	0461737
1 May 45	Capt. Leroy F. Smith	01300406

L Company

1 Jan 44	1st Lt. Frederick M. Wooster	0387640
1 Feb-7 Apr 45	Capt. Paul P. Price	01295595
1 May 45	Capt. Erskine Wickersham	0416046

M Company

1 Feb 44	1st Lt. John H. Yeager	01296789
2 March 44	Capt. George L. Ware	0446760
1 Apr 44	Capt. Ernest F. Golden	0423107
24 Aug 44	1st Lt. Arthur Decker	01300137
8 Sep 44	Capt. Ernest F. Golden	0423107
1 Jan 45	1st Lt. Arthur Decker	01300137
1 May 45	Capt. Arthur Decker	01300137
13-31 Jul 45	Capt. John Caddle	0366365

99TH INFANTRY—395TH INFANTRY REGIMENT

Battle Babies came to stay on November 9, 1944
The 3rd Battalion moved on line,
We were greeted with propaganda leaflets
Saying "welcome ninety nine."

We returned the welcome
With a thunderous artillery roar,
I guess it made us wonder
What really was in store.

As all the men adjusted
To the weather, so bitter cold,
We were about to make history
Years later to be told.

I'll never forget that morning
On December sixteen,
The enemy thought that we would run
Because, as combat troops, we were green.

I guess we suddenly realized
This was the real thing,
We didn't have time to wonder
What the future might bring.

For a time that seemed an eternity
We struggled night and day,
Finally the enemy realized
The battle babies had come to stay.

During the fiercest fighting
We finally had them on the run,
It makes war seem a mystery
When you use an enemy's gun.

The enemy had us surrounded
But we continued to give our share,
When the battle had subsided
The 3rd Battalion was still there.

We knew the end was near
And proud we had stood the test,
Of course victory doesn't come easy
For so many comrades lay at rest.

But when final taps have sounded
There will be no need to pray,
Then the 3rd Battalion will re-assemble
Where the "Battle Babies have come to stay."

Bob Gordon
K Company

HEADQUARTERS 395th INFANTRY AJM/agh
Camp Barkeley, Texas

17 June 1944

SUBJECT: Commendation

TO : The 395th Infantry Regiment

I have always felt that when soldiers do a commendable job, they should be informed of that fact. Therefore, since I cannot personally tell each man in the Regiment, I take this means of informing him that I am tremendously pleased with his work on the Camp Barkeley Reservation.

The Regiment, plus attachments, was sent to this area by Major General Lauer to act as the enemy detail in a test of an organization which greatly outnumbered us. You did a splendid job. Once before, as you may recall, this Regiment was commended for a splendid defensive position. That was when Lieutenant General McNair commended us during the Louisiana Maneuvers.

I am very happy that you have not been content to rest on your laurels. When the job was given you to do, you did it in a superior manner. You dug holes in ground which was said to be too hard to dig in. You set up a defensive position which completely balked a superior force. You worked hard. The Commanding General of XXIII Corps, Major General Craig, told me "I am highly pleased with your Regiment in every respect". The Commanding General of IV Army, Major General Lucas, told me "It's a pleasure to inspect troops like these".

You have established a reputation which will be difficult to maintain. You can keep it only by remembering that you are constantly on parade. Continue to maintain the same high standards of military courtesy and discipline, and I know you will hold the reputation you have established.

Let me say in closing that I am thrilled with the privilege of commanding such a Regiment.

A. J. MACKENZIE
Colonel, 395th Infantry
Commanding

Distribution:

1 ea Off
1 ea EM

HEADQUARTERS 99TH DIVISION

APO 449

United States Army

GENERAL ORDER)
:
NUMBER   16)   6 March 1945

Battle Honors—Third Battalion Three Ninety Fifth Infantry

Under the provisions of Section IV, War Department Circular 333 (1943) and Section VII, Circular 2, Headquarters First United States Army, dated 4 January 1945, citation of the following unit, as approved by the Commanding General, First United States Army, is announced. The citation reads as follows:

The Third Battalion, Three Ninety Fifth Infantry Regiment, is cited for outstanding performance of duty in action against the enemy during the period 16 to 19 December 1944, near Höfen, Germany. During the German offensive in the Ardennes, the Third Battalion, Three Ninety Fifth Infantry Regiment was assigned the mission of holding the Monschau-Eupen-Liege Road. For four successive days the battalion held this sector against combined German tank and infantry attacks, launched with fanatical determination and supported by heavy artillery. No reserves were available to the battalion, and the situation was desperate. Disregarding personal safety and without rest the men fought vigorously to hold their positions against hostile penetrations. On at least six different occasions the battalion was forced to place artillery concentrations dangerously close to its own positions in order to repulse penetrations and restore its lines. On other occasions, men came out of their fixed defenses and engaged in desperate hand-to-hand fighting in order to repel enemy assault teams. The enemy artillery was so intense that communications were generally out. The men carried out missions without orders when their positions were penetrated or infiltrated. They killed Germans coming at them from the front, flanks, and rear. Outnumbered five to one, they inflicted casualties in the ratio of eighteen to one. With ammunition supplies dwindling rapidly, the men obtained German weapons and utilized ammunition obtained from casualties to drive off the persistent foe. Despite fatigue, constant enemy shelling, and ever-increasing enemy pressure, the Third Battalion, Three Ninety Fifth Infantry Regiment prevented the German break-through from extending to the Monschau area, guarded a 6,000 yard front, and destroyed seventy-five percent of three German Infantry regiments. The courage and devotion to duty displayed by members of the Third Battalion, Three Ninety Fifth Infantry Regiment, in the face of overwhelming odds was in keeping with the highest traditions of the military service.

The Third Battalion, Three Ninety Fifth Infantry Regiment, is entitled to the citation streamer. The individuals assigned or attached to this unit on the occasion for which citation was awarded are entitled to wear the Distinguished Unit Badge. Individuals subsequently assigned or attached are entitled to wear the Distinguished Unit Badge only so long as they remain with the unit.

HEADQUARTERS SEVENTH ARMORED DIVISION
Office of the Commanding General
APO 257, U.S. Army
23 April 1945

Major General Walter Lauer
Hq, 99th Infantry Division
APO 449, U.S. Army

Dear General Lauer:

I wish to express my appreciation for the fine service rendered by the 3rd Battalion, 395th Infantry while attached to this division during the reduction of the Ruhr pocket. They assisted materially in the success of the operation. Their capture of GLEIDORF and subsequent repulse of a determined counterattack made at night to recapture the town is deserving of high praise.

Please accept my thanks for the loan of such a fine unit and convey to its officers and men my appreciation and that of my division for the excellent work done by them.

Sincerely,
/S/ R. W. Hasbrouck
/t/ R. W. HASBROUCK
Major General, U.S. Army
Commanding

1st Ind.

HEADQUARTERS 99TH INFANTRY DIVISION, APO 449, U.S. Army, 28 April 1945

TO: Commanding Officer, 3rd Battalion, 395th Infantry

Thru: Commanding Officer, 395th Infantry

It gives me great pleasure to receive and forward this commendation. I add my appreciation for a job well done.

/S/ Walter E. Lauer
/t/ WALTER E. LAUER
Major General, U.S. Army
Commanding

2nd Ind.

HEADQUARTERS 395th Infantry, APO 449, U.S. Army, 6 May 1945

TO: Commanding Officer, Hq, Third Battalion, 395th Infantry

I am pleased to forward this note of appreciation from the Commanding General of the 7th Armored Division and endorsement from General Lauer. I can well understand why they appreciated your courageous work. You have done an exceedingly fine job.

/S/ Thomas N. Griffin
/t/ THOMAS N. GRIFFIN
Commanding

GENERAL ORDERS)
No. 43   )

DEPARTMENT OF THE ARMY
Washington 25, D.C., 19 December 1950

GENERAL   Section
LIST OF UNITS AND CITATIONS   I
RESCISSIONS   II
                                                      III

I. GENERAL. - 1. Confirmation.- The following list of units of the United States Army to which decorations have been awarded by cobelligerent foreign governments during World War II, together with the citations therefor, is confirmed in accordance with current regulations.

2. Wearing of foreign decorations.- The wearing of foreign decorations by individuals will be in accordance with AR 260-15 and the following:

a. French and Belgian Fourrageres.- Normally, two citations are required before a unit becomes eligible for the award of the Fourragere. The award of the Fourragere is not automatic, but must be specifically authorized by decree of the respective foreign government. A citation in orders or award of the Croix de Guerre to a unit does not authorize the wearing of the decoration by an individual. Likewise, no award of the Croix de Guerre to an individual will serve to constitute eligibility to wear the Fourragere. The Fourragere may be worn permanently by individuals who participated with the unit in both actions for which the unit was cited. The French Fourragere may be worn temporarily by individuals assigned to the unit subsequent to the time the award was made, but only so long as they remain with such unit. The Belgian Fourragere is not authorized to be worn temporarily.

b. Netherlands Orange Lanyard.- The Netherlands Orange Lanyard may be worn permanently by individuals who participated with the unit in the action for which it was cited and temporary wearing of the Lanyard is not authorized.

99TH INFANTRY DIVISION

CITED IN THE ORDER OF THE DAY of the Belgian Army, by Decree No. 2509, 17 June 1946, by Charles, Prince of Belgium, Regent of the Kingdom, with the following citation:

During the period from 18 November to 16 December 1944, the division and attached units entered into action along the border of the canton of Malmedy. During that period the division endured the test of combat and developed the technique which proved itself in the campaign of the Ardennes. An offensive directed against the Siegfried line met with success, when the great German offensive was launched on the morning of 16 December 1944.

CITED IN THE ORDER OF THE DAY of the Belgian Army, by decree No. 2509, 17 June 1946, by Charles, Prince of Belgium, Regent of the Kingdom, with the following citation.

During the period from 16 December 1944 to 20 February 1945, the division and attached units showed a stoical determination and an extraordinary heroism in facing, checking and finally pushing back the German offensive of the Ardennes. The division took a defensive position on the Elsenborn crest and checked all the enemy attacks under extremely difficult climatic conditions until 30 January 1945, when the division was again able to take the offensive.

BELGIAN FOURRAGERE (1940) awarded under Decree No. 2509, 17 June 1946, by Charles, Prince of Belgium, Regent of the Kingdom.

CITED IN THE ORDER OF THE DAY of the Belgian Army, by Decree No. 1891, 20 November 1945, by Charles, Prince of Belgium, Regent of the Kingdom. (For citation, see "9th Infantry Division", second citation only.)

Hq & Hq Co, 99th Inf Div
99th Cav Rcn Troop (Mecz)
324th Engr Combat Bn
324th Medical Bn
393d Inf Regiment
394th Inf Regiment
395th Inf Regiment
Hq & Hq Btry, 99th Inf Div Arty
370th FA Bn (105 How)
371st FA Bn (105 How)
372d FA Bn (155 How)
924th FA Bn (15 How)
Hq & Hq Co, Sp Troops, 99th Inf Div
99th QM Co
99th Sig Co
799th Ord Light Maint Co
Band, 99th Inf Div
MP Platoon, 99th Inf Div

395th Inf Regiment, 2d & 3d Bn
(Atchd to 9th Inf Div)

9TH INFANTRY DIVISION

CITED IN THE ORDER OF THE DAY of the Belgian Army, by Decree No. 1391, 20 November 1945, by Charles, Prince of Belgium, Regent of the Kingdom, with the following citation:

From 20 December 1944 to 26 January 1945, in the course of the German offensive in the Ardennes, the 9th Infantry Division of the United States and the attached units received the mission to defend the north flank of the counter-offensive led by the V Corps of the United States Army in the sector of Eupen (Belgium) Montjoie (Germany). Facing an obstinate defense, it attacked without respite. The enemy counterattacked but was unable to enlarge the breach caused by its breakthrough. After thee enemy attack was unsuccessful, the 9th Infantry Division and the attached units attacked and forced the German Army to retreat and abandon the Belgian Territory in that region.

BELGIAN FOURRAGERE (1940), awarded under decree No. 1391, 20 November 1945, by Charles, Prince of Belgium, Regent of the Kingdom.

HEADQUARTERS 393RD INFANTRY
APO 449, U.S. Army

9 July 1945

SUBJECT: Night Attacks
TO: Major de Forceville, Senior French Liaison Officer, Third U.S. Army, APO 403

1. In reply to your request on reports concerning night attacks, I first thought that I would outline what basic facts are necessary for a night attack to be successful; secondly, the control that is necessary; thirdly, three different types of night attacks that use these basic principles.

2. a. For a night attack to be successful, the following basic elements must exist.

(1) Limited objective, or if objective is not limited, there must be a series of limited objectives designated prior to the final objective.

(2) A night with enough moonlight to give fair visibility, especially during the time the attack is going on. This is not essential for the troops to move into position prior to the attack but must exist during the attack.

(3) The final objective must be a dominating piece of terrain which when taken will control the entire surrounding territory.

(4) There must be sufficient time for the battalion commander to make a reconnaissance, give his order to his company commanders and for the company commanders to make a reconnaissance prior to darkness. It is not essential, however, that the platoon leader make a reconnaissance but they must have a thorough and comprehensive briefing of what they are to do and full knowledge of the situation prior to the operation.

(5) Higher echelon must designate what supporting weapons as well as supporting fire will be available for the attack.

(6) Control of the operations must be under one man and should not be larger than one battalion.

(7) The plan of attack must be simple.

a. All elements must attack on parallel lines.

b. All unit commanders understand in detail what they are to do.

3. The control of any night attack is without doubt one of the largest factors necessary for a successful operation. As my attacks have all been the unit size of the battalion, I will deal chiefly with this type of operation. For control, the battalion commander must do and accomplish the following items.

a. Reconnaissance for the attack prior to darkness.

b. Issue orders to his company commanders on the ground during daylight pointing out where they are to go and what they are to do so that he can be assured that the attack will start in the right direction and all unit commanders know what they are to accomplish.

c. He must designate what identification will be used by his troops. I have found that a white armband on each arm has been very satisfactory.

d. If the objective is some distance from the line of departure, he must designate some limited objectives prior to his final objective and see to it that his units stop and reorganize and do not move forward to continue the attack except on his order. In addition to this, he must designate some check points to be used, not only for control, but also to be used in giving information in the clear whether it be enemy or friendly when so desired by company commanders or a battalion commander.

e. He must let the company commanders know where they can find him at all times. I have found that the best position was to move behind the leading company, not more than 200 meters from the leading elements at any time. This, incidentally, may see rather far forward for a battalion commander to be but it has paid me large dividends in every night attack that I personally have ever commanded because the company commanders were able to find me and talk to me when they ran into difficulties without having to move more than 150 meters from their own location.

f. He must lay plans and see that they are carried out, to have his unit close on the final objective, and set up an all-around defense prior to daylight. This is extremely important due to the fact that a large number of enemy troops will invariably be either by-passed or not eliminated during the attack and come daylight you cannot be sure from what direction a counterattack will hit your unit. Sometimes you even have a counterattack hit from the rear.

g. If the battalion commander is given support of artillery, I strongly recommend that he has as large a concentration placed on his initial objective as possible, allowing him to designate the time as to when this concentration is to be fired so that his unit will be able to follow the artillery in without loss of any time whatsoever once the fire is lifted. The effect of the artillery fire in my experience has been as follows. It has dazed and confused that part of the enemy that is on the alert watching for an attack and that part of the enemy that is asleep has been so used to artillery fire dropped upon his position that he would not wake up regardless of the quantity that was thrown into the area. The result was that those on the alert were dazed and those not on alert were never aroused in time.

h. In case armored vehicles in the form of tanks, half-tracks, etc. are to support the attack, it is advisable to hold them far enough in the rear so that the noise of their approach does not tip off the pending attack to the enemy and yet to arrive in support of the unit once the attack is launched in minimum time. I have found that tanks moving quietly generally get within two or three kilometers of the enemy without disturbing him unduly.

4. The three different types of night attacks are attack on town and vicinity, attack across river and mountainous country and attack on a narrow front driving deep into enemy territory to destroy rear installations. I will take them up in the order as named.

a. The attack made by my battalion, the Third Battalion, 395th Infantry, on Bergheim, Germany, ran as follows. My battalion was given the mission to attack parallel to Erft Canal, capturing Bergheim, Germany, and vicinity and clear all enemy from that territory. The attack was to jump off at 0300 the following morning. I had time to make a reconnaissance of the area, decide on the line of departure, direction of attack and was informed that a large concentration consisting of eight battalions of artillery would be fired on my objective commencing at 0245 in the morning. My company commanders arrived prior to darkness and I was able to show them the direction of the attack, the formation they were to use and the identification the troops would wear, which was white armbands on each arm. The plan of operation consisted of two companies attacking abreast, the boundary between them being the road running parallel to the Erft Canal and through the center of town. My reserve company was to follow the two leading companies echeloned to the right rear at four hundred meters and clear out the area between the town of Bergheim and the canal. I was to follow in the rear of the right leading company and be parallel to the reserve company. The attack went off as planned. The heavy concentration completely disorganized the Germans who were to resist our attack going into the town, and the Germans in the town were either so disorganized or did not wake up and the result was that we were in the town before they could get organized. As soon as the leading companies arrived at the town they immediately started clearing buildings and moving forward to the first check point that I had designated which happened to be the center of the town square. This operation was accomplished prior to daylight. The reserve company had moved forward and I had them stopped about four hundred meters short of that first check point. By this time the leading elements had moved approximately four kilometers. The operation was quite successful because first we had caught the Germans completely by surprise and gotten into town without organized resistance. By stopping at the crossroads in the center of town and controlling this area we cut off any route of escape by those Germans who were pocketed by the elements in town and the reserve company between the town and the canal, and by stopping when we did we were able to move up our tanks and tank destroyers into the town, mop up small pockets of resistance, and protect ourselves from a counterattack which came later that morning by approximately 300 troops trying to escape from the trap which had been sprung. The result of the operation cost the Germans approximately 150 killed and about 300 captured, and two tanks knocked out. The reasons for the success of the operation I attribute to the following factors. A moonlit night which gave enough visibility for control, heavy preparation of artillery concentration that was followed up immediately by infantry once it was lifted, catching the troops on the alert still in a dazed condition, the aggressive spirit on the part of the infantry to reach the center of town thereby cutting off the route of escape for those who had been bypassed, the battalion commander staying close enough to the forward elements so that when the company commanders ran into a situation they were not sure of, they actually made personal contact and talked the situation over with the battalion commander, and lastly the battalion stopping on a dominating feature until daylight thereby having control of the entire area. The losses of my battalion in this operation were negligible.

b. The next attack involved the crossing of the Wied River and capturing the high ground approximately 1 1/2 kilometers on the other side. My battalion was designated to capture four pieces of terrain which dominated the area but was on a three kilometer front. I was given a maximum amount of artillery support for the initial attack and the rest of the fires were on call when I designated later. We had sufficient time prior to the attack so that I was able to have down to and including my platoon leaders of each company come up and look over the area from the battalion CP during daylight. My plan of attack was as follows. Have one company move across the river on my extreme right flank, capture a high piece of ground approximately one kilometer on the other side of the Wied River and protect the flank of the adjacent regiment. I was to maintain contact with them by radio. We agreed upon a series of check points in that vicinity so that we could talk in the clear and the enemy would be unable to obtain any worthwhile information. The remainder of the battalion moved across the river in a column of companies approximately one kilometer north of the first company's crossing. I was to follow the leading company at two hundred meters. The leading company was to move quickly across the river, clear out a small settlement just on the other side and then gain control of a dominating piece of terrain approximately 1 1/2 kilometers inland. The reserve company was then to pass on the right of the leading company and move on to our final objective. The attack went as planned for the crossing of the river by the main part of the battalion. The lead company was able to move forward and get the initial objective. The reserve company ran into trouble. They first made contact with the enemy and had a small fire fight. Once this had been eliminated they moved forward in the heavy woods in the area, became confused and moved in a big circle ending up after hours of effort at the location they started from. It was at this point that if it had not been for my location being well known and close to the front, the whole operation might have fallen down, as I was able to talk by personal contact to both of the company commanders, change my plan of attack and move the lead company forward to take the final objective and which had originally been given to the reserve company. The reserve company, in the meantime, was allowed to move onto the initial objective and reorganize and the company commander gathered his unit back under his control. While this was going on the company which was operating by itself at approximately one kilometer to our right had crossed over the Wied River, run into heavy opposition, and on finding a small indentation in the ground, moved single file under the final protective line of two German machine guns and gained their objective, consolidated their position and then at daylight attacked the German defensive positions from the rear eliminating the entire pocket. By daylight I had all three companies on the objective and prepared for a counterattack which might come. The result of the operation was as follows. A successful crossing of the river, killing approximately 150 Germans, knocked out 2 armored cars and one tank and the capture of approximately 300 prisoners of war. The success of the attack I attribute to the following items. The aggressive spirit of the infantry, a moonlit night which allowed the company commanders to keep control of their companies even though they moved through heavy woods after crossing the river, my location close to the front lines so that when the company commanders became confused they were able to come to see me and find out what to do and the consolidation of the position on dominating pieces of terrain so that after daylight we were able to attack the strong pockets of resistance from their rear. This attack was incidentally one of the most difficult operations I have ever had to command due to the fact that not only was it a night attack but it also included crossing the river, moving approximately 2 kilometers through heavy woods and controlling a frontage of three kilometers once we had taken our objective.

  c. The third operation involved the battalion attacking on a narrow front and breaking through the German defense, moving to their rear echelon approximately six kilometers behind their front line and captured the dominating terrain in that area. This attack was to be made down a narrow gorge. Here again I was given sufficient time to make my reconnaissance and go over the plan of attack with my company commanders during daylight hours. The plan of attack was simple. We were to attack in a column of companies. I was to follow directly behind the leading company. We were to attack a strong point. Once this was cleared to move rapidly, gain our objective and be prepared to hold territory gained once daylight arrived. As for the other attacks, it was a nice moonlit night, and for identification I used white armbands, one on each arm. The attack this time did not go as planned. The lead company ran into more resistance than was expected and if it had not been that I was near front, control would have been lost. The terrain was such that at that point you could only attack on a platoon front. I gained contact with the company commander and the leading platoon leader. I informed them that they would have to move on the resistance with marching fire and overwhelm the German resistance by fire power alone. Maneuver was impossible and we could expect losses accordingly. The platoon carried out my order efficiently. When they opened up with their automatic weapons all at once, the effect on the enemy was astonishing. We killed approximately ten Germans outright, wounded a number of others and the remainder left. From then on it was a fast moving situation with the platoon leading the entire way. The final objective was taken prior to daylight and with maximum surprise upon the enemy. During this operation the battalion captured four towns, knocked out three armored cars and two Mark IV tanks and captured approximately 400 prisoners to include the entire German regimental command post in that area. This command post, incidentally, was far enough behind the line and felt secure enough so that they did not have any local security around the CP. The consolidation and reorganization of the final objective prior to daylight was accomplished and was essential as armored counterattacks tried to dislodge us the remainder of the morning, only giving up when the remainder of my own regiment and the adjacent regiment had come up on line with my location. I attribute the success of this operation to the following factors. A good moonlit night to afford maximum control, the aggressive spirit of the infantry who moved in on the enemy regardless of their position, the location of myself close to the front line so that I could push the attack and give orders once we had run into trouble. The close in on the final objective prior to daylight and consolidating that position so that we were able to repulse any counterattacks that came the next day. These counterattacks included two armored cars supported by infantry, attacking my own location from the rear.

/S/
McCLERNAND BUTLER
Lt. Col. 393rd Inf

HEADQUARTERS THIRD U.S. ARMY
French Liaison Mission
APO 403

26 July 1945

Lieutenant Colonel McClernand Butler
Headquarters 393rd Infantry Regiment
APO 449

Dear Colonel Butler:

I have received two copies of your report addressed to me, subject "Infantry Night Attacks in The U.S. Army."

I have sent one copy to the General Staff in Paris and the other one to the personal staff of General De Lattre de Tassigny, Commander-in-Chief of the First French Army.

I am now directed by both these authorities to express to you their deep appreciation for the valuable document you handed me, and also their heartiest congratulations for the gallantry and ability displayed by you personally in the therein described action.

May I be permitted to add my own thanks with warmest personal regards.

Very sincerely yours,

/S/
PHILLIPE de FORCEVILLE
Major, Artillery
Senior French Liaison Officer
Third U.S. Army

INDEX

Allen, LTC Jack 3
Allison, MAJ Luther 22, 59
Anthony, Warner 65

Barnes, Ralph 49
Bartow, William 31, 41, 61, 89, 130, 152, 154, 166, 180
Belefant, Martin 49, 51
Bivings, Isaac 45
Blasdel, William 24, 43, 83, 129, 138, 145-146, 148, 150, 174, 179, 180
Boyden, LT Robert H. 199
Broadbent, Edward 49
Buchanan, BG Kenneth 24
Burgin, CPT Charles 26, 30, 32, 95, 100, 105, 121, 180, 199
Butler, LTC McClernand 2-3, 22, 27, 30, 32, 35, 37-38, 42-45, 48, 53-55, 59-61, 69, 88, 96-98, 100, 104, 107-108, 112-113, 116-117, 120-122, 127, 139, 141, 143-144, 147-148, 150, 152, 154, 161, 164, 168, 172, 176-177, 180-181, 187-189, 197, 199, 218-219

Caddle, CPT John 200
Chiodi, LT Ernest 48
Craft, Robert 48-49
Craig, MG Louis 5, 24, 116
Crewdson, James 22, 29, 33, 66, 76-77, 79, 84, 86
Crist, Robert 48-49

Decker, LT Arthur 47, 55, 90, 200
Denhard, Howard 47, 146
Dunkin, Doyle 46-47

Fabianach, CPT Keith 26, 199
Ferris, Hugh 70, 97, 175

Gallagher, LTC James 5, 86, 199
Gangway, Donald 41
Gibney, COL Jesse 24
Gibney, Samuel 32
Golden, CPT Ernest 27, 55, 113-114, 121, 199, 200
Gorby, Richard 18, 85, 88, 96, 112-113, 131, 138, 146, 152, 169-170, 174
Gordon, Robert 202
Griffin, Thomas N. 207
Groff, CPT William 40

Hallman, Joe 25
Hare, LT James 48, 60, 95-96, 98, 100, 105
Harmon, William 78
Hartwell, LTC Oliver 173, 199
Hasbrouck, MG R. W. 156, 206
Herman, Herb 128, 130-131, 135, 155, 159, 166, 171
Huebner, MG C. R. 63
Huffman, William 43, 46, 68
Humphrey, Leo 113, 121-122

Kissinger, Homer 12, 17, 28, 160
Kreuger, Robert 68, 71

Laird, John 102
Larson, Pap 25
Lauer, MG Walter 2, 32, 63, 108, 206
Lawrence, BG Thompson 1
Leming, LT Elroy 105

Lewis, Thomas 124
Lintman, Grant 88
Lipshitz, Harvey 36-37
Llewellyn, LT Stanley 56
Looney, CPT George 56, 67
Lucas, MG John 5

Madura, LT Victor E. 199
Malekos, George 120
Martakos, James 146
Martin, John 31, 49, 58, 144
Mattix, John 45
McClendon, CPT Mack 144, 147, 199
McKenzie, COL A. J. 3, 5, 203
Mills, Richard 42, 62, 67, 97, 99-100, 107, 115, 127, 129, 132, 139, 141, 143, 149, 172, 175, 178, 191, 194
Mizrahi, LT Ralph 54
Montgomery, GEN B. L. 40
Musser, LT Jack 105, 115-117, 143-144

Neill, George 26, 65
Noonan, John 78
Nothwang, George 65

O'Brien, John 64
Orr, MD Herbert 46, 67, 70, 76, 91, 102, 105, 107, 109, 148, 156, 168, 172

Parks, Robert 14, 33, 41, 52, 56, 84, 109, 175, 180
Peterson, LT W. E. 105
Phillips, CPT Horace 27, 143, 199
Piersall, Thornton 35, 58, 62, 99, 192, 194
Prager, George 42, 63, 104, 112, 122, 153, 177
Price, CPT Paul 27, 143, 199
Putty, Paul 3, 24, 117

Randall, Jack 26, 115, 133, 155
Rohrs, LT Robert 34

Sandbergen, Harry 146
Satler, Rollin 97
Schnitzer, Alfred 127, 181
Scott, Euart 71
Shipman, Duane 78
Shulz, Lambert 127, 133
Simba, George 146
Smith, CPT Houston D. Jr. 199
Smith, LT Leroy 146, 199
Smythe, COL George 55, 79
Snead, George 146
Snevily, Robert 23, 65, 105-106
Stalcup, LT Gene 105, 199
Stallings, SGT 148
Stone, Willie 44-45
Sullivan, Dan 115, 120, 144, 149, 168, 172, 176, 180

Tabb, John 17, 25, 34, 65
Thomas, Henry 89
Thompson, Fred 91, 106
Tutt, Giles 96-97

Vicari, Angelo 34, 37, 47

Walker, LT John A. 199
Ware, CPT George L. 200
Waterman, Bruce 112
Wells, LT Paul E. 199
Wesson, LT Benjamin L. 199
Whalen, James 73
Wickersham, LT Erskine 78, 199
Williams, CPT J. W. 37, 45, 199
Williams, LT James W. 199
Willis, Junior 107, 146
Wilson, Warren 2, 181
Wooster, LT Frederick M. 199
Worley, LT William 73

Yeager, LT John H. 200

Zellers, William 63
Ziegler, SGT 62
Zioncheck, Edward 154, 156, 166

❖ ❖ ❖

To order additional copies of this book, please use coupon below.

Mail to:

Brunswick Publishing Corporation
ROUTE 1, BOX 1-A-1
LAWRENCEVILLE, VIRGINIA 23868

Order Form

Please send me _____ copy(s) of *Butler's Battlin' Blue Bastards*, by Thor Ronningen, ISBN 1-55618-132-9, LC 93-9515, at $19.95 per copy plus $4.00 shipping and handling for the first copy, 50 cents for each additional copy. Virginia residents add 4.5% or 90 cents sales tax per copy.

❏ Check enclosed ❏ Charge Orders — 804-848-3865
❏ Charge to my credit card: ❏ VISA ❏ MasterCard
❏ American Express

Card # _____ Exp. Date _____

Signature: _____

Name _____

Address _____

City _____ State _____ Zip _____

Phone # _____